Dr. Manisha Kshirsagar,
BAMS (Ayurveda, India)
Esthetician with
Megan M. Murphy, CAP

Enchanting Beauty

Ancient Secrets to Inner, Outer & Lasting Beauty

New Age Books
New Delhi (India)

ENCHANTING BEAUTY

ANCIENT SECRETS TO INNER, OUTER AND LASTING BEAUTY

ISBN: 978-81-7822-487-9

First Indian Edition: Delhi, **2016**
First English Edition: 2015

(Published by arrangement with the Lotus Press, USA)

Published by
NEW AGE BOOKS
A-44 Naraina Industrial Area, Phase-I
New Delhi (India)-110 028
E-mail: nab@newagebooksindia.com
Website: www.newagebooksindia.com

Library of Congress Cataloging-in-Publication Data
Kshirsagar, Manisha
ISBN 978-81-7822-487-9
Includes foreword, author's note, appendix, resources, references by chapter, acknowledgements, glossary of terms
Ayurveda/Beauty

For Sale in South Asia Only

Printed and published by
RP Jain for NAB Printing Unit
A-44, Naraina Industrial Area
Phase-I, New Delhi-110 028. India

TABLE OF CONTENTS

Table of Contents

Table of Contents

Foreword

BEAUTY AND ANANDA

Saundarya, the blissful form of inner beauty is every woman's celebration! Beauty manifests as splendor, magnificence, exquisiteness and loveliness of the heart, mind, body, soul and spirit. Since time immemorial woman has celebrated the art of beauty, unfolding its finer nuances on the canvas of her soul.

Everything arises from Ananda or bliss in yogic thought, which is the creative power behind the entire universe, and comprises the inner essence of all life. Everything is meant to be beautiful, not as a mere expression of human vanity but as a manifestation of Divine joy and the Divine love that pervades all eternity.

If our sense of happiness dwells within us, that true happiness will be transmitted outwardly as graciousness, a natural beauty and luster of face, flexibility of the body, and grace in movement. If our sense of happiness is on the outer side the stress and strains of our desires and expectations will negatively impact how we feel, how we move, and how we appear to others.

The body is meant to be beautiful but in a natural way, the same way we find beauty in trees and flowers, the Earth, water and skies. This true beauty of the body is only possible when we have peace in the mind, a receptivity of the heart, and an inner connection to our own immortal soul and spirit.

SHAKTI AND BEAUTY

Shakti is the cosmic force of the Divine feminine that keeps all forces in nature moving and transforming. It is the healing and nurturing power of the five elements - Earth, Fire, Water, Ether and Space. Shakti is the dynamic cosmic power behind the seasons and the growth and fertility cycles of all creatures, great and small. Inwardly this Shakti aids us in healing, creativity and the unfoldment of a higher awareness and unity consciousness.

Each one of us has some portion of this Shakti of nature and can develop it further through special practices, as taught in Yoga and Ayurveda. This Shakti is mainly reflected in the power of what is called in Yoga, the Akarshana Shakti, the capacity to attract and draw things to you at the level of the heart. It can also draw to us nature's special healing powers and allow us to transmit these to others, as well as to benefit from them on our own.

In every indigenous or ancient culture the Divine feminine beauty and power was revered through sacred rituals and special offerings. Worshipping the Mother Goddess or Shakti is pivotal to experiencing the bliss and abundance of beauty. Early revering of the Mother can be dated back to the spring celebrations to honor Rhea, the Mother of the Gods in ancient Greece, with offerings of honey-cakes and flowers.

In ancient traditions, beauty was a reflection of the five great elements understanding the sacred energy of fire, wind and water wafting through endless space manifesting earth's bounty of plants, fruits and flowers.

As beauty reflects the revelation of the Divine in nature, yogic wisdom is a doorway to the greater universe of consciousness that both embraces and transcends all forms of bliss. Satyam Shivam Sundaram epitomizes the yogic view of beauty where satyam is truth which creates the Shiva stillness in our being of harmony experiencing all of life as beauty and bliss.

Rejuvenative Ayurveda and Beauty

The greater part of rasayana or rejuvenation is not the body but of the heart, mind and spirit, which requires that we align ourselves with the cosmic forces of bliss, creativity and vitality. Ayurveda unfolds the ancient Vedic wisdom of rejuvenation and immortality reflecting every aspect of health and beauty. Rasayana begins with the skin which forms our first line of contact with the outer environment and sensitivities. The skin often reflects the nutrition of the body as a whole, the condition of our plasma and of the digestive tract as well as our emotional temperament.

The face and skin holds a certain Tejas or luster, reflecting the glow of our vital energy. The face has the highest number of nerve endings in the body which must be cherished with tender loving care. The scalp, head and hair allow us to absorb sensations and oils that can directly affect the brain and nervous system. Gentle nurturing and handling of the face and skin is not about mere cosmetics but about optimal inner and outer well-being.

Sacred Sankalpa for Beatific Bliss

The unfolding of our blissful nature as beauty is the result of a deeper Sankalpa or sacred intention. Sankalpa must resonate the deeper bliss which encompasses our wishes, desires, and will power. Everything we attempt in life rests upon our motivations in one form or another. We are the manifestation of our personal sankalpa, wishes and intentions.

For every seeker of beauty, the harnessing, nurturing and cultivation of Sankalpa is essential for inner growth on a beautiful fulfilling Yogic path. To discover the purity of our soul, the inner Shakti of beauty, we must first create a strong Sankalpa or sacred intent, unveiling the depths of our soul beauty.

Inspiring The Art of Yoga Shakti

Over the past several decades I have been sharing and teaching women the yogic secrets of harmony and happiness, through various books, programs and retreats throughout the world, inspiring the art of Yoga Shakti. We see a lot of restlessness and sadness in women today, owing to the great expectations put upon them to be successful in a career, but also to have a good family life, and to remain ever beautiful and attractive.

The cosmetic business has filled this expectation of beauty for women with a vast array of products that are difficult for the average woman to navigate through. It is easy to observe that many of the cosmetics women take have side effects and are not good for them long term, often containing various deleterious chemicals. That is why a natural Ayurvedic alternative is so helpful and necessary for cultivating and nurturing a blissful and beautiful heart-mind-body and spirit. These involve not only cosmetics but an entire life-style to promote health, beauty and ananda encompassing the grace of Shakti.

Enchanting Beauty
Is a must read for every enchantress!

Manisha Kshirsagar is a highly respected Ayurvedic doctor and author from India, living in the United States, and has an extensive practice and teaching career. Her husband Dr. Suhas Kshirsagar is a similarly highly regarded Ayurvedic author, teacher, and practitioner. Manisha brings into her writings special secrets of Ayurveda from her background in India and her many years of clinical work in India and the United States. I have been fortunate to know her for a number of years, witnessing her skill as both a teacher and a healer.

Manisha's book Enchanting Beauty discusses the important role of beauty in Ayurveda, India's traditional natural healing system, for both health and happiness, which is seldom examined properly or in a modern context. She offers many practical tools and insights to enhance natural beauty and inner well-being, including special plans and programs for improving our lives on all levels.

Yet her book is much more than an examination of physical beauty. It helps us understand the feminine spirit and the important issues and stages in a modern woman's life from childhood to old age, when so much is expected of women both in the family and in society. Her book is a good reference guide for women's health from a holistic perspective.

Manisha takes a broad view of her subject helping us understand both inner and outer beauty, not only in how we appear but how we feel and express ourselves, enabling us to gain the optimal beauty possible for our own unique body and personality. Her book explains how we can create a foundation for a beautiful life in a proper Ayurvedic life-style that starts with diet but extends to our entire life experience. She guides us in bringing greater beauty and grace into the world in which we live, which is certainly needed today and without which social harmony is not possible.

In short, Enchanting Beauty helps us reclaim our true nature of bliss and beauty. Manisha shows that there is a viable and effective alternative to some of the modern day cosmetic treatments and plastic surgery, through inculcating the wisdom of Ayurveda in our daily lives. Manisha inspires us in the direction of transformation through cultivating our inner beauty to heal ourselves and the world at large.

My heartfelt prayer today is that we embrace the Yoga Shakti or inner power of Yoga to draw us once again into our Divine source, where we all celebrate the natural flow of beauty and bliss through aligning ourselves with nature's healing powers and divine grace.

Yogini Shambhavi Chopra

Author - Yogini: Unfolding the Goddess Within and Yogic Secrets of the Dark Goddess (www.vedanet.com - Shambhavi.yogini@gmail.com)

Santa Fe, New Mexico

[illegible] old [illegible] in the body and in society. Her book is a broad reference guide for optimal health from a holistic perspective.

Mandhata takes a broad view of her subject helping us understand both inner and outer beauty, not only in how we appear but how we feel and express ourselves, enabling us to gain the optimal beauty possible for our own unique body and personality. Her book explains how we can create a foundation for a beautiful life [illegible] [illegible] beauty and [illegible] grace [illegible] in the world in which we live, which is currently needed today and without which social harmony is not possible.

In short, Enchanting Beauty helps us reclaim our true nature of bliss and beauty. Mandhata shows that there is a viable and effective alternative [illegible] modern [illegible] treatments [illegible]

[illegible] lives. [illegible] the [illegible] and [illegible]

My heartfelt prayer today is that we [illegible] the [illegible] of inner power of Yoga to draw us once again into our Divine source, where we all celebrate the natural flow of beauty and bliss through aligning ourselves with nature's healing powers and divine grace.

Yogini Shambhavi Chopra

[illegible]

[illegible]

Santa Fe, New Mexico

Author's Note

I was born and raised in India. I had a happy childhood. Even though we did not have a big house and we were not rich, we were content living together in our joint family. My father had a job, which required frequent traveling. Changing neighborhoods and schools made me and my brother patient and flexible. In spite of the challenges in our family, we learned to "move on" nonetheless.

In my growing years, my grandmother always had a natural solution for pimples and rashes, eye irritations or problems with our hair. She pulled remedies we needed right out of her kitchen cupboards! Later, when I went on to study Ayurveda professionally, I realized that everything I had learned from her was in line with Nature.

After I got married I began traveling with my husband to many different countries teaching Ayurveda and Yoga. It was a total cultural shock! The vast differences in cultural customs were mind-boggling to me. I began to probe deeper into what I was feeling and asked myself some serious questions about what life meant and plight of being a woman. Little did I know, that many years later, these inquiries would become the foundation for the book that you now hold in your hand.

In my clinical practice I contemplated questions like: "Why did women feel that they were somehow unworthy after the menopause?" "What made young ladies have fears around their appearance and such a lack of self-esteem?" "Why did women feel vulnerable in their relationships? "Why were they so stressed?" In my view, women hold such an important and valuable role in society. They are the ones who breastfeed all of humanity and civilizations are cradled in their laps. So how did these women not know and understand this about their nature?

That was when I realized that the message of *inner beauty* needed to be heard. I wanted women to remember their innate worth and beauty. I wanted them to be able to cultivate peace, forgiveness, gratitude and compassion in their lives so that their relationships could heal. I wanted them to understand the *true* beauty within themselves and others so that they could live their lives with confidence.

As an Ayurvedic doctor, many women come to see me complaining about their menstruation, dry skin, wrinkles, headaches, hair loss, eye problems and so much more. I realized that although the modern world is highly developed with a technological growth, the art of the natural living was still missing! In spite of the wealth of resources available in the west, women don't know that they are abusing the laws of Nature. They just don't know how to take care of themselves. As a result, their bodies suffer. This is when I knew I had to share my concept of *outer beauty*. I wanted women to have simple, natural, go-to solutions at their fingertips.

Finally, my concept of *lasting beauty* was developed out of the need for women to practice prevention and anti-aging strategies as soon as they possibly could! In my practice I see women who have plenty of resources to buy organic food, go to yoga classes, exercise at a nice gym and learn meditation, but nevertheless, they fail to do these things. Even if a woman is fortunate enough to be endowed with good health and external beauty, if she does not proactively take care of herself in her younger years, then as she ages, her beauty will not endure. Women are neglecting the lifestyle that is needed to prevent illness and maintain *lasting beauty.*

If women want to add quality years onto their lives and ensure that their beauty endures throughout time, then they must learn to abide by the rules of longevity that Ayurveda has set forth. They have to empower themselves with knowledge and discipline. Money can't buy them health. Expensive anti-wrinkle serums are of no use if women wait until their 40's and 50's to start paying attention to how they look. Health is not in a bottle or cream. It is not an exotic herb. It is found in a positive mindset and a lifestyle that exudes *enchanting, lasting beauty*.

Finally, I want to offer a message about simplicity. Somehow in our modern lifestyle, we have forgotten our priorities. We need to simplify our lives as much as possible. Uphold strong morals and values in your household and place simple, nourishing food on your tables. Give your loved ones the space and support they need to realize their *inner beauty*. And finally, simply return home to the *inner beauty* that lies within yourself and you will become a role model of *enchanting beauty*.

May we all be beautiful
May we all learn to appreciate the beauty in everything
May we all radiate enchanting beauty forever...

With love,
Manisha Kshirsagar

Enchanting Beauty

Chapter 1

BEAUTY

Looking Deeply at the Nature of Beauty

The Wisdom of Beauty

Real beauty has been buried, entombed, confused and forgotten in our modern day climate. Excessive glamour, razzle-dazzle and airbrushing have lead to serious misinterpretations of what beauty means, where it comes from, and how to get it. The media has overwhelmed our instinctive connection with the nature of authentic beauty so that we are left with only a veneer of beauty's character. What we need to recover is the *wisdom* of beauty – the timeless, universal and absolute *truth* that exists in our palpable, sensual experience of beauty. I want to share this with you, and remind you of what you already know deep inside. I want you to taste the sweetness of the *real* beauty that exists within yourself so that you can then come to see it in others and in the world as a whole. When you find this precious gem of beauty, your life will be filled with magic and magnificence because you'll remember, finally, the truth of who you are and the miracle of your life.

It is our birthright to experience this profound understanding of beauty, but in a world of so much pretending, masquerading and twisting beauty into something other than what it truly is, we need somewhere to turn to that harbors the truth. We need a practical, step-by-step, guide that will show us how to go about unwatering the real beauty in our lives. That's why I would like to share this book with you. In the coming chapters, I will present you with three simple stages that will lead you through exactly how to uncover the genuine beauty that exists within you and all around you.

To begin with, the first and foremost stage out of the three entails a personal process of allowing our *inner beauty* to resurface in our awareness. *Inner beauty* encompasses all of our virtuous qualities that stem from a strong sense of self worth, value and respect. Then, after a secure foundation based in *inner beauty* has been established, a natural and healthy inclination to care of our *outer beauty* or physical body ensues. Finally, with the ongoing care of the *inner* and *outer* aspects of our beauty, we are organically inspired to make an even deeper commitment to living a wholesome, balanced life. In doing so, we approach the mastery of beauty or what I like to call *lasting beauty.*

These are the three platforms upon which I expound on the nature of real beauty as it exists as an expression of truth, virtue and love. Each of these three steps is rich in wisdom and infused with the insights from the ancient, holistic medicine of India known as *Ayurveda* . As a doctor of Ayurvedic medicine myself, and a devoted esthetician, I aim to impart to you both the sacred and profound principals of beauty, alongside with its more tangible, and practical applications as well.

Finally, to further enrich our journey together, I set out to interview over twenty women, eighty years old and above, from all over the world. Each of these women have generously shared with me their pearls of wisdom on life, love, happiness and beauty. Their words are priceless - infused with the kind of knowledge that can only come from a lifetime of experience. You'll find their messages scattered among these pages, cheering you on and reminding you of what's really important along the road to enchanting beauty.

Waking Up to Beauty

Before we dive into our exploration of the concepts of *inner, outer* and *lasting beauty,* I'd first like to invite you to come with me on an early morning walk. It's the walk I take almost every morning. It is here that we will begin our journey into discovering the wisdom of beauty together.

The air outside is crisp and laden with moisture. It is quiet. No one is up yet. The clouds in the sky are like blankets wrapped around the homes that line the streets, keeping everyone tucked warmly in their beds, peacefully sleeping away the early hours. There is something exhilarating about being up before anyone else and hearing only the sound of silence on the streets. Satisfied, you take a deep breath and listen to the sound of your feet on the pavement. Then, slowly, a slight smile crosses over your face and you find that your pace quickens. You're beginning to feel the inspiration that lives inside the newness of this day. The morning is *alive* and you are *alive* with it.

As you continue to walk, your energy only builds. You can feel the strength in your body as you decide to approach the mountain ahead. Inhale, exhale, inhale, exhale; your breathing is in rhythm with your steps. Your chest expands and contracts. Your lungs are lifted out of their cage, as if they've grown wings to fly you up the mountain. As you turn the corner, nearing the peak, you find yourself slowing down. You can sense that what is just beyond the bend is going to take your breath away. And surely, it does. A stunning view of the eastern sunrise settles over your eyes. Vibrant colors flood the sky summoning the coming of a new day - blood oranges, crisp reds, and shy lavenders with bold punctuations of bright yellow, against a pale blue backdrop. As you stand there in total awe, your hand instinctively moves to cover your heart. Sweet tears swell in your eyes, for what you behold in this moment is like nothing else. You feel yourself overtaken by the miracle of life unfolding before you, and finally, you understand the meaning of beauty.

Now, coming out of this picture of our beautiful morning walk together, I want you to consider an alternate scenario for a moment. What if we go on the same walk, with the same type of stunning sunrise, but this time, on a different morning? At 5:45am you wake up to the blaring sound of your alarm and begrudgingly roll out of bed. You're tired and you've worked overtime this week. As you force yourself to put on your sneakers and begin your morning walk, you feel as though you're already at work. Your mind is swimming with all the projects on your to-do list and churning over the words you'll use to approach your boss about that raise and summer time off. Physically you're there, walking along the street, but really, you're somewhere else entirely. You take no notice of the day as it is innocently beginning all around you. To you, the only things that are real are the thoughts swirling inside of your head - anything else takes second place. So finally, as you approach the top of the peak and turn slightly towards the east as you always do, you don't even care to look up at the sunrise. Your brow remains furrowed down, looking at the ground in discontentment and aggravation. But even if you were to pause for a brief moment and look up at the sunrise, to you, it would we bare. Its colors would be dulled, its performance merely mediocre, and whole event nothing more than mechanical. To you, in this moment, there is no measure of beauty that could ever impress; for you are lost in your mind's illusions and you are host to your own oblivion. You are blind to beauty.

Ask yourself:

"Where am I missing the beauty in my life?"
Might I be overlooking beauty in myself or in someone around me?

I have experienced both of these morning walks – the one that heralds beauty from the mountain top and the other that clouds it despite the incredible vista. As you put yourself in my shoes, you might have been able to palpably experience the contrast between the two walks I am so familiar with.

In the first scenario you woke up present in your life and in your body. You were available for beauty to expose itself to you on your walk, and it did. In the second scenario you arose in a tight knot, constricted by the worries and fears of your mind. You were closed off to beauty of the sunrise that was begging to be let in. In either case the sunrise was spectacular; the only difference was in your perceptivity.

This is why fully knowing and understanding beauty in its essence is an art form. It takes being present and connected to both yourself and to the universe as a whole. When this happens there is a dynamic harmony that flows between you and the objects of your perception. It is as if whatever you shed your eyes upon unfurls itself in exquisite, delicate beauty. This most definitely was true in the case of our first walk together. Objectively speaking (if that is really even possible), it is quite likely that there were many other sunrises that year that had deeper shades of red, more radiant purples and better, shinier golds. But on that morning, none of that mattered to you. The sunrise you witnessed before you was like none other. You let yourself be vulnerable to the essence of its beauty so it penetrated your being and touched your heart.

Recognizing real beauty takes the ability to look deeply. Only when we use our whole bodies, minds, spirits and senses can we see through the superficial and attain the kind of vision that reveals the truth of beauty. That's because beauty is something that reaches far beyond what can be seen by the eyes alone. It travels into the realm of experience where it imparts a sense of connection to life, and therein engraves its signature onto our hearts. According to Webster's Dictionary, beauty is "the quality in a person (or thing) that provides the highest pleasure to the body, mind and senses." According to this definition beauty is an actual *sensation.* Our sense of touch, smell and sight are nourished when they are open to receiving the pleasure of a morning walk. The engagement of the senses therefore, results in an overall *feeling* of beauty. When we see a rose in full blossom, we find it to be beautiful because of its intoxicating scent, the perfect texture of its soft petals and the shape of its bloom. When we see a peacock, we find him to be beautiful not just because of his magnificent colors but also because of how he moves with such grace and dances while he so confidently displays his array of feathers. Our appreciation and observation of all of these various attributes collectively compile to give us the experience of beauty, *if* we are available to notice. When we allow our senses to fill with the energy of life and creation, that's when our eyes are opened and the magnificence of beauty can finally be revealed.

Sadly, often it isn't until we are at the edge of life, perhaps battling fatal illness or recovering from a serious accident, that we finally allow ourselves to be open enough to let beauty come in and fill up our senses. Most of the time, it's just too easy to inadvertently dismiss the beauty of our lives, our loved ones, and ourselves; even if only by way of meaningless distraction. A child however, lives with total availability to the impact of beauty. If you've ever spent time around a child, you know that their mind is in awe and wonder of life. They find magic everywhere, in everything. With the innocence of their hearts and the purity in their minds, they are able to see what we so often forget to look for – *real* beauty. We get confused, thinking beauty is simply the way something or someone looks. Yes, we can see beauty with our eyes, but t*rue* beauty can only be seen from our hearts. For instance, say there is a mother of a 3 year old child who happens to forget to apply her makeup. She may feel self-conscious, thinking that she is not as beautiful today as she was yesterday. To her young adoring child however, there is no difference in the beauty of his mother. She is no less extraordinary to him today than she was yesterday. That's because her son looks at her without judgment, preconceptions

or expectations that she should be anything other than exactly how she is. How could he? For to him, she is everything that beautiful could ever be. Her beauty comes from his love for her – something makeup could never replace. Those eyes made of innocence and inspired by love, wonder and awe, are the only kinds of eyes that are fit to see the truth of beauty. They are the eyes that we all need to adopt if we want to restore the beauty within ourselves and the world.

Tri-Beauty

Beauty as an Expression of Value

For most of us simply saying the word "beauty" conjures up a myriad of images in our minds. Most immediately, we might think of a strappingly handsome young man or an elegant woman in a long red dress. We also could have called to mind the image of a delicate white rose or pale pink sunset. Indeed, all these things are in fact beautiful, but as we've begun to allude, the term "beauty" itself means so much more than what we might see at first glance.

In my experience as a Doctor of India's traditional medicine *Ayurveda*, I've seen many women in a clinical setting. I hear their stories and I'm saddened at just how many express fears at being disregarded by their employers or husbands if they do not keep their body fit or remain "attractive enough." What is even more disheartening is that these women are not without reason for their concern. Research shows that overweight women tend to earn less than women who are within the normal range for their weight-height ratio. Interestingly enough, this applies to women only; the same is not true for men. In fact, it is exactly the opposite. Overweight men tend to earn more money than men of normal weight. I think this paradox is a reflection of how we value the sexes. Men are valued for putting in long hours at the desk and women for their physical appearance. It is a tragedy that such long term commitments like employment or marriage should be contingent upon a woman's outer representation alone. Is there no value a woman holds in society beyond what just meets the eyes? We are failing to see the extraordinary value that women bring to all of their engagements – professional and personal.

Sincere

In all that you do, make it come from the heart. People around you will sense your genuinity and they'll be comforted in your presence.

Unfortunately, if society under-appreciates any aspect of a women's beauty, then she herself risks starting to feel as though she is not beautiful. She may sense she is unworthy because her *outer beauty* doesn't meet the superficial standards imposed upon her by cultural expectations. Suddenly she begins to question her value as a wife or employee because her skin is starting to sag, her buttock is not firm enough or her bra size is too small. If women equate their value to their external appearance, it is a tragedy beyond compare. The consequences range from problems like eating disorders, to major depression or even suicide.

"Women should never look outward for approval."

~ *Lora Boswell, born 1931* ~

It is not a coincidence that a women's sense of value is equated with her feeling of being beautiful. It is hard to separate the two perceptions. When we feel appreciated in our lives, we feel valuable. When we feel valued, we feel beautiful, because we feel confident that we have something worthwhile to offer to the world. So beauty is merely a reflection of the value we believe we have. I have seen that a woman receives her sense of value (and thus beauty) from two places: both her internal awareness and the external, cultural messages she receives from soceity.

First, let's take a look at the external information a woman gets from her environment. For instance, if her husband is appreciative of her and she feels his love, affection and gratitude and if she also has children who adore her and think highly of her as the "queen of the household," then this woman will likely have a solid sense of worth. She will understand her own value because she is treated with admiration and respect by those around her. Naturally, this translates into a secure sense of being beautiful. Her environmental input has penetrated into her internal sense of beauty. In this case, she is a by-product of the value placed on her by her community. Feeling this value and appreciation, she will flourish in life.

In the opposite situation, there may be a woman who is abused by her husband and disrespected by her children. Even if this woman is quite lovely on the outside, it is unlikely that she will feel very beautiful at all. This is because her external world does not give her the message that she has any value, and without value it is difficult to feel beautiful.

Love

Love is the basis of beauty. Live with love for yourself and for others and beauty will be yours.

The Three Levels of Beauty

Beauty is so much more than having a pretty body, a lovely face, or nice hair. Although those features are indeed valuable, they are only *part* of the picture. Take for instance the experience of meeting someone who may not immediately appear outwardly attractive but their personality makes them an extraordinary delight to be around. We're drawn to being in their company because *who they are* is attractive. Their *inner beauty* shines forth and it lights up their external features, making them appear beautiful. On the other hand, it is just as likely that we've had the experience of encountering someone who is strikingly gorgeous, but awful to be around! In this case, their beauty only runs skin deep and we would prefer not to spend our time with them. You see, when our perception of someone is positive because we genuinely appreciate who they are, then we are opened up to seeing their true beauty. This is what I like to call seeing the *inner beauty* in someone.

> When asked, "What is the definition of a beautiful women?" *Phyllis Katz, born in 1918 in Minneapolis replied,*"What you think inside and what you do for other people. That's what makes you beautiful."

Attractive

When you view yourself as beautiful from the inside out and you know your value, then others will begin to see that in you as well. No matter what your outer appearence, you'll become attractive because of your inner radience, confidence and kindness!

As you can see, if our *inner beauty* is strong, then we will naturally see a change in the way people interpret our external beauty. That's why when we give love to others, we expose our *inner beauty* and seamlessly, we become more attractive to them. Plus, as we offer our inner virtues of compassion and kindness to others, then we organically end up doing the same for ourselves as well! One way that this manifests is in our physical bodies. As we nourish our bodies, we further enhance our *outer beauty* and the *inner beauty* we cultivated will light up our features. After all, what is a pretty face without a glow? As you can see, cultivating *inner beauty* is a win-win situation. But wait, it doesn't even stop there! Once both our inner and *outer beauty* are continually reinforcing one another, then we inevitably stumble upon a type of beauty that is ageless. It endures throughout antiquity and sticks with us for the long haul.

I like to call this beauty *lasting beauty*.

"I BELIEVE THAT BEAUTY COMES FORM WITHIN – RADIATING A SENSE OF KINDNESS, CARING, INTELLIGENCE, INNER CALM."
~ Juneva Lanser born 1930, San Francisco, CA ~

In sum, there are three levels of beauty to consider throughout the conversation we'll be having together in this book: (1) *inner beauty*, (2) *outer beauty* and (3) *lasting beauty*. Out of these three, as you'll come to see, *inner beauty* is the primary, most fundamental and pivotal piece of the puzzle - without which the other two components could not be realized.

Inner Beauty {Gunam}	Personal sense of self love and value which manifests through the exemplification of virtuous qualities.
Outer Beauty {Roopam}	Physical beauty as an expression of healthy, vibrant physiology.
Lasting Beauty {Vayastyag}	Enduring beauty that comes from a healthy, balanced lifestyle and the continual maintenance of both *inner* and *outer beauty*.

Inner Beauty

I'd like to first consider the internal component of a women's sense of value and thus, beauty. The inner qualities that she herself cultivates have the capacity to give her profound beauty, whether or not she looks like a super model on the outside. This is the kind of beauty that comes from the inside and radiates outward. If a woman is forgiving, kind, caring, confident, loving, strong and good-man natured, then her internal beauty will shine through the character that she presents to the world. As a result, the external world comes to value and respect her even more! Her virtuous behavior allows her family, culture and society to appreciate her for who she really is.

"A beautiful woman is someone who is conscious of her presence and gives off an aura of confidence in herself and her actions. She may or may not be well groomed or well dressed, but it feels good to be around her."
~ Dhaj Sumner, born in 1930, New Zealand ~

Kindness

Take the time that is needed to offer a warm "Hello" to your neighbor, or to bring some soup to a sick friend. Even the little things make a big difference.

We might be able to think of some good examples of men and women in the media today who might not meet the typical standard of beauty in modern society, but whose redeeming personalities have given them great beauty in the eye of the world. They are seen as highly attractive and are sought after worldwide just so people can be in their presence. These people could be talented actors or actresses; they could be talk show hosts, religious saints, philanthropists, or even esteemed doctors and healers. Whoever they are, the common denominator among them all is a profound inner strength, passion and love that emanates from them, out into the world. Their personalities are magnetic. People flock to be around them because they feel good in their presence. It is clear that these people recognize the good within themselves. They appreciate their own value and what they have to offer to the world. Because they see this beauty in themselves, it is easier for others to notice it in them as well. They reflect externally what they feel about themselves internally. Plus, just by virtue of being accustomed to seeing the positive qualities in themselves, they'll automatically find it in others as well.

"IF MONEY IS LOST - NOTHING IS LOST.
IF HEALTH IS LOST - SOMETHING IS LOST.
BUT IF CHARACTER IS LOST - EVERYTHING IS LOST."

Hindu Proverb
Quoted by Kulkarni, born 1931 India

This is how the cultivation of *inner beauty* acts as a system of positive feedback. As we've seen, inner qualities of self respect broadcast externally through acts of kindness and meaningful connection with others. This creates a positive response from the environment (like people wanting to spend more time with you) which feedsbacks to reinforces your own inner beauty. The more we value ourselves, the more the outer world will value us as well. As a result, we end up feeling even more beautiful all the time! We all want to be a part of this positive feedback loop! It is the chain reaction that leads to long *lasting beauty*.

COMPARE AND CONTRAST: INNER, OUTER AND LASTING LEVELS OF BEAUTY

Inner beauty will always grow as long as we genuinely respect and love ourselves. We may not be in control of how we look on the outside, but we do have jurisdiction over the inner qualities we cultivate. *Inner beauty* is real, authentic beauty. It radiates from our inner state of being through our consciousness. Ancient Vedic wisdom says that true beauty is expressed by the purity of the words that come from your lips:

> "KEYURA NA VIBHUSHAYANTI PURUSHAM....
> VAGBHUSHANAM BHUSHANAM...."
>
> *~Niti-shatak ~*

> "RARE FLOWERS, ARMLETS, ORNAMENTS, PEARL NECKLACES, JEWELS, CEREMONIAL BATHS AND PASTES LIKES CHANDANAM ARE NOT THE TRUE ORNAMENTS TO A PERSON; THE REAL DECORATION THAT BRINGS OUT THE BEAUTY OF A PURUSHA (MAN/WOMAN) ARE THEIR WORDS."

If we value who we are in essence (on the inside) then naturally we will take good care of our *outer beauty*. In other words, if we truly appreciate ourselves, we are more likely to eat a good diet, keep good company, manage our stress, nourish our skin and keep our bodies active. As you cultivate your internal beauty you feed the innate drive to properly take care of your external body. In this way, our *outer beauty* truly becomes a mirror of our *inner beauty*. Conversely, when our efforts to maintain *outer beauty* don't arise from a sense of self-love, we might do things like get multiple cosmetic surgeries or spend an extensive amount of money on makeup and hair-dye. However, when we are authentically caring for ourselves from a place of self-love, we produce a kind of beauty that is durable, long lasting and self-perpetuating.

To sum it up: the secret of *outer beauty* is good food, water, fitness, sleep, and activities. The secret of *inner beauty* is bliss, contentment, and peace. And finally, if you can maintain both of these at all times, you can reverse the aging process and maintain *everlasting beauty*.

> "A beautiful woman is one who is at peace with herself; settled and contented with life."
>
> ~ *Ann B. of Los Angeles, CA born in 1929* ~

Level of Beauty	Sign	Maintenance and Care
Inner Beauty {Gunam}	A mind and heart that are in harmony. A person who is loving, caring, sharing, kind and courageous	Use techniques like self-reflection and journaling, meditation and qi-gong or support groups and time in nature. All of these things sooth your spirit and align you with the divine Goddess within.
Outer Beauty {Roopam}	Hair and nails are strong. Eyes are bright and skin is pure, smooth and clean. There is grace in movements and posture.	Maintain a strong metabolism (or 'agni') by regular exercise and meal times. Ensure proper digestion and the resulting purity of your blood and skin will ensue. Your health comes from balanced physiology.
Lasting Beauty {Vayastyag}	A long, healthy, vibrant life well into the later years (a.k.a. healthy aging)	Live into the fullness of your unique constitution. Always honor the transitions in your life and your inner Divine power. Changes with the seasons. Use your senses wisely. Develop good lifestyle habits.

Personal Application

You may be asking yourself:

"Where do I stand in my own heart and mind within the spectrum of inner, outer and lasting beauty?"

As a woman, this is a worthwhile question to genuinely reflect upon. To take a survey of how you really feel, check out the quiz below. Then, check out the feedback according to the answers you've chosen.

Please note that however you answer the chart below, you must remember that your personal perception of your own beauty is dictated by three things: (1) the environmental stimulus you receive, (2) what physical characteristics you may find beautiful according to your cultural background, and (3) your own degree of self-love and acceptance.

Question 1	Yes?
Do you feel you were born with *outer beauty*?	☐ See 1A
Do you wish you were more physically attractive?	☐ See 1B
Question 2	**Yes?**
Do you feel you have strong *inner beauty* because of who you are as a person?	☐ See 2A
Do you feel your value as a person is lacking? Does it seem like you're just never good enough no matter what you do?	☐ See 2B

Question 3	Yes?
Are you maintaining a balanced state of physical, emotional and mental health?	☐ See 3A
Do you think you've failed to maintain either your inner or *outer beauty* through the years? Do you have a physical or emotional hang up that is sabotaging your *lasting beauty*?	☐ See 3B

Survey Responces

1A

EXTERNALLY BEAUTY ABOUNDS:

You are fortunate enough to be born with external beauty. Because of that, it is important to be aware that you could be at risk of underestimating the value of your internal beauty.

If your answers indicate that you feel you do have external beauty, then it is your job to make sure your inner qualities do not go unattended. It is too easy to rely on external beauty alone to make up the perception of your value (after all, our culture supports this kind of beauty as the only one that really matters). It is more important to let your worth shine from within. Make this a priority. Kindness, friendliness and sincerity naturally attract people to you. No matter how beautiful your appearances may be, if you are still uptight, tense, or irritable, people will steer clear of you.

2A

EXTERNAL BEAUTY IS LIMITED:

You are at risk of forgetting your value as a person and misunderstanding external beauty to be the only way to be and feel beautiful.

Even though everyone is beautiful in his or her own way, sadly many of us are insecure about the way we look. If your answers show that you do not feel you have much external beauty then please do not be discouraged. If your physical features are less than what you think of as perfect, I suggest starting to change the angle in which you're viewing yourself. Instead of focusing on the outward appearance, look through a deeper lens and cultivate inner qualities (or *gunam)* like kindness, softness, love and compassion. Then, supplement these natural qualities with beautiful physical qualities (or *roopam)* like graceful movements, good posture, a relaxed manner and calm voice. Put your attention on cultivating internal beauty of character and let that emanate outward. When you do this, you will be highly attractive in the best possible sense and you'll start feeling truly beautiful!

2A INTERNAL BEAUTY ABOUNDS:

You have a strong sense of internal beauty and likely that translates into outer beauty as well.

In this situation you can breathe a sigh of relief. You have been blessed with a healthy and enduring perception of your beauty and value in this world. Many women struggle to find this, so count your blessing that you already have a grasp on it! No matter what your age, occupation, or status, you have the tools you need to maintain a true beauty that lasts. Keep your sights on your internal landscape so that you continue to care for your body mind and spirit, and your beauty will never end! Let your light shine on!

2B INTERNAL BEAUTY IS LIMITED:

You are not seeing the beauty that lies within.

Be tender with yourself. Learning to appreciate your inner virtues is a personal journey that doesn't always happen overnight.

To support your efforts, make sure to surround yourself with people in your environment who will lift you up and remind you of your true beauty. Consider becoming part of a group that shares similar morals and values as you do. This way you can feel appreciated for what you believe and who you really are. Along the same vein, it would be wise to remove yourself from relationships in your life in which you are not fully valued. Finally, make sure to fill your senses with images of women whose beauty comes from the inside out, and seek to emulate them.

3A LASTING BEAUTY ABOUNDS:
You have achieved the utmost beauty.

Congratulations! You have beauty that lasts – a kind of beauty that will endure across all time and space. Your mind and your body are in harmony with one another, which is something we all strive to achieve. You have been blessed with a strong sense of self worth and value and that translates into radiant health and a glowing personality. Your skin shines, your mind is clear, and your heart is open to the world. You fully love and appreciate those around you, and in return, you are fully loved and appreciated as well. You're living within the positive feedback loop of beauty that we all hope to experience: the more you live from your *inner beauty*; the more you see what is beautiful in others; the more you are loved and supported by others; and finally, the more enduring your beauty becomes!

We know that this hasn't always come easily though. You've spent years working hard to care for yourself and cultivate your inner and *outer beauty*. But now you can celebrate knowing that finally, all your introspection and self care has paid off!

3B LASTING BEAUTY IS LIMITED:

You may need to pay more attention to either your inner or outer beauty.

It is easy to neglect an area of self-care in our lives It is not usually the case, but sometimes even when we take good care of our inner lives we may ignore our outer lives. For instance, sometimes people can have a flourishing connection to their Higher Power but never lift their pinky toe to exercise. If our bodies are ignored, then we'll never achieve a beauty that lasts because we are fundamentally unhealthy.

The opposite can be just as true as well. Many times people focus externally on caring for their physical bodies by working out, doing seasonal cleanses or eating well, but they forget to look inside. The state of our minds is what maintains *inner beauty*. If you have a turbulent mind or one that has forgotten its self-worth, it is difficult to achieve *lasting beauty*, even if our bodies look and feel great. At some point, something will break down because the quality of our mind inevitably affects the health of our bodies.

Conclusion

Remember in its truest sense, our beauty is nothing less than a reflection for how we appreciate and value ourselves. At the end of the day, no matter what your view of your current level of beauty happens to be, what is always most important is to focus on your *inner value*. How are you unique? What gifts do you have to offer this world? How can you express yourself more fully? When you live into the answers of these questions, the external world will begin to give you the respect that you deserve as a woman. Then, when that happens, the whole world changes for the better!

Chapter 2

INNER BEAUTY

The Messages of Beauty Seen and Heard

Perception as a Choice

Few of us are aware of the sheer power of our own inner perception. "Inner perception," as I am calling it, is a force that has a pervasive affect on every aspect of our day to day lives. It has such an omnificent influence is in our lives because it is the lens through which we visualize reality. Our inner perception lays the foundation for our interpretation of reality – the way we see the world.

Essentially, our inner perception consists of the collection of beliefs that we have (whether conscious or unconscious) about anything and everything in our lives - including ourselves. Each of these beliefs will affect the way we view any given circumstance, situation, person, place or thing. They selectively determine the information that we ascertain about our reality. They colors the choices we make and even the kinds of experiences we have. Our inner perception drives us to pick the pink shirt instead of the green, or to take that job instead of this one, or even become friends with him, and not her.

I know this all might sound a bit abstract, but stay with me here for a moment. I'll give an example of a story of two lovely ladies; one named Jane and the other named Susan. Both Jane and Susan look at the same box. Jane finds the box to be unappealing and designed poorly. Susan, on the other hand, sees the box as brilliantly crafted and perfect for what she needs. As the day goes on, Jane and Susan both leave the box and go on their merry ways. Unconsciously, each of them has stored an impression of the box in their memories. In their impression, they each have a belief about the quality of the box. Jane possesses a distasteful image in her mind, while Susan has an amicable one. Naturally, as a result of their differing impressions of the box, each of these women will respond differently when they next encounter it. Jane will steer clear of it and Susan will rush to use it. Their perceptions of the box determine not only their beliefs about the box but their future actions in relation to the box as well.

Why is this important? Well, because the same is true of our perception of ourselves. Consider yourself akin to the box. Your inner perception of yourself could then be similar to either Jane's or Susan's. If your perception were like Jane's you would see yourself as less-than worthy. If it were like Susan's, you'd have a clear appreciation for your worth. What matters here is that although the box is the same, the perception is different.

Ask yourself:
"What is my inner perception of myself?

Do you see yourself like Jane sees the box? Or
Do you see yourself like Susan sees the box?

The way we see ourselves is imprinted deep within our minds. Our inner perception of ourselves contains the beliefs we have about our value and worth as women in the world. The foundation of our inner perception determines the actions we take on our own behalf and how we show up in life. It is the foundation for our *inner beauty* because it is a reflection of our sense of self-worth and value.

The good news is that if we become aware of our inner perceptions we automatically have the power to change them. We can take off the glasses that don't work for us and put on new lenses so that we see ourselves more clearly.

Like Susan, we can choose to cultivate beliefs about ourselves that are appreciative instead of self-demeaning. We can ask our Jane-like perception to step back and reconsider for a moment. It is up to us to uncover the negative beliefs we haev about ourselves. This way we can begin to plant new seeds of self-love which will allow our *inner beauty* to grow and flourish.

MENTAL CLARITY

STAY ACTIVE, EAT WELL AND TEND TO YOUR INNER PSYCHE. ALL THESE THINGS WILL ENSURE YOU MAKE GOOD CHOICES IN YOUR LIFE BASED ON PROPER DISCRIMINATION.

THE MESSAGES WE SPEAK: THE POWER OF THE MIND-BODY CONTINUUM

Every day we get asked the question, "How are you?" numerous times; maybe even hundreds of times depending on our vocation. Most people give little thought to their answer. They automatically respond with a blanket, "Fine, thank you." But others may actually consider what the question is really asking and respond with something more like, "I'm having a bad day; everything is going wrong," or just plain, "I'm awful." Still another group of people might seriously consider the question but respond instead with, "I am great," or "All is well; I have nothing to complain about." We have (1) the responder who numbs-out, (2) the responder who answers negatively and hopelessly and (3) the responder who answers positively. In each of these three scenarios, the responder is repeating their answer to the question, "How are you?" all day long, every day, each day of the year.

FOOD FOR THOUGHT:

BEFORE WE MOVE ON, TAKE A PERSONAL INVENTORY. FOR A MOMENT, ASK YOURSELF HONESTLY:

"Which type of responder am I?"

DO YOUR RESPONSES VARY DEPENDING ON YOUR MOOD?

DO YOU RESPOND TO SOMETHING SEEING

"The glass half full or half empty?"

When I was young, if I ever answered the question "How are you?" with a negative response, my mother would always encourage me to try a different, more positive response. No matter what was going on in my life, she always suggested I respond with, "Yes, thank you; I am well." At first I thought she was asking me to do this to please other people and learn to be 'a good girl,' but later I realized that it wasn't about other people at all. In fact, it was solely about me.

Here's why: if I said over and over again to myself throughout the day, "I am not doing well. I feel sad, I'm full of aches and pains and just don't think life is worth it," how do you think I'd feel by the end of the day? You better believe I would feel depressed, sick and tired! If I tell everyone around me that I'm doing horribly, day in and day out, I'd literally be giving fuel to the flame of inflammation and oxidative stress in my body. My words would be sending information to my body that would reinforce the pathways of malaise and depression within me. The effect of this would stifle my *inner beauty* and compromise the health of my *outer beauty* as well.

> "See and think good thoughts."
>
> ~ *Lois Hanneman of Hollywood CA, born in 1916* ~

On the other hand, if I changed my response and spoke positive words out into the world (and thus, to myself) I would be reinforcing good patterns in my body and mind and bolstering the strength of my *inner beauty*. My mother knew that I had the choice to give either a life-supporting or life-depleting message to myself by simply responding to the question, "How are you?" I could predispose myself for health or for illness, depending on the programming of my mind.

SMILE!
IT'S EASY, NATURAL AND BEST OF ALL…
IT'S TOTALLY FREE!

LET MY SOUL
SMILE THROUGH
MY HEART AND MY
HEART SMILE
THROUGH MY EYES,
THAT I MAY
SCATTER RICH
SMILES IN SAD
HEARTS.

~ *Paramhamsa Yogananda* ~

A WOMAN
WHOSE SMILE
IS OPEN AND
WHOSE EXPRESSION
IS GLAD HAS
A KIND OF BEAUTY
NO MATTER
WHAT SHE
WEARS.

~ *Anne Roiphe* ~

WHAT DOES IT TAKE FOR US TO SMILE?

Really, why can't we? It takes fewer muscles for us to smile and more muscles for us to frown. So come on… take the easier route! A smile is an expression straight from our heart. It is a sign of emotional and mental health and satisfaction. If we smile, it changes our physiology and the whole atmosphere around us. When we smile, we generate happy molecules in our own body and to boot, we make other people happy too! Smiles are contagious. Smiling is the only 'cosmetic' that you'll really ever need. It is sure to enhance your beauty throughout your entire life!

Appreciative

> An attitude of gratitude is the key to a long, healthy life. Focus your attention on just how fortunate you really are and you'll begin to recognize all the plentiful blessings in your life

Every day my patients walk in the door of my clinic and I ask them the question "How are you?" Mind you, these people are not just coming into my office to share a cup of tea and talk about the weather. They often have a major physical crisis that they're coping with. Nonetheless, if they respond negatively to my question, I gently remind them of another option. I explain to them the power of their words and how language is not just a collection of letters and sounds, but a meaningful message to ourselves and the world.

Our words act as prompts to our physical bodies. In fact, the Vedic sciences of India teach us that there are even particular primordial sounds that reverberate deeply within our bodies and have the power to create changes in our physiology. These are called *mantras*. If *mantras* can do this, then certainly the words we speak aloud or silently to ourselves, every day, all the time, will also have a profound effect on our physical health.

In response to the question "How are you?" I encourage my patients use phrases that are life-affirming like, "I'm well and I'm grateful for every day of my life." At the moment they speak those words, right then and there before we've even started our appointment, my patients have taken the first steps on their healing journey. The words they've said out loud send a wondrous message of healing and love directly into every cell of their bodies. That is the power of cultivating *inner beauty* and inner perception.

We need to become aware of the words we are speaking both to ourselves inwardly, and outwardly, to others in reference to ourselves. Our self-talk can be a potent medicine or poison depending on the selection of our words. If *inner beauty* is strong then our messages become medicine, but if it is weak, they become poison.

Honest

Speak words of truth to yourself and to others. Over time, others will begin to have confidence in your integrity and see that you are trustworthy.

The effect of our inner perception is our internal self-talk. In other words, our beliefs about ourselves give way to our own personal, internalized language.This has never been more clearly demonstrated than in autoimmune disease. Studies have shown is that childhood stress and trauma increases the likelihood of developing an autoimmune disease later in life.

One study reported that the stress children endured took on the form of physical, emotional, or sexual abuse; growing up in an environment in which mom or dad is mentally ill or incarcerated, or even just witnessing a tumultuous divorce. In this study, out of a sample of 15,357 people hospitalized for an autoimmune condition, 64% reported at least one of these "adverse childhood experiences," or "ACE's." Furthermore, the numbers of hospitalizations for autoimmune conditions in the person's lifetime directly corresponded to the number of traumatic incidences they endured as a child. In other words, as ACE's increased, so did the emergency visits to the hospital. Therefore, we can conclude that intense childhood stress can actually be a predictor for autoimmune disease developed decades later in life. Likely this is due to the complete disruption of the development of *inner beauty*, or the person's coherent sense of self-worth, and positive self-talk.

Food for Thought:

"Either aloud or silently, what do I say to myself every day?"

Do I hear myself speaking messages of love and support to my body and mind?

or

Do I hear myself speaking harmful messages that are self-degrading?

As children, we look to our environment to determine our place, our role, and our unique value in life. When our environment is inconsistent and full of fear or distress, a child easily can become lost. Indeed, it would be hard to find your way if you grew up receiving negative messages about your worth and identity from the adults and authority figures in your life. Whether or not these messages came directly in the form of words or inadvertently through actions, the information was relayed nonetheless. These children may have heard messages (either aloud or 'in between the lines') like: "You're worthless," "You're not good enough," "You're not important," "Look how ugly and stupid you are," "No one will ever love you," and more. Hearing these kinds of negative messages during such impressionable times, undoubtedly leaves its mark.

Adults afflicted with early childhood trauma may find it difficult to access their sense of sincere, true, *inner beauty*. Self-acceptance and self-love was sabotaged for them at a young age. This makes them blind to their own inner value and their inner self-perception becomes skewed. To make matters worse, the emotional memory of the trauma is buried deep inside them for decades at a time. Those negative messages lodge themselves within the very tissues of their physical bodies. Thus, it is no surprise when these adults develop conditions in which their body sees itself as the enemy and attacks its own cells - an autoimmune condition.

Stress induced autoimmune disease is a profound example of the powerful affect our self-perception and *inner beauty*, can have on our lives. Clearly it not only impacts our minds, but our bodies as well. For better or for worse, the messages we hear and repeat in our minds set the stage for either prosperous health or deleterious disease in our bodies.

The Story of the Ugly Duckling: The Transformation of Inner Perception

Fortunately, we have the power to change our inner perception. We can transform our sense of value, worth and beauty for the better. Think for a moment about the classic story of "The Ugly Duckling." I find it to be a beautiful parable about the transformative power of our self-perception. In India we have a song we sing that recounts the journey of this young, lonely "duck." Every time I sing it, tears come to my eyes because it touches something deep inside of me. It is a potent reminder about how the perception of ourselves determines our sense of self-worth, value, and thus, beauty. So, in case it's been a while since you've heard the great story, I thought it would be worth it to give you a little refresher. Here's how I remember the story of "The Ugly Duckling:"

Once upon a time, before he had even hatched out of his egg, a little baby birdie accidentally got mixed up into the nest of a family of ducks. Obviously, the family of ducks was not his own, but he didn't know this.

All he knew was that he was very, very different from the other young ducklings that had hatched around him. He didn't look the same, sound the same or act the same as the others. Although he so longed to be a part of their family, he couldn't. He was chastised, ridiculed, and rejected. He just didn't fit in and no one wanted him around.

He knew that a big part of why the others didn't like him was because of how he looked. When he gazed into the water to see his own reflection he was horrified. He didn't appear to be like any of the other birds he had ever seen! He believed he must have been born horribly deformed and disfigured. Heartbroken and alone, he despaired. He sadly thought to himself, "I just don't belong anywhere!"

Just when he'd given up completely and could barely see through the tears of his sobs, he suddenly noticed something out of the corner of his eye. Along came a family of white swans. He couldn't believe his eyes – they were just like him! They made the same 'quack,' had the same feathers, and played in the water just like he did! This was a joyous occasion for the ugly duckling!

But the ugly duckling still couldn't believe that he'd ever be good enough to be accepted into such a beautiful family of swans. Just as he began to swim away and return to his lonely life, the mother swan reached out her beautiful white wing and pulled him close to her. He immediately felt the warmth of her motherly love and he knew he had finally found his home.

The ugly duckling was simply elated. He had never wanted anything more than to belong somewhere! At last he had a family of his own who loved him just as he was. He let out a big sigh of relief and satisfaction as he swam down the river alongside his new brothers and sisters.

Later, when he ran across his old family of ducks again (the ones who treated him so poorly), he proudly puffed his chest, lifted his head and paid them no mind. Now he knew he was a worthy member of nature's society and no longer deserved to be mistreated. They

couldn't hurt him anymore because he knew who he truly was and he felt beautiful from the inside-out.

As the years went by, our dear friend the ugly duckling grew up to be a confident and handsome young swan, who was known across the land for his kindness to all and for his extraordinary grace.

This is simple but poignant story in our discussion about the meaning of beauty and inner perception. We can see the transformation that occurred in the ugly duckling's self-perception. When he was outcast and underappreciated he believed he was not good enough for anyone; not even for the family he actually belonged to. His *inner beauty* was crushed. But when he was finally accepted and loved by his new family, he learned to appreciate himself. The famous ugly duckling realized that in fact, he wasn't really ugly at all!

At last he understood that he was among the tribe of some of the most beautiful and graceful birds in all of nature. Most importantly though, he realized that he was worthy of love and that he need not be any different than who he really is – now *that* is *inner beauty!* From his foundation of *inner beauty,* our little friend the ugly duckling was able to step fully into his confidence. He could see the value he offered to the world. With this new understanding, he went on to flourish as a regal and humble swan.

Consider this:

"Who in my life lifts me up and reminds me I am beautiful – inside and out?"

And

"What kinds of people, places or things do I expose myself to that are not healthy for my self-perception?"

Industrious

> Make things happen! If you want something to be different in your life, then put your mind to it and create the reality you're looking for.

The story of the ugly duckling is powerful because it is our story too. The negative messages we may have been exposed to in our upbringing might have made us feel unworthy for whatever reason. For instance, if you are a woman growing up in the USA like my own daughter, you were inevitably exposed to countless advertisements in mainstream media. You inevitably heard the message that unless you looked like Barbie, you wouldn't be worthwhile as a woman.

Much like the ugly duckling, you might have thought you could never be good enough. These messages of unworthiness are received so strongly for some women that although they could look much like the spitting image of Barbie (which is not healthy to begin with because Barbie's dimensions are totally unrealistic) they *still* can't see themselves as beautiful! This is because their connection to their *inner beauty* is severed by the messages of the media. They are told that how they look on the outside is the only thing that matters and sadly, they believe it. If these women do not have any sense of value coming from within, then no matter however "perfect" they look on the outside, their minds will still trick them into thinking they've fallen short. External beauty can never make up for the authentic beauty that comes from within. If we can't hear the voice of our *inner beauty*, self-love and acceptance, then we're at risk to develop illnesses like bulimia and anorexia-nervosa.

Susan Schmidt, born in 1934 gives us wisdom from her perspective that "The negative impact of the media is in all the images of slim women. This causes eating disorders and low self esteem because young girls don't measure up to the ideals."

As adults we have the opportunity to expose ourselves to environment that will promote the development of our *inner beauty*. We need to find people in our lives who accept us as we are, just like the ugly duckling did when he discovered his new swan family. Often these kinds of people will have similar values, morals and views as we do, and we feel a sense of belonging in their company. Spending more time with them, we start to see that we too are beautiful for reasons other than our pretty "tail-feathers."

If we surround ourselves with uplifting friends who reflect our own *inner beauty* back to us, and if we expose ourselves to healthy media that makes us appreciate our bodies, then we will begin to see that truth in ourselves. This kind of external support and validation let's our *inner beauty* thrive!

Majorie Pally, born in 1921 in Detroit MI wants to tell young women to "Have confidence in yourself. Look at yourself realistically. Most kids are good and they should realize that."

To conclude, I believe it is time that we reignite the appreciation of the true beauty in all women of every color, shape and size. When their *inner beauty* is validated, alongside with their own, personal understanding of their worth, then they can shine unabashedly with pride and grace, just like our little friend the ugly duckling. So go forth and shine!

"YOUNG WOMEN SHOULD AVOID IMITATING ANYONE ELSE. JUST BE YOURSELF!"
~ *Fruma Kit Endler, born in Russia 1920* ~

THE MESSAGES WE SEE: THE FORCE OF THE MEDIA

Since a woman's environment has such a great impact on her ability to feel beautiful, it behooves us all to take a good long look at our media exposure and the effect it may be having on our self image. We all learn to behave by example, so we have to make sure the role models of *outer beauty* that we're exposed to are: (1) realistic (2) wholesome and (3) healthy, instead of: (1) airbrushed (2) sexualized and (3) sickly.

This is never more important to pay attention to than during the time of young adulthood. The teenage years can be a vulnerable time and many young ladies are insecure and don't understand the nature of real beauty. Mass media focuses heavily on external beauty so that they can make money off of products which claim to ensure a more appealing physical portrait for young women. Girls start to believe that their ticket to beauty lies in purchasing that new brand name purse or sporting flashy designer clothing.

My daughter herself was surrounded by girls like this in her high school. They bought into this idea because they were trying to mimic an image of "beauty" that they'd seen on TV. They fell victim to the propaganda of the mass media that was designed to exploit their insecurity surrounding their self-image - and it worked.

> "The media defines happiness as things outside of the self, so true satisfaction and happiness is never achieved."
> ~ *Juneva Lanser (Taffy), born 1930* ~

Thankfully, because I had raised my daughter to know her own *inner beauty*, she did not feel pressured from her peers. She knew it was not necessary that she wear expensive jeans or put on exorbitant amounts of makeup in order to be "beautiful." She understood that clothes, jewelry and makeup only satisfy temporarily and do not truly reflect the virtue of who she is as a person. She didn't need anyone else's approval or any amount of material things to be good enough. The strength of her *inner beauty* was unwavering. I am very proud of my daughter. She is a simple, humble and an absolutely beauty young lady.

Compassionate

> Look beyond the surface until you see the suffering that all beings experience. With this view, you will develop a true understanding of the plight of your fellow brothers and sisters and can genuinely offer them mercy and forgiveness.
> Then, turn this same eye of understanding towards yourself and the challenges you face.

I would highly recommend to all mothers of young daughters to watch out for these sorts of concerns during the teenage years. It is a vulnerable time for the self-image of young ladies and they need all the support they can get. If you want to be proactive about this, the best thing you can do for your daughters, nieces, or any of the other young ladies in your life, is to allow them to see you as an example of *inner beauty*. Young women need healthy modeling for what beauty really means, and I believe it is our responsibility to emulate that for them.

After we've done our part as role models, we can also bring in the help of progressive beauty campaigns. These are conscious media movements that show real women's bodies that are not cosmetically altered, airbrushed or overly thin. They picture healthy women in healthy bodies at normal, healthy weights with normal, healthy curves in realistic proportions! One company that is currently running these kinds of advertisements is Dove, but there are others as well. In sum, we have plenty that we can do to lift up the young women in our lives and support them in discovering and holding true to their *inner beauty*.

> "THE MEDIA CHANGES ITS PERSPECTIVE ALL THE TIME...
> DON'T CHANGE YOURS!"
> ~ *Fruma Kit Endler of Russia, born 1920* ~

On that note, I'd like to suggest that we don't forget to support one other as women. We are all sisters in the same boat, struggling to find and maintain our *inner beauty* against the current of society's confounding messages. Too often we become overly competitive with one another and we lose our innate, nurturing feminine energy in the process. So please, help each other. Give to each other what you can. Believe in one another. Remind your fellow woman of her *inner beauty* so that she can learn to see it deep inside herself. Then overtime, she will begin to recognize that same *inner beauty* within all the women in her life as well. In the end, that is how we can make a difference – one beautiful woman at a time.

Women in Society, Family and Professional Life

Inner Anchor

After I graduated from medical school at 24 years old, I told my parents I didn't even want to talk about the subject of marriage! I wasn't interested in actively pursuing a husband or being bothered by dozens of suitors. Plus, even if I were to be married, I required that my husband be a doctor of Ayurvedic medicine, as I was. I figured that if we were both doctors, we would share the same values and be able to have stimulating conversations over dinner!

Well, it turned out that after a little while of my parents nonchalantly being on the hunt for a good match, they found out about a handsome young doctor named Suhas Kshirsagar. After a thorough investigation of his background, family, education, health, hobbies etc., my family finally decided he had good potential.

I agreed to go over to his home to meet him and his family - after all, he did meet my main condition of being a doctor. When I arrived, it was a full house. Suhas' grandparents, parents, siblings, their spouses and their children, were all there staring right at me! They proceeded to ask me and my family some questions. In return, we asked plenty of our own questions as well! This went on for quite some time until his grandparents finally asked me the ultimate question, "Can you cook?" In Indian culture, if you can make a certain kind of stuffed *chapatti*, kind of like a fancy calzone, then you can do anything! And lucky for me, I wasn't half bad in the kitchen and so I could truthfully reply, "Yes!"

Once we arrived back home, my parents said that they would give me three days to consider taking this man as my husband. They also gave me the option to meet with him again and learn more about him. Honestly, I felt satisfied and confident. I really wasn't worried. He met my main requirement and I quite enjoyed our somewhat lengthy introduction, so I said "Yes! I will have him as my husband." Luckily, on his side, he also agreed to take me as his wife and we were soon married.

Shortly after that we had our first son. He stayed at home with my grandparents, brother, brother's wife and all their children while I went to work at a local Ayurvedic clinic. Without the support of my family, there would have been no way I could have continued my career.

Then, one fateful night, Suhas and I got a call coming in from the clinic. It was from Holland. We had been selected to go abroad and practice Ayurveda with the Maharishi Mahesh Yogi movement of Transcendental Meditation. They invited us to pack our bags and come. But at that point we hardly even knew where Holland was on the map! I had never boarded a plane in my life and neither of us had our passports! So initially we said, "No, absolutely not. We have our clinics here and our families are here in India." But then after some time thinking, we reconsidered. After all, it was a pretty incredible, once in a lifetime opportunity!

Nonetheless, the truth was that we had no idea what would be in store for us overseas. We were unsure about what exactly what our new work would entail or just how demanding it would actually be. Would we be traveling a lot? What would the quality of the food be wherever we went? Or even more basically, were we prepared for the changes in weather? There was so much we didn't yet understand. Our families recognized this and pleaded with us, "Go wherever you please, but you must leave your child with us. We will take good care of him while you're gone." And we too, wanted to protect our son from all the unexpected possibilities of life abroad, so we agreed.

It was excruciatingly difficult for us to leave our two-year old son behind with our family, but we knew he would be well loved and taken care of in our absence. For this, I am forever grateful to my family. In our greatest time of need they were willing, and even insistent upon stepping in to support us in the pursuit of our dreams. Without them it is hard to say what we would have done or how different our lives would look today.

Fortunately, we loved our work in Holland. Our aim was to bring awareness to the world of Ayurveda and her sister science of Yoga. We were so inspired by the Maharishi movement that after a trial of one year, we decided we wanted to stay. We immediately went to get our three-year old son and to everyone's surprise, brought him with us on the road! With him by our side, we did Ayurvedic consultations for local people in hundreds of different locations worldwide.

> "Women need to be independent.
> I used to travel whenever I wanted to and
> I traveled with people younger than me.
> I was in my 60's and my [traveling] group was 20 years
> younger. It's good to be around younger people.
> Sometimes I left my husband at home to travel.
> It's important to be independent!"
> *~ Phyllis Katz, born 1918 ~*

After about five years of traveling to numerous different countries with the movement, we had our second child, my beautiful daughter. When I look back on it now, it is almost unbelievable. With two children, one newborn and the other only in grade school, we traveled to almost thirty different countries over the span of about eight years! During this time, we acquired some serious life education. We learned so much as we traveled, but I think the most valuable skill we picked up was "the art of adjustment." My whole family, including the kids, had to learn to navigate constant change. Just as soon as we would settle down somewhere, we'd have to pick up again, only to settle down temporarily somewhere else! It wasn't easy. That's why I refer to it as an art. Maintaining a sense of poise and grace through the turbulence of change is an art because it requires strong self-awareness and creativity to skillfully navigate.

> "BE ON GOOD TERMS WITH YOUR PARENTS AND YOUR PARENTAL BACKGROUND – WHERE YOU CAME FROM. DON'T RUN AWAY FROM WHERE YOU CAME FROM."
>
> *Ann B., born in 1929*

Although it was challenging, I am grateful that my kids, my husband, and I, all got "properly schooled," shall we say, in the art of adjustment. Today my children are young adults, and for their age, they are surprisingly adaptable. They know how to "roll with the punches," so to speak. They also know exactly who they are and where they stand in life. Their *inner beauty* is strong because they know the value they bring to the world. You see, they had to develop resilience and adaptability early on in order to handle all the different schools, friends and cultures that they encountered. Today I see that they've kept these skills alive and put them to good use when confronted with the various challenges that kids face growing up.

FLEXIBLE

> CHANGE IS AN OPPORTUNITY TO CONNECT WITH YOUR *INNER BEAUTY*. BE WILLING TO ADJUST YOUR COURSE IF LIFE IS CALLING FOR IT. YOU NEVER KNOW WHAT WONDERFUL SURPRISES MAY BE IN STORE FOR YOU!

I also learned some important lessons myself as I traveled. I was confronted with so many different environments and new cultural traditions as we moved around, that I quickly became aware of something deep inside me that I hadn't necessarily noticed before. It was my connection to my Self. I found that it was vital to my survival in the face of constant change. Outwardly, in my world, everything moved and changed, but inwardly my journey was constant. I never lost sight of who I was as a woman, where I came from, or what my work in the world was meant to be. I had an inner pillar of strength and I never let go. In fact, I hung onto it for dear life. It anchored me to my inner Truth. When I held firmly to this internal anchor, I made choices that were in integrity with my Self, even if it meant going against the grain of others around me. It was as if I had a built-in internal compass that whispered to me where to go and what to do in tricky situations. I trusted it, which meant that I trusted myself.

"Rely on yourself. You have to find your personal strength inside. I had nobody to help me but I found my personal strength inside."

~ Frida Reich, of the Czech Republic, born in 1932. WWII Auschwitz concentration camp surviver ~

I am sure that had my inner connection not been so solid, I would have easily become lost in the storm of change – forgetting who I was in the face of so many new people and places. Fortunately for me however, my inner life was as firm and stable as my outer life was fluid and variable. It's a good thing too, because the truth is: change is unavoidable. We're all faced with sudden changes and challenges in life, but the good news is that we all have the resources we need to stay true to ourselves in spite of it.

Inner Beauty

> "Be flexible – not so set in your ways that you are not open to new ideas. Understand that you were not promised a 'rose garden.' Life's choices are often demanding. The courage to face them is up to you."
>
> ~ *Juneva Lanser (Taffy), born 1930* ~

In each and every one of us, no matter how imperfect, there exists a wellspring of love that flows deep within. Sadly for many of us, access to this oasis of internal strength is blocked. Either because of deep wounds from the past or simply because no one ever showed us the way to get there, we haven't been able to find our own personal gold mine of internal beauty and riches. But this treasure is our birthright to reclaim. Without it we become depressed, anxious, angry or fearful. Then we develop diseases which reflect our psychological malaise. We need an anchor of fortitude and *inner beauty* to give us the strength we need to handle the challenges that life presents.

If you feel you have forgotten the way to your inner anchor of truth and self-love, then it is my sincere desire to be the one to help guide you back home. I want to show you how to rediscover and reignite the personal, *inner beauty* that inherently lies within you. All you have to do is remember how to find it.

If you will, I'd like to share with you a little more about how I came, through my cultural background, to realize the depth and strength of my own *inner beauty*. It is my hope that in hearing about the context of my upbrining, that you too will be reminded of the power and beauty that lies deep within you.

The Life of a Family

In India, we all lived together – me, my husband, our children, our parents, and our grandparents. For many westerners that probably sounds like a living nightmare. How could we all possibly get along, have enough of our own space and not drive each other completely mad? Coming from the background of a culture that was born out of the values of independence, individuality and freedom, these are worthy concerns! In the United States, establishing yourself apart from your family is not only a primary objective (some can hardly wait until they're 18 to do it), but also a reflection of personal success.

For my family though, it was the opposite. When we moved to the USA and left our joint family it felt painful and isolating to live without them. Having their presence in the home was an inherent part of life in India. Without it, something major was missing – there was a hole in our home and in our hearts.

Good Listener

> The best way to show someone that you love them is by giving them your full attention. When they're speaking, it is your job not to just hear the words they say, but to truly understand their message.

Outside of all the emotional benefits of being surrounded by people that we loved and who loved us in return, the joint family also provided us all with major practical support for our everyday living. In a joint family all the overwhelming responsibilities of life can be shared together and distributed among many people instead of solely on the mother and father.

Marriages existing in the context of joint families are often less strained. There are very low rates of divorce in India, in part because the man and wife's relationship is traditionally supported by the elders in the family unit. If a marriage is in jeopardy, the grandparents or great-grandparents intervene. They play the role of the modern day counselor excpect that their advice is both free and full of pure wisdom. Plus, there is the added advantage that they have known either the husband or wife since they were a child, and so easily understand the subtle contours of their personalities. Overall, they are well poised to provide invaluable words of guidance to the struggling couple.

Grandparents also relieve the parents of some of the household and child rearing burdens. Parents are thus more likely to have the mental, physical and emotional reserves to connect with one another in a loving way. For example, say mom and dad come home tired and weary after a long day of work, and grandma has left a hot, fresh, home cooked meal on the table for them. Surely, all houshold relations, including husband and wife, will be more aimiacable when everyone is well fed! Without that kind of support, it is exhausting to begin to cook dinner from scratch at the end of a long day. Tension and stress can arise between all members of the family as people become increasingly hungry. To avoid this, it is often much easier for families just to go out for fast food. In the process however, the quality of both the food and family time is sacrificed.

When generations of families live together, children never have to doubt that someone will be there ready to embrace them when they return home from school. There will always be a family member there to greet them and help them with their homework or afternoon activities. The idea of paying a babysitter or day-care service, or even having a child arrive home to an empty house, is foreign to cultures using a joint family system. Plus, children in joint families also learn to respect their elders and are taught to cooperate, share and serve their family from a young age. Their *inner beauty* is strengthened through this upbringing.

And the grandparents benift too. Grandparents have confidence that their grandchildren would be willing to offer them a ride should they ever need to run an errand or visit a friend. They know that they'll never be put into a home for the elderly, painfully isolated from their loved ones. They know that there will always be someone to take care of them, come what may. Furthermore, being a part of the joint family gives grandparents purpose and meaning well into their later years of life.

Recent even research bolsters the idea that living in a joint family has its benefits. Members of joint families live longer than their single family counterparts. Likely this phenomenon is due, at least in part, to the reduced levels of stress found in joint families. Stress decreases when there is so much communal support. Knowing that people are there to help, the nervous system can relax. When the fight or flight response is turned off, there is less fear, isolation, depression and worry. Anxiety lessens because the family structure provides a continual, built-in, support system to help each member cope with the struggles of life. The joint family is a durable, reliable groundwork that lifts everybody up. Each member of the family is there for one another. Everyone pitches in and participates for the betterment of the family unit as a whole. The result: everyone benefits.

Thoughtful

Consider others. Take into account their wants, needs and desires when making choices in your own life. Do not act in a way that dismisses another person's well-being, but instead aim to be as considerate as possible.

India is not the only traditional culture that has used the joint family system through the ages. Italian, Mexican, and South

American families (to name only a few), also historically cohabitate in a similar way. If you've heard the common phrase, "it takes a village," it is true. We evolved this way – in small bands and tribes. Why? Because it's just too hard to do it alone. My heart goes out to those women and men who struggle to raise their children single-handedly and in an economy that demands so many hours at work just to make ends meet. It is no easy task. I am so grateful that in India I naturally had my village built into my joint family. For me it served as a tremendous source of love, connection, community and support growing up.

When I came to the United States, without my joint family I felt lost. Separating from them when I immigrated to the USA was not only heartbreaking but also incredibly stressful. I felt the pressure of being a working woman and a mother of two without the traditional support network I was accustomed to. In our economy today most often both parents need to work to provide for the family. This means that from morning to night a woman juggles her various duties at work and home. Most often she becomes exhausted this way because her schedule is unsustainable. I knew that even with the help of my husband, if I were to work full time, I couldn't maintain a solid family life and uphold the values that I believed in.

Our family is vegetarian so I needed to be available to cook food for my children so that they were not left without options at the school cafeteria or at home for dinner. I also wanted my children to know that their mom was happy, healthy and fully present for them at home. In order to do these things, I knew I would have to make a compromise. So I began to work just part time. With my new schedule I could always pick up my children from school and be with them for the afternoons and evenings.

Then, to make the situation even better, I invited my own parents to come from India to stay with us for six months out of the year. For the other half of the year, my husband's parents came to do the same. We made a make-shift joint family! Our kids ended up growing up with their grandparents as a part of their daily life. It was beautiful. The times my children had with their grandparents are priceless and I wouldn't trade them for anything. And for me, knowing the extended family was there at home was a great relief. I finally felt I could settle in and relax.

Aspects of *Inner Beauty* Cultivated in Family Life & Community Cooperation

Sharing * Clear Communication * Listening
Non-judgment * Respect of elders
Responsibility

Women and Vedanta

Beeing a part of both worlds/cultures, I've witnessed the role of women in the west. It seems strained and undervalued to me. We are expected to "do it all" and "have it all," and for the most part, all on our own watch. Today it is not uncommon for a woman to be balancing everything from a failing relationship with to her husband to a full-time career, gym membership, and her three children - all at once! Our society even praises a women who can do all of these things. But even if she is managing, a woman cannot possibly inhabit her full potential when she is spread so thin, taking on so much all by herself and playing so many different roles.

A women's role is
"To be a good example of truth and love for children."
~ Ruth Runze of Germany, born in 1929 ~

In ancient India, women were not pushed to the brim like this. They were supported and respected in their communities and did not have to bear the weight of the world on their shoulders' alone. For example, if they chose to be a mother and/or wife, their decision was not viewed as less-than when compared to others working outside the home. Today, a woman may feel a sense of guilt if she "only" stays at home. She may feel as though she should be contributing financially as well (as if the work at home isn't enough)! Women back then had the support of their families and their culture to do as they pleased. Whether they desired to go after academia, motherhood, philosophy or theology, they were respected.

There are many records of women in ancient Indian society holding roles of leadership and authority. Both married and single women alike were *Rishis*, or enlightened and highly regarded "great seers of wisdom." In other words, they were some of the authors who inspired the writings of the sacred *Vedic* (or ancient Hindu) scriptures. At that time women were esteemed teachers, sages, philosophers, doctors and politicians and were free to share their wisdom with the world. In one of the oldest ancient texts of India, the *Artharva Veda* we see the role of women in society outlined: "women should be valiant, scholarly, prosperous, intelligent and knowledgeable. They should take part in the legislative chambers and be the protectors of family and society." Another text called the *Rig Veda* states that "the wife and husband, being the equal halves of one substance, are equal in every respect; therefore, both should join and take equal parts in all works, religious and secular."

Women were welcomed to participate in all aspects of life, and were not seen as inferior to their male counterparts.

Humility

Be grateful for who you are and what you've been given."

Women have fought hard and made tremendous strides in society today by obtaining numerous rights and opportunities that were lost to them for hundreds of years. The 19th century Indian saint Swami Vivekananda sums it up when he says, "Woman has suffered for eons, and that has given her infinite patience and infinite perseverance." While we have transformed our suffering into virtuous qualities, it is comforting to know that it wasn't always the case that women were so gravely undervalued in society and ubiquitously disrespected. If we go back further into history, we see that the culture of ancient Inida was not only very supportive of women's rights but also acutely aware of the uniquely feminine virtues they offered to the world. By no means was ancient India the culture in which women were subjugated and controlled by harsh discriminations as they sometimes are today. It was a virtuous time in our past in which women were more clearly understood and deeply respected.

We can look to this exceptional era for guidance and wisdom. We can use their example not only as an inspiration for the future evolution of women's status in society at large, but also as a personal reminder to ourselves about the inherent value we naturally posses as women. When we finally start to recognize our own innate value, we will begin to open our eyes to our true nature and the authentic beauty that lies there within. Then, we can learn to see ourselves in a different light –one of love, respect, acceptance, appreciation, admiration and compassion – and in the end, we will shine with beauty from within.

Inner Beauty

In ancient India it was believed that women contained a potent energy called *Shakti*, or a kind of divine feminine energy. It was said to be a force of nature that only a woman could posses and which was responsible for the creation of the entire universe. This creative power was visualized in the form of the great Hindu Goddesses *Durga, Parvati, Kali, Lakshmi* and *Saraswati*. An ancient Hindu text called the *Manu Samhita*, writes that "where women are honored, the gods are pleased. Where they are not honored, no sacred rites yield rewards." This speaks to the power of *Shakti!*

Simply by virtue of being a woman, a young lady in ancient India had an elevated status because she was seen to contain the strength and groundedness of the Mother and the power of the Supreme Creator. Her place in society was honored. On certain occasions, people, including her own parents, would even come to wash her feet as a sign of respect and acknolwedgement that she is Goddess incarnate. Women were worshiped by others in their communities because they were the keepers of *Shakti* and it was commonly recognized that the well-being of society at large, depended on this potent energy.

Another one of the ancient scriptures of India, the *Rig Veda*, describes the value women offer to society by saying, "The entire world of noble people bows to the glory of the glorious woman so that she enlightens us with knowledge and foresight. She is the leader of society and provides knowledge to everyone. She is a symbol of prosperity and a daughter of brilliance. May we respect her so that she destroys the tendencies of evil and hatred from society." Clearly the *Shakti* within a woman was seen as a force so powerful that it could even overcome evil and bring about good for the whole of civilization. In fact, I love what Swami Vivekananda says about the value of women in society: "There is no chance for the welfare of the world unless the condition of women is improved."

Intelligent

> Take every opportunity you can to educate yourself.
> Exercise your mind and keep it sharp.
> It is a great tool that if properly cared for will serve you well for many years to come.

Furthermore, if a women of ancient India so desired, she would be supported in perusing academic endeavors. Her scholarly contributions would be equally as valued, if not more valued, than that of a man's. The text of the *Yajur Veda,* expounds upon an academic woman's impact in society by saying,"The scholarly woman purifies our lives with her intellect. Through her actions, she purifies our actions. Through her knowledge and action, she promotes the virtue and efficient management of society." That is why Swami Vivekananda says that "The best thermometer to the progress of a nation is its treatment of its women." In this perspective, a woman's knowledge is seen to benefit not only herself, but the whole of culture and society as well.

Remembering *Inner Beauty* Through Ancient Culture

Divine Feminine Energy (Shakti)
Women as *Goddesses*
Women as *Holders of Intuitive Wisdom*
Women valued as *Scholars*
Women valued as *Philosophers*
Women valued as *Mothers & Creators*
Women valued as *Wives*
Women valued as *Sages & Priests*
Women valued as *Teachers*

In ancient India, if a woman preferred to focus her efforts on the home by taking on the role of mother and wife, she was no less valued then the woman who pursued academics. Being a mother and wife did not mean that she would acquiesce to a life of subservience. In fact, within the context of a society and culture that deeply valued and respected the role of a woman in the home, the opposite was true. The aforementioned *Artharva Veda* explains that a married woman "rules there [in the home] along with her husband, as queen over the other members of the family". Clearly being a mother is not a diminished position but an elevated post revered and respected among the family unit.

> "KNOW YOURSELF, LIVE UP TO YOUR POTENTIAL, BE HELPFUL TO OTHERS AND CONTENT WITH YOUR LIFE."
>
> ~ *Katherine Kronert, born 1929 Pennsylvania* ~

A mother is a child's very first guru or teacher, and her guidance trumps all others. There is even a special word in Hindu that describes the relationship of the mother as the first and most impactful teacher - *matru devo bhav.* And, in the Mahabharata, (an ancient epic moral tale of India) it proclaims that, "the teacher who teaches true knowledge is more important than ten instructors. The father is more important than ten such teachers of true knowledge and the mother is more important than ten such fathers. There is no greater guru (teacher) than mother." The words of wisdom uttered by a mother are clearly the most valuable of all, even over fatherly advice. This is because the mother possesses strong feminine energy which gives her special insight that is unmatched to all else.

Caring

The archetype of the Great Mother is the one who nourishes all. She offers loving attention and tender care to all those in need. Ask that the qualities of the Great Mother be invoked within you as well.

Generally in the west, women who concentrate their energy on being a mother are not valued in the same way as women working outside of the home. Perhaps that is because there is a perception that external endeavors mandate more skill and demand a certain level of competency that is not required in the home? If this is in fact the reasoning behind our culture's dismissal of the work women do in the home as mothers, it is far from accurate. The role of a mother is excruciatingly laborious to say the least. It is a career that is challenging on all levels – physical, psychological, emotional, intellectual and spiritual. In fact, no other job is as demanding. As a mother you never get to clock-out. You are on duty 24-7.

Mothers have the pressure of upholding the most critical job in all of society. Without a mother who is able to be present for her children, the proper psychological and emotional development of her child is at stake. In general, lack of proper mothering leaves children to grow up without the guidence they truly need. Downstream, this cumulitively makes for a negative impact on society as a whole. But nonetheless, the unseen work of a mother and wife remains highly underappreciated in today's world.

"A woman has an imporatnt role in soceity and the family as a nurturer. She has to accept her dual responsibility. She needs to be strong, have a good sense of self worth and find satisfaction through her own self expression doing what she enjoys.

All the while however, she also has to nurture her family. A lot is asked of us women."
~ *Susan Schmidt, born in 1934* ~

According to the Hindu code of ethics, the *Niti Sara*, the proper role a wife or mother is explicitely outlined. So as not to leave any room for ambiguity, it clearly describes six desirable attributes that any proper householder should supply. Below is a list of each of the qualities described in their original language.

'Karyeshu Mantri, Karaneshu Dasi; Bhojyeshu Mata, Shayaneshu Rambha, Roopeshu Lakshmi, Kshamayeshu Dharitri, Shat Dharma Yukta, Kuladharma Patni'.

To break down this phrase:

Karyeshu Mantri	Works with the heart of a servant
Karaneshu Dasi	Advises like a minister
Bhojyeshu Mata	Nourishes like a mother
Shayaneshu Ramba	Makes love like the heavenly beauty Rambha
Roopeshu Lakshmi	Is beautiful like the Goddess Lakshmi
Kshmayeshu Dharitri	Has patience like the Earth
Shat Dharma Yukta	A woman who has these six virtues
Kula Dharma Patni	Is a good wife

Out of these six virtues there are several that stand out and which would do well to be explained. First of all, when this verse speaks about a woman having patience "like the earth," it is referring to her as having the quality of patience for the whole world. The earth is enduring. It calmly holds everything within its bosom for centuries and without a single complaint, it continues to give. It is all encompassing, unconditionally forgiving and full of sustenance. A woman is just like this and can be likened to a manifestation of Mother Nature. There is a reason we do not refer to Nature as being fatherly. The earth is our birthplace and the source from which we derive our nourishment; it is therefore an expression of the Feminine.

The quality of "advising like a minister" encourages women to share their advice with others. In this way a woman becomes the moral and ethical backbone of her community and society. She takes responsibility for those needing care, she mediates among disputing parties, she teaches her children how to be good citizens and she provides guidance to her community as a whole.

Forgiving

> Holding onto anger if someone has wronged you will only poison your own heart. The best thing you can do for yourself and for anyone else, is to give up hope for a better past, and move forward into the future with a clean slate.

In India we say that the greatest quality of a woman is forgiveness. I think this has to do with the virtue a woman inacts when she is able to let go of negative emotions that come up around the sacrifices she makes in her marriage and family. As the leader of the household, a woman often gives up her personal desires for the benefit of the family as a whole. She thus, "works with the heart of a servant." Any good leader demonstrates this quality of selflessness but in order for resentment not to build up, women must forgive those they are making sacrifices for. If a woman wishes to avoid grudges between her and her children or if she hopes for her marriage to not be poisoned with resentment, she must always practice forgiveness.

> "WOMEN SHOULD THINK ABOUT WHAT THEY HAVE – NOT WHAT THEY DON'T HAVE."
> ~ *Katherine Kronert, born 1929 Pennsylvania* ~

In ancient times a 'housewife' was a highly regarded position in society and was understood to be necessary for the health of the community as a whole. This is because women were seen as the ones who "breastfed all of humanity," so to speak. It was in their lap countless civilizations were cradled and nourished into existence. Hence, back then, there was a collective sense among society to be humbly indebted to the mothers of the world for all their sacrifices and the selfless work they provide. In that way, the quality of "nourish[ing] like a mother" is the most important aspect of womanhood; for surely motherless children, nations and families are bound to suffer without the love and guidance they need.

Our ideal housholder is also referred to as being "beautiful like the goddess Lakshmi." Lakshmi is the goddess of wealth and abundance. Traditionally, she is said to offer prosperity and good fortune to any who worship her. She is certainly a beautiful goddess externally, but her internal beauty radiates even more profoundly. Just as a woman who knows her own beauty imparts joy, grace and kindness to her community, Lakshmi's presence too, brings about blessings to all those around her. Along the same lines, the woman described in the *Niti Sara* also "makes love like the heavenly beauty Rambha." Rambha is a mystical and strikingly beautiful queen known for her multitude of talents in dancing, music, art and...love making. The alluring sensual powers of women were beseeched by men centuries ago just as they are today – some things never change.

Natural Lover

A woman who is beautiful from within exudes love wherever she goes. Her heart is open and her instinct is to pour affection onto all those she cares for

Ultimately, women are valuable to the world when they see their own beauty from within and then allow it to be shared with the world. The qualities listed in the *Niti Sara* are mostly all internally derived virtues that would be inherent in any woman or wife who has diligently cultivated her *inner beauty*.

Hard working

Apply yourself fully to all that you do in life, no matter what the situation is or how great or small the reward. Invest your energy and effort into producing top quality work for the greater good of all.

Overall, what we can see through all these examples of how the traditional culture of India acknowledged and appreciated women, is that their value was not limited to their external appearance or their work outside of the home. Rather, women were valued for their internal qualities of wisdom, grace and knowledge and were given respect in all of the roles they played. Unfortunately, in modern culture we have lost this kind of deep respect for women. Nowadays their value seems to lie in their external appearances and/or accomplishments outside of the home. I am not saying that having *outer beauty* is not valuable or that keeping a career is not a fabulous option for some women – because it is. Rather, what I am hoping to convey is simply that there is far less appreciation for the unseen qualities and hard labor of women in the home today. Knowing this, it is crucial that we as women learn to keep returning to the foundation of our *inner beauty* so that we can recover our value and strength in spite of our society's frame of reference.

MARRIAGE AND DIVORCE

Women who spend their time in the home as wives and mothers need to remember the profound value they offer to the homestead. They are the root of the household, providing it with the strength and nourishment it needs to thrive.

If women are experiencing any level of abuse in their home or if the bond of marriage is somehow dishonored, then I would encourage them to readjust their lives in a way that ensure they are highly regarded and loved and they deserve to be. If they do not, these women will live a life consumed by chronic stress. This kind of ongoing unhappiness is horribly taxing on both the mind and the body. To cope with this stress, women often times end up making unhealthy choices in lifestyle and diet. As a result, both their *inner* and *outer beauty* suffer - lines of worry, fear and anger etch themselves onto their faces and their hearts grow cold and weary. No longer can they exemplify beauty because it has been stripped from their lives. In these cases, it may be necessary to leave a marriage.

Contrarily, there are many incidences in which a decision to divorce is taken too flippantly. Couples separate for simple reasons that could be resolved with only a little more effort, forgiveness, gratitude and care. Seeing the *inner beauty* in yourself and your partner is key to making a marriage work. Unfortunately, today it is rare that couples are able to do this. So few stay together for a lifetime. In the celebrity world it is not uncommon to see superstars get married just as often as we see them get divorced! Where is the depth to these relationships? Where is the reverence for the commitment of marriage? Have we forgotten that entering into the bond of marriage is sacred? And what about the other people involved? Divorces impact the families of the man and woman as well as any children they may have had together. It is too easy for people to become absorbed with their own wants and disregard their family's. There is great responsibility that needs to be taken here, but I do not see this recognition reflected in the skyrocketing divorce rates.

"DON'T ASSUME YOU ARE RIGHT.
RELATIONSHIPS ARE TWO WAY STREET."
~ Juneva Lanser (Taffy), born 1930 ~

Sometimes I wonder if people are getting married just for the fantasy surrounding the ritual of marriage– the proposal, the ring, the invitations, the wedding dress and the attention from family and friends. But marriage is so much more than that. It is a lifelong journey. Sometimes the journey might not be easy, but that doesn't mean that we should quit.

"TREAT YOUR HUSBAND LIKE A KING.
RESPECT HIM AS A MAN, AND LOVE HIM LIKE A LITTLE BOY."
~ Aurelie Zachary, from Saskatchewan Canada, born in1922

If we're looking for our happiness externally, we are bound to be disappointed. We might think that buying the latest electronic devise or fancy car will fill the void in our hearts, but it only satisfies temporarily. We'll have to keep on purchasing over and over again until we are likely to reach bankruptcy. The same is true with our relationships. It may be that after some years we want a "new and shinny" partner to fulfill all our fantasies and desires (and possibly even improve the image we have of ourselves); but often we're simply missing out on the depth of our "oldies but goodies." Just because something is less thrilling and more familiar, doesn't mean we get to toss it out. The grass isn't always greener! Seeking external beauty, fantasy or thrill from another person will never take the place of knowing the *inner beauty* that exists within your spouse.

Patient

> Have patience with the imperfections in yourself and in others. Making mistakes is part of being human and learning takes time. Understand this and you will have far more peace in all of your relationships – including the one with yourself!

These days it seems that many men and women are unwilling to make compromises for one another in their relationships. Perhaps this is due to the individualized nature of modern culture. Nonetheless, it is tearing countless marriages apart. Too many people get married for themselves, but marriage is for the partnership, and partnerships take compromise. There is nothing wrong, weak, or even unfair about making adjustments to our own agenda for the sake of our loved ones – whether that person is our husband, parent, good friend or child. When we honor the vows of marriage we are promising to yield, bend, and be of service to the other person. So long as the relationship is based on love, the sacrifices we make for one another are some of the most heart-opening experiences we can have as humans. If we're truly loving our spouse unconditionally, then compromise won't feel like a chore. We want to do things that will put the other person first. Ultimately, this is the place we need to be in, and from here, cooperation is effortless. That's why the qualities inherent in *inner beauty* like: selflessness, love, forgiveness, kindness, flexibility, patience and compassion, all must be present in order for any relationship, especially a marriage, to work.

> "For a healthy and happy relationship, be willing to compromise."
>
> *~ Hilda Richards, Frankfurt Germany, born in 1917 ~*

In marriage we must give our absolute best effort to see and appreciate the inner virtues or *inner beauty* of our partner. It is far too easy to focus on the negative in our spouse. When we get in that mindset, the people we actually love will never be 'enough.' They won't be good enough simply because they'll never meet our expectations for 'the perfect partner.' You see, the models we have in our heads about how the perfect partner should be are most likely unrealistic. Everyone comes with pros and cons. Each of us is a mixed bag. Nobody is perfect. If you are trying to find the perfect somebody - sorry but they don't exist. What does exist though, is opening your eyes to the beauty of the person who is right in front of you instead of looking elsewhere for your happiness. In lieu of focusing on what you wish your partner would be like, concentrate on all that they do offer. What do you love about your partner as he is right now?

Focus on the positive qualities of your loved one, and you may find your relationship begins to blossom all over again. Feeling all that genuine appreciation coming from you, your partner might actually start reciprocating your energy! If each person in the relationship focuses their attention on the inner virtues of their partner, it will be easier for them to rediscover the unique and lovable person standing right before them as their husband or wife! That's how the magic of *inner beauty* really works. When we recognize the *inner beauty* in another person, it has the power to heal and restore our most important relationships.

"Listen to each other. Speak what you think and don't let anyone run your life for you."
~ Phyllis Katz, from Minneapolis, born in 1918 ~

Finally, whether a marriage is between a man and a woman, a woman and a woman, or a man and a man, is not what is important. What matters is the love, respect and commitment that lies there within. It needs to be authentic. Whatever choices we make around marriage (who, how, and when) should not be taken lightly. We need to go into our marriages without having the lingering thought in the back of our minds, "Well, I could always just get a divorce if it didn't work out..." While divorce is certainly called for at times, it needs to be used only when absolutely necessary. The sanctity of marriage needs to be restored in our society at large, and it can be done with the cultivation of *inner beauty*.

If we appreciate the beauty within ourselves, we automatically embody the right kinds of qualities that it takes to make a relationship work. What I mean is that as we see the worth and value in ourselves, we are more likely to find the *inner beauty* in our partners as well. We need to get married with great mindfulness, and if we are to get divorced, it should be with equal consciousness and never first without the consideration for the *inner beauty* within ourselves and our spouses.

> "I always say a good sense of humor for a healthy realtionship!"
> ~ *Majorie Pally, from Detroit MI, born in 1921* ~

Conclusion

Overall my message is that women in our culture and around the world need to be upheld in society and seen clearly for the value we offer to the world. The light of our beauty shines no matter what role we play in life or what age we may be. A woman's beauty lies deep within in the form of the Goddess who reflects the Divine Feminine which is essential to all life. It is time that we all recognize Her sanctity and lift Her up in all her endeavors and the weight of the responsibility She bares for the world. And individually, we as women need to have faith in our own personal value and confidence in our *inner beauty*.

Transitions in a Woman's Life

THE MOON AND THE FEMININE

A woman's energy has an ancient and deep tie to the moon. The Feminine, like the moon, is cooling, round, changeable, sensitive, dark, quiet and soft. It does not give off its own light but reflects the brilliant light of the sun. A woman too, has a highly reflective and intuitive nature which is inwardly drawn in its essence. A man's energy on the contrary, is tied to the sun. The Masculine is heating, sharp, abrasive, forceful, charismatic and bold. The sun rises and sets each and every day without fail; it is always consistent. The moon however, waxes and wanes in the lunar cycle, forever transforming. Both men and women have solar and lunar energies within themselves but for a woman, the moon-like energy dominates and for a man, the solar energy prevails.

Nevertheless, men are still affected by the moon – not to the same extent as women - but they are impacted by its presence even so. In fact, humankind's psychology at large is connected with the changes in the moon. The root of the word "lunatic" is after all, *luna*, meaning moon. There are more accounts of epileptic and schizophrenic episodes or violent crimes during either phase extreme of the moon - full or new. Along similar lines, there are more pregnant mothers who deliver on the full moon when they can be supported by the brilliant energy of the bright night sky.

The changes in human psychology based on the patterns of the moon are evident in our everyday lives as well. We may find it more difficult to sleep on the night of the full moon, or we may want to stay indoors when it's a dark night with only a new moon in the sky. There is no question that our bodies respond to the vibration of the brilliance of the moon.

Vibrant

Let the joy and excitement you feel for life expand into all that you do. Allow your enthusiasm to bubble up from within and overflow out into the world. Your radiance will be contagious.

For centuries humans measured time through observing the changes that took place in the visible moon. The words "moon," "menses" and "month" all come from the same root word meaning *to measure.* The changes in the moon correspond with the movement of the ocean tides and the cycle of a woman's menstruation. A women's cycle typically ranges from 28-30 days and the cycle of the moon is 29.53 days on average. During the approximately fourteen days prior to ovulation (the proliferative phase), a women's energy is aligned with that of the full moon. As the moon is growing, so is the lining of her uterus. Typically during this time she is more inclined to be extraverted, vivacious, dynamic and creative. She has more power and energy than at any other time during her cycle. This is because estrogen dominates during this phase giving her unctuous, fertile physiology, and driving her to go out and find a mate. After ovulation however, during the secretory phase of a women's cycle, her energy shifts again with the moon. As the moon wanes, it hides behind the earth letting only some of its magnificence shine. Likewise, a woman generates less and less desire to expose herself to the world during this time of her cycle. Her hormones are dominated by progesterone and she is given the biochemical dynamics needed to hold and nourish a potential embryo if impregnated. No longer is she out seeking a mate but she is inward, supporting the possible implantation of her to-be child. If she is does not become pregnant however, the entirety of the cycle resumes again with menstruation at the new moon.

THE WISDOM OF 1,000 MOONS: CULTIVATING *INNER BEAUTY* WITH AGE

Throughout her life, a woman moves through many moons and plays many different roles in her life. From a baby girl to a grandmother or from the onset of menstruation as a preteen, to the years after menopause, a woman grows and transforms. She may be a daughter, sister, mother, grandmother, and wife, or become a teacher, monk, priest, activist, executive or entrepreneur. In any case, she evolves emotionally, physically, psychologically and spiritually. I feel as a society, we need to honor and embrace each of these transitions for women. In this way, we honor the *inner beauty* that she has cultivated in order to successfully pass through each successive rite of passage.

One way the *inner beauty* of a woman can be "measured" is through all the wisdom that she has garnered throughout the years of her life. A woman (or man for that matter) with plentiful life experience has what the Vedic tradition refers to as "the wisdom of 1,000 full moons." They mean this literally. The actual sighting of the 1,000th full *(Sahastra Chandra Darshana Shanti)* moon is said to be the third milestone in a man or woman's life. Out of these three, the first milestone occurs at age 60. Many people are able to reach this level of wisdom, but only some move on to attain the next milestone at 70 years, and even fewer realize the turning point of the 1,000th full moon at 80 years of age. The select few who are fortunate enough to have good health, a proper environment, and an active lifestyle, actually see 1,000 full moons by the time they turn 80! Sighting 1,000 full moons is by no means a small achievement. It requires good health, strong *inner beauty*, a sound mind, and many supportive contributions from family and community.

Traditionally the waypoint of the 80th birthday is christened by a wondrous celebration! At a large family gathering, the energy of deities are formally invoked, holy water is sprinkled on the grandmother (or grandfather) and later, a sumptuous feast brings the event to a climax. What is perhaps the most significant aspect of this celebration is the fact that the younger generation seeks the blessing of the woman crossing the milestone. If they receive this blessing, it is considered a rare privilege. It is a coveted experience for the youngsters because the woman of 80 years has become what we call a *Vruddha*, or Elder. The status of Elder reflects not only age but also knowledge and wisdom and thus, *inner beauty*. With the cooling energy of 1,000 full moons, an Elder's psyche is calm and peaceful and her *inner beauty* thrives. At this age, she is enormously valuable to the community and culture because she exemplifies the picture of *inner beauty*.

Peace loving

> Create relationships with family, colleagues, and friends that put cooperation, compromise and understanding as a priority over everything else.

Respecting and honoring the elder is a rewarding experience for both the wise woman who has seen 1,000 moons, and for her younger protégé who has seen only a realtive few. Sadly, in this modern day culture we dismiss our elders as useless and burdensome. It seems that women are disregarded as less valuable after they've passed through the fire of menopause and cease to cycle with the moon through their menstruation. Although they are older, they are still deeply connected with the Feminine energy of the moon. Society however, no longer views them as 'sexy' because they are not in their fertile years. To make matters worse, once a woman gets to retirement age, she is further dismissed because she is no longer a part of the work force.

Inner Beauty

These days, the dominant habit is to quickly and thoughtlessly throw out something old in exchange for the newer, bigger, better thing. We're told by the media that we need that shinier, fancier product, because what we had before is now useless and obsolete. We may waste our money on such ventures, but we must not treat our women in this way as well. Women need to be treasured for their *inner beauty* at all ages, and especially as they enter into the mature years of their life.

> "To be sucessful in life you must find satisfaction and not become greedy."
>
> ~ *Nirmala Aaphale, born 1932 India* ~

Just because something or someone gets older does not mean it is less valuable. In fact, the opposite is true. As a good bottle of wine gets sweeter and more well rounded with age, so does a woman. Her *inner beauty* grows with time as she continues to gain wisdom and alchemize the challenges she faces in her life through the years. In modern-day culture it is difficult for us to see this value in our elders. But the truth is that they hold a myriad of experience from the past and a plethora of sagely discernment for the future. Plus, spending time with our elders, we can discover things about the history of our lineage that we never knew. Perhaps we find out that our great-grandmother had an uncanny intuition, or that her sister was an esteemed mathematician. Either way, we can gain insight into the *inner beauty* that runs through the women in our family trees. Then we can then look to our own lives to see how we too, can lead by example and carry on the qualities of *inner beauty* for the generation that will follow us into our own 1,000th moon.

Recognizing our Differences

As women, our experience in life is different than men's, however, we don't always make any allowances for those differences. Standard Feminist theory tells us we should be able to do everything a man can do, and then some. We should be able to be a full time business executive, patient mother, sexy lover, good sister, loyal daughter, loving wife...the list is endless. The fact is, we *can* do all of these things, and we *do*! But my question is: *at what cost?*

Sweet

Choose gentleness and love in your interactions with yourself and with others.

Many women who come into my office are from California's so called, "Silicon Valley," a major hot spot for high tech, big name corporations like Google. In a way, these women have been trained out of their femininity in order to survive. They've had to learn to do business like a man so that they can succeed in such a highly competitive, cut-throat working environment. This means that when they're menstruating they never stop – there's no "time outs" allotted for painful cramps, fatigue or heavy bleeding. Then, when they're pregnant they continue working 60 hours per week until the day before they're due. After they give birth, within another couple of weeks they're back in the game, flying across the country for another major conference. They work this way because they feel the pressure to keep up with the pace of the men around them who are scrutinizing their competency and upholding masculine standards for their performance. They are allotted no difference in time, space or respect for being a woman because the overarching value in the working environment is *equality.*

Inevitably, through the process of equalizing, these women end up sacrificing aspects of their *inner* and *outer beauty*. In today's world there is little value placed on the softness, gentleness, forgiveness and sweetness that are inherent in the feminine *inner beauty*. Furthermore, the aggressive relationship we have with the delicate feminine body makes our health suffer and we wind up compromising our *outer beauty* as well. Is that really what the Feminist movement intended and worked so hard to achieve?

Transitions in a Woman's Life: Opportunities for the Cultivation of *Inner Beauty*

The transitions a woman goes through in her life are seen by both men and women alike to be hindrances to productivity. But what if we gave ourselves an allowance to be different from men? What if we recognized that as a beautiful thing instead of a disadvantage or inconvenience? It is intriguing to think about what it would look like if society saw a woman's life cycle as filled with glittering opportunities for personal evolution and transformation. What if women were actually supported during these vulnerable moments of transition, because there was a collective understanding that they were the perfect occasions for her to cultivate her *inner beauty* and wellbeing?

> Have a daily routine. Even if only for 30 minutes.
>
> Do something for yourself.
>
> *~ Pauline Mitterhammer born 1926 Vienna, Austria ~*

Imagine an ideal world where this would be the case: a woman is praised when she has her first period and is initiated into adulthood; a menstruating woman automatically gets to stay at home from work to rest when she is bleeding; a new mother basques in all the time she needs to bond with her newborn knowing there is no threat that she'll lose her job; and finally, a woman in menopause is given extra care and attention by all. This is a world in which every woman is appreciated and respected for being feminine. Each of the various phases of her life would thus be equally honored and given ample space to unfold in their unique timing. Although this is a far-fetched vision for our modern world, it acts as a beacon of light to illuminate and shape our lives as we move forward in cultivating our *inner beauty*.

Naturally, most women these days are responding to societal pressure and speeding through these precious transitions in their lives without taking the time to really even notice them. They are not to blame for this; society has taught women that there are more important things to do in life than listen to their bodies. The major happenings of the female life experience, like menstruation, pregnancy, birth, postpartum and menopause, are extraordinary events but too often they are just "fit in" on top of a woman's already overwhelming schedule. Other obligations in life take precedence over these sacred moments. In fact, to many modern women these transitions are seen as irritating annoyances at best.

The truth is though, that giving our bodies the time and attention they need to go through their various metamorphoses is one of the rare privileges of being a woman. You see, these transitions are doorways to our *inner beauty*. They offer us opportunities to balance our bodies, minds and spirits so that we can deepen our connection to ourselves. Every transition in a woman's life is thus, a mandate from Nature to honor her femininity and cultivate her *inner beauty*. The gentleness of the feminine energy is what opens the door to connecting with the Self. Therefore, these moments of transition are the perfect opportunity to get to know and appreciate ourselves in the midst of our vulnerability. They are propitious moments put here for you by Nature so that you can learn to love and accept yourself *unconditionally*.

Aspects of *Inner Beauty* Cultivated in The Transitions in a Woman's Life

Patience with the body
Nonviolence with the body
Love towards the body
Harmony with the body
Mercy with the body and Self
Cleanliness with the body
Compassion towards the body
Kindness towards body

The more compassion and understanding you generate for yourself during these times, the more your *inner beauty* grows. Then, because of your positive mindset and increased mindfulness, without even trying, you will be much more likely to have a pain free menses, a gentle menopause, and a smoother conception and delivery. However, if these times of transition are not respected, they can do the opposite - induce pain and suffering and inhibit the qualities of our *inner beauty*. Therefore, it behooves us to stop and pay attention so we can move through the transitions in our lives with mindfulness. If we do not, we risk the health of our bodies and minds, and in doing so sabotage God-given opportunities for us to cultivate our *inner beauty*.

Non-violent

Live your life in a way that inflicts no harm to the emotional, physical and spiritual well-being of all living creatures (including yourself).

In the following pages, I'll be discussing each of the major markers in a woman's life that define the chief transitions she experiences in her lifetime. Some are physiological transitions that happen no matter what, and others are transitions that are made by choice. I call these: mandatory and electivetransitions, respectively. Regardless of their nature, all of these transitions are milestones in a woman's life that provide sacred opportunities for healing, and transformation and thus, the evolution of *inner beauty*.

Transitions in a Woman's Life

Mandatory Female Life Transitions	Elective Female Life Transitions
Menarche	Marriage
Menses	Motherhood: pregnancy, birth, postpartum
Menopause	

Menarche

As a woman transitions from childhood into adulthood she reaches menarche, or the difining moment of her first menstruation. Culturally, Inida offers up some rich traditions in recognition of the archetypal Goddess or divine feminine, so as a woman reaches menarche she is worshiped. This is an expression of the cultural understanding of a how a woman's *inner beauty* is enhanced during the transitions of her life.

Before a woman's menstruation first begins she is seen as containing unmanifest *Shakti*, or the female principal of divine energy. With the onset of menstruation, that *Shakti* finally becomes manifest. At that moment, she steps into her divine expression of the feminine. In her honor, she is given a ceremony so she can symbolically embody this major life transition and further understand her value or *inner beauty*. Elderly woman wash her feet, a coconut is used to represent her womb, and with this ritual she is formally initiated into womanhood. Can you imagine receiving such a ritual as a young woman? It seems unreal for most of us to think about our first menstrual cycle as celebration, much less a signal that the Goddess within has awoken! For most women the onset of menstruation is certainly not experienced as a moment of pride. Many women have horror stories about their first period – when and where it happened, how bad their cramps were, and how embarrassed they felt about the fact. What I am suggesting is that if young women knew of the virtue that abided in the onset of their first menstrual cycle, then I am sure that they would have a far better understanding of the royal and honorable *inner beauty* that they inhabit as a woman.

When a young lady's body initiates the commencing shed of the uterine lining, it is the first major transition in her life. Now, while it would be beautiful to hold a ritual or ceremony in her honor, it is not necessary to go to such lengths in order for her to feel supported. What is necessary however, is the comfort, guidance and respect she receives from those around her as she navigates the change. This effort of support and love can take on any form, it doesn't have to be a distinct ritual. Your support could be as simple as a hug, a good talk, lighting a candle, running a warm bath, preparing a hot meal, or making a cup of ginger tea for the newly christened woman.

Additionally, when speaking with her about the event, use words that convey your respect and honor for her transition into womanhood. Allow your language to lift the shadows of shame and embarrassment and replace them with a sense of pride and celebration. This is how menarche becomes an opportunity for developing *inner beauty* instead of a chance to squander it.

Positive

See the glass as half full, not half empty. Your perspective is your choice so why not make it an optimistic one?

This type of additional support is especially important if the young woman begins her transition into womanhood at an earlier age. She will need extra tender loving care so that she can withstand what will inevitably feel like an overwhelming adjustment and altogether ridiculously complicated ordeal! Many young ladies are starting their periods earlier and earlier these days. Girls as young as eight and nine are reaching menarche. Nature did not intend for girls to begin their fertility cycle at these ages. They are not yet emotionally equip to endure the transition into womanhood and thus, the quality of their *inner beauty* is at stake. They may feel shame around the event or they may not know how to manage the fluctuations they feel in their hormones. Together, these factors erode the foundation for *inner beauty*, or the sense of her self-worth.

The sad truth is that our modern lifestyle is disrupting the hormone systems of young women, diminishing their potential to manage their *inner beauty* and disturbing Nature's clock. Things like the bovine growth hormone (found in inorganic meat and dairy products), xenoestrogens (found in plastics), and excess adipose or fat tissue (due to the overconsumption of nutrient poor calories found in processed food), all play a part in the early induction of a woman's menses. We must do our best to protect our women, young and old, from the threat of these pollutions and the problems they pose to their hormones, and hence, their ability to uphold the qualities of a woman with true *inner beauty*.

Menstruation

It is too easy in our world of scientific and technological innovation to think that we can outsmart Nature. The idea that our intelligence can prevail over the superior omniscient laws of Nature (that we don't even fully comprehend yet) is misguided. Unfortunately, one of the places we see the application of this faulty logic is in the field of women's health. Thanks to the invention of Hormone Replacement Therapy and birth control, women can now manipulate the timing of their menstrual cycles as they please. They may alternate between wearing a synthetic estrogen pack for three weeks, only to remove it for one week while their body attempts to naturally menstruate. It is difficult for a woman's body to swing between unnatural and natural hormones like this. It taxes her because she is forced to go against the grain of natural law and in doing so, forces her body and mind out of their natural propensity towards God-given *inner* and *outer beauty*.

Personally, what I have seen in my practice, is that trying to control Nature with synthetic hormones only leads to worsened PMS, weight gain, acne, migraines, mood swings and menstrual cramping in my patients. As a result, they are unhappy both physically and emotionally and as a result cease to continue the self-care that is needed to maintain their *inner* and *outer beauties*.

It is a far better choice to let the wisdom of Nature regulate our patient's hormones in lieu of imposing technologically manufactured replacements. The reality is that these synthetic hormones can only mimic Nature's perfection and in their attempt, they often cause damage and harm a woman's potential for *inner*, *outer* or even *lasting beauty*.

Menstruation is a natural monthly detoxification process and a sacred transition that women alone have the privilege of using to their benefit. Too often however, this virtue of the menstrual cycle goes underappreciated and a woman's menses is manipulated to be delayed or even purposefully eliminated altogether. This is not a good thing because if a woman misses the opportunity to menstruate in her younger years, toxins will inevitably accumulate and be transferred into the next phase in her life. Furthermore, not having a menstrual cycle is also a stark indication that hormonal imbalance is present in her body.

The aggregate effect of excess toxins combined with imbalanced hormones, makes it so that this woman is sure to not feel beautiful from the inside, out! The toxic build-up in her body likely manifests as acne on her skin, (undermining her *outer beauty*) and the hormonal dysregulation prevents her from behaving virtuously (diminishing her *inner beauty*). Bleeding regularly helps a woman to maintain her "cool," literally and figuratively. With regular menses she nourishes the "cool" qualities of her *inner beauty* like: patience, peace, centeredness, serenity, and harmony. If she does not have her menses, due to synthetic hormones or other hormonal imbalance, then she will more likely accumulate symptoms of excess heat like: anger, hostility, irritability, criticism, and violence – quite contrary to the aims *inner beauty*! This is how dishonoring the transitions in our lives compromises the integrity of our beauty.

One time a month a woman has the option to either honor this mini-transition as a sacred time of release or to disregard it as a mere annoyance. If she chooses the former, she may be able to hear the whispers of her instinctive energy telling her to take time to rest, eat lighter meals, avoid over-stimulating activities like sex and heavy exercise, and maybe do some inner reflection. Perhaps even if she couldn't take a day or two off of work altogether, she would choose to limit the amount of extracurricular activities she does or even just ease up on her pace at work. The more she respects herself she intentionally waters the seeds of her *inner beauty*.

CLEAN & ORGANIZED

> KEEP YOURSELF AND YOUR SURROUNDINGS CLEAN, PURE AND FREE OF CLUTTER. THE EXTERNAL APPEARANCE OF YOUR HOME, YOUR CAR, YOUR BODY AND YOUR PERSONAL ATTIRE ALL REFLECT THE INTERNAL CLARITY OF YOUR MIND.

In some small villages in India women still, as they used to in the olden days, go into separate dwelling places to bleed, and remain there during the entirety of their menstrual cycle. There, they do not cook, clean or do work in any capacity. They simply rest and let their bodies menstruate. Furthermore, they take the time they need to be in stillness and sit in quiet meditation. That's how they work through all their emotional and mental turmoil that has built up over the month. It is as if they schedule a designated time every month to tend to the health of their *inner beauty*. They cleanse the state of their minds so that the virtuous qualities of their *inner beauty* go unobstructed and they support their *outer beauty* by taking care of their bodies.

Of course, at "that time of the month" we can't all go into "red tents" like women in ancient India did, but we can still do our best to minimize our activity as much as possible and take care of ourselves. Menstruation is the perfect transition for us to start to back up, slow down and take it easy. It is not the time to push or fight, but to let go of the old so that we can welcome in the new qualities of *inner beauty* that arise in the process of connecting with ourselves.

Another way we can support ourselves during this transition

is getting in the right kinds of good quality, nourishing foods. For example, sipping on hot liquids and eating fresh, warm, soft foods will assist in our body's ability to metabolize and release toxins. We can favor things like vegtables soups and lentils both of which are nourishing and easy to digest. Conversely, food and drink that will be hard on our systems are things like: iced water, cold, caffeinated beverages and dry foods like popcorn and crackers. These are all displeasing to a body that is menstruating because they tend to inhibit the proper movement of the menstrual flow through the channels of the body. Giving ourselves the proper types of foods during menstruation is one way that we can practice honoring our bodies. This way we will be more balanced and able to promote the virtuous qualities of our *inner beauty* within ourselves.

Menstruation

Make time for reflection

Enjoy a gentle walk in nature

Nourish yourself with warm food

Stay warm and cozy

Take a break from sexual acitvity

Relax into your monthly detox

Understand the nature of your body

Accept yourself as you are

Transfer your energy inward

Ensure you get emotional support

Marriage

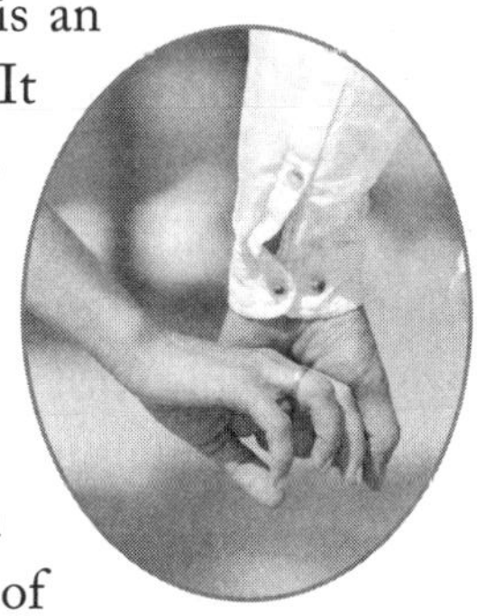

Marriage is a beauiful ceremony and ritual. It is an important, yet optional transition in a woman's life. It can be integrated if a woman so chooses and desires. This sort of "elective transition" should take place only when and if a woman is ready. Marriage is no small commitment. It requires each partner to give up their personal, individual agenda in favor of a unified, collective mission. Each must make the transition from their own sense of individuality, into a shared sense of unity for their new family in the making. Undoubtedly, this requires compromise, adjustments and letting go – clearly not the transition for the faint of heart! It is a choice only for a woman who has strong, well established *inner beauty*.

Whatever the transition in a women's life may be, ritual is there to act as a confirmation for the milestone she is crossing. Creating an intentional ritual is a powerful way to outwardly express the presence of an inner transformation. This is why we see people suddenly decide to cut their hair after ending a relationship, or completely rearrange their living room when they're grieving the death of a pet or loved one. In all of these cases there is an intangible energetic shift the person has experienced and they're now yearning to express it outwardly. My point is that this is the place from where the desire for a marriage should arise. It needs to be inspired by an internal transformation, not by a fantasy about cupcakes, twinkle lights and ball gowns. The marriage ceremony is meant to be an outer reflection of a substantial internal change marking the transition out of individuality and into union. This is the kind of change that occurs when our *inner beauty* evolves to a new level – moving from a desire to live only for the self, to a desire to live for the whole of both you and your partner.

In India there is a custom to be married with seven steps and seven vows (*saptapadi*, it is called). The steps are taken as a part of a ritual around a fire. The fire is sacred because it symbolizes the ultimate Truth. It can also be seen as the flame of the couple's *inner beauty*. As they encircle the fire, they are held accountable to the maintenance of their respective moral and ethical virtues, or *inner beauty*. Walking around a fire in a Hindu wedding is like taking a vow with your hand upon the Holy Bible in a western courthouse – it ensures and morally obligates honesty.

Additionally, as bride and groom take their steps around the fire, they pledge their allegiance to one another for their entire lives. With the addition of each new step they recite oaths and make vows to uphold their promises. These steps are the first they take together as husband and wife and are said to set the stage for happiness and prosperity for their lifetime. The bride and groom take these steps not just for their own endowment of good fortune, but for their family's as well. This is because the union of bride and groom is understood to also be a union of two families. The blessings in the couple's ritual are thus extended to each of their mothers, fathers and grandparents as well. Again, we see that the purpose of the wedding is so much greater than any personal agenda or gain; it is done for the greater good. It is a ritual designed to bring affirmation and blessing not only to the transformation within the couple, but within their families as well. That is why the marriage it is an expression of the couple's familial, collective *inner beauty*.

Now, to go a little deeper into the picture of this wedding , imagine the bride. Surely if you've ever witnessed a Hindu wedding, you'd know she would be lavishly adorned with ornate jewelry. She would shimmer with gold hanging from her head, falling down her arms, glittering from her ears, and sparkling on her nose. As she approaches the temple to be wed, her whole being would glisten with gemstones and fine gold or silver.

Inner Beauty

Looking at the bride, you might assume that her jewels are there to make her feel as though she were a Goddess radiating with beauty on her wedding day. While the jewels indeed accomplish this mission, they also do something more. With only a superficial glance, we might not know that these jewels also relay a deeper meaning. Each ornament worn comes attached with a blessing from the father of the bride, to the groom's family. For example, the bracelets she wears are said to bestow her with the calling to do good things. Similarly, her earrings bless her ears so that she may listen well, and the rings placed on her fingers remind her to have loving touch. Everything beautiful that she wears corresponds with an equally beautiful intention to bring blessings to her new family. In sum, the virtues of her *inner beauty* are emboldened by every jewel she wears.

Coincidentally, as it turns out, the famous Audrey Hepburn also had the same idea that external beauty is only significant when complimented by internal good intention, or *inner beauty*. She is quoted saying:

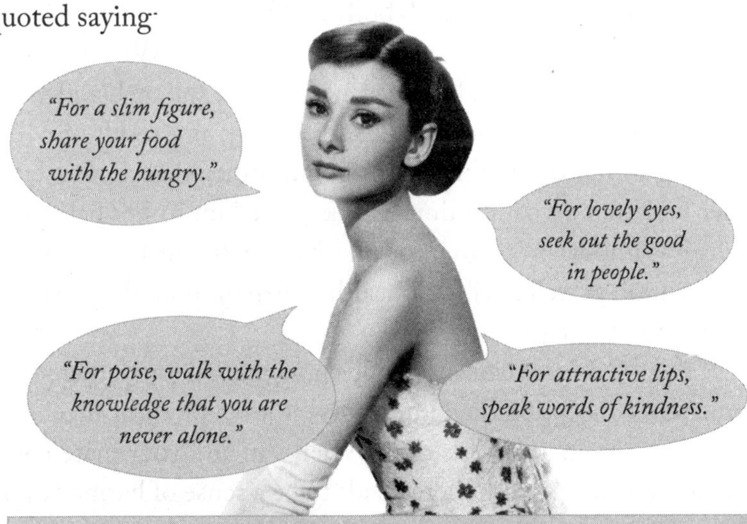

"As you grow older, you will discover that you have two hands; one for helping yourself and the other, for helping others." ~ Audrey Hepburn ~

Fertility & Conception

Each and every woman has within her the energy of creation. In the ancient Vedic scriptures of Inida, this is referred to as *Shakti* or the divine feminine. *Shakti* is a force of creation unique to a woman alone and is the essence of her femininity. It is both the seed and fertile soil from which all life is germinated. Just like a seed, *Shakti* contains the potential for new life and just like rich soil, it nourishes that potential into fruition. In other words, *Shakti* is the energetic principal needed to transform the meeting of sperm and egg into a human being. Without *Shakti* there can be no creation (or procreation for that matter). Without *Shakti*, *inner beauty* is lifeless.

When a woman lives her life with fear, stress and anxiety she inadvertently disturbs her *Shakti* and thus, her *inner beauty*. If her *Shakti* falters altogether, she will have difficulty conceiving. On the other hand, if her *Shakti* is just diminished or somewhat taxed, she may still be able to conceive but unfortunately, not without consequences. Both a woman's body and her developing baby will be taxed if her *Shakti* is compromised in any way. With too little reserve, mama's system will be burdened and the toll on her physical body will be felt by baby as well. Additionally, as a result of Mom not being in her optimal health, any impurities that accumulated in her body before conception will be passed on to her baby. This is why it is important to go into conceiving with great mindfulness and intention as well as vibrant health – thereby upholding a strong foundation of *inner beauty*.

If there is no consciousness enlivening mother and father at the moment of conception then intercourse is just a physical, mechanical process aimed at procreation. When you and your mate come together to create a baby, there needs to be a sense of harmony and greater purpose within each of you. Ayurveda says that the union of sperm and egg is a sacred moment when a new soul is invited into the world. It is meant to be a cherished act of mindfulness. Then, when both partners are completely present, balanced and healthy, they will impart the energy of consciousness and *inner beauty* on their soon-to-be child.

Spiritual

> Having a spiritual practice attunes your life to a greater meaning. It allows you to live with intention instead of mindless indifference. If you don't already, try doing a small practice of meditation to remind you of the unity that exists in all of life.

The moment the sperm and the egg successfully meet is significant not just because it makes a pregnancy possible. Each of the gametes coming from mother and father carry with them a set of qualities that will impact the nature of the zygote. According to Ayurveda, the qualities of the sperm and egg are reflections of the mother and father's diet, lifestyle, emotional state, exercise routines, stress levels and/or physical problems. Another way of looking at this is through the lens of epigenetics. Epigenetics describes the way our environment affects the expression of our genes. It looks at which genes are turned on or off depending on the way we live and what we're exposed to in our lives. If we have strong *inner beauty*, we turn on "good genes." If we have weak *inner beauty*, we let the negative forces in our lives take over and we're more likely to encourage our "bad genes" to light up. Therefore, the state of each parent's *inner beauty* is subtly embedded into their gametes just as their respective degrees of physical health or disease (*outer beauty*) also impact the seeds they bear.

If you are hoping to begin planning for a baby in the future, I highly recommend that you start preparing now. Make the proper adjustments in your life that will enable you to be the most balanced version of yourself with the strongest degree of *inner beauty* possible. When you are in a healthy state and working within the harmony of Nature's timely support, then you will find the best possible moment to conceive a truly beautiful and blessed little one.

Motherhood: Pregnancy

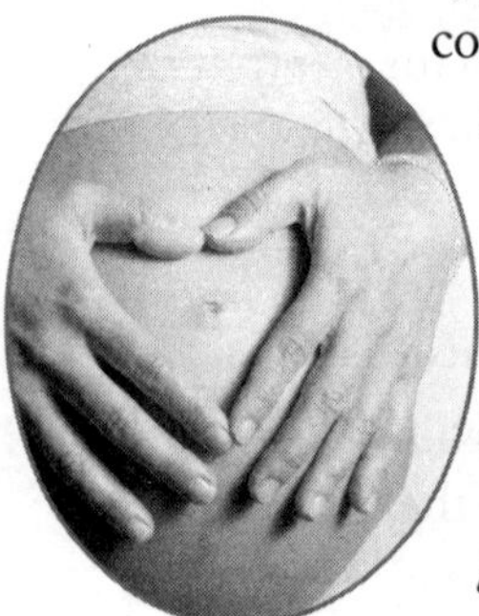

Many women are afraid that their *outer beauty* will become compromised in the process of gestation. They fear they'll never recover the fit, youthful appearance they once had prior to their pregnancy. They think that they'll be left with saggy skin on their bellies, atrophied abdominal muscles, stretch marks and weight that just won't come off. It is understandable that women have such fears around their figures changing. Society emphasizes *outer beauty* first and foremost and thus, many women feel discouraged about getting pregnant, nursing and giving birth because of the effect it will have on their physiques.

I once had a famous Hollywood actress come into my office for an Ayurvedic detoxification method called panchakarma. During our time together she expressed to me her deep desire to have a child. At the same time however, she was concerned that the pregnancy would change her figure and compromise her career. Hollywood sets the standard that a women's body should never change, so sadly, this actress felt nervous to bear a child. She wanted to know how quickly she would be able to recover after her delivery. I explained that recovery time has everything to do with age. Nature supports women in recovering from their pregnancy best before the age of 30. At that age, it takes only about 1 year to completely restore the body and mind to their prenatal conditions. After 35 years old however, it takes around a total of 5 years to recover, and beyond 40 years old, it is difficult to recover at all.

That being said, no matter what your age is when you become pregnant, the most important thing for you to do during this time is focus on your *inner beauty*. If you maintain a robust *inner beauty*, then your physiology will naturally be more balanced as a result. In that way, you'll be able to avoid some of the enduring physical scares of childbearing and "bounce back" more easily.

As you can see, the responsibility mom faces to foster plentiful *inner beauty* does not stop with a successful conception. Her commitment to maintain a quality life filled with *inner beauty* must follow her through her entire pregnancy (and beyond in fact). A new mom must hold her child mindfully in her womb.

Discipline

> You cannot be fully free without being fully disciplined. Ironic as it may seem, it is true. Freedom comes only after practicing persistence, diligence and devotion – all qualities inherent in discipline.

Earlier we discussed the concept that according to Ayurveda, a mother's egg is infused with the qualities of her *inner beauty*. The same concept applies to her gestation. The time the fetus spends in utero is the single most important time of their entire lives. The developing child is at its most vulnerable state during pregnancy and is highly susceptible to all external and internal environmental input. Even simple things like Mom's choices in food, her daily routine, and the way she manages her emotions are all highly influential on the little one she holds in her womb.

It is fascinating to think that thousands of years ago the ancient scholars of Ayurveda knew just how important it was for mom to be happy, healthy, and filled with the virtues of *inner beauty* during her pregnancy. They understood that gestation is a critical stage in which the growing child receives potent cellular information that has a profound effect on their life as an adult. These acute observations lead the Ayurvedic sages to craft specific antidotes that would ensure that Mom could maintain a healthy level of *inner beauty* during her pregnancy. Their suggestions range from deeply nourishing foods, to calming spiritual practices like meditation, all aimed at securing the balance and harmony of the mind and thereby strengthening the mother's innate *inner beauty*.

MOTHERHOOD: BIRTH

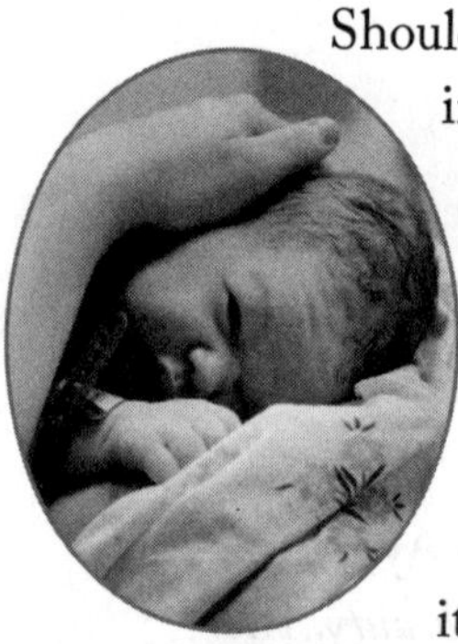

Should a woman decide to bare children, the moment of truth in her life is the moment she gives birth. Her body mind and spirit are put to the test and after holding for nine months she has to let go. The concept of giving birth can sometimes feel like an insurmountable and even physically impossible task! The entire preparation and anticipation of the event is akin to setting sail at midnight – you'll never really know what it will be like until it is actually happening! It is a monumental transition in a woman's lifetime and the perfect opportunity to cultivate qualities of *inner beauty* like faith, trust, and relaxation.

Perhaps in an effort to make the birthing process feel more "sane" and lessen the feeling of being so out of control, there has been a recent trend for women to schedule cesarean sections for their births instead of waiting until "Nature calls." In this way they'll know at exactly what time and date the baby will arrive. Certainly this is has an understandable advantage. Mom won't be caught off guard, grandma and grandpa will know when to come over, dad can take the day off of work, a babysitter can be arranged for any siblings, and all will go as planned. The only problem with this is that both Nature's timing and Nature's way are being dismissed. As we've seen before, there are consequences when this happens.

There are times when c-sections are absolutely warranted. They can save the lives of both baby and mama in many cases of emergency. However, elective c-sections are very different. They deny Nature the opportunity to do its brilliant work and they leave mom with compromised *outer beauty*, as she is nursing back to health a body that has endured major abdominal surgery.

If at all possible, having a natural delivery is more balancing to the female hormones and thus supports the propensity towards upholding *inner* and *outer beauty*. Plus, a mother will be doing her baby a favor too. As it turns out, part of Nature's design in birth is to transfer healthy microbes to the baby via the vaginal canal. Mom's vaginal mucosa is teeming with these good bugs and the baby needs them to establish a healthy immune system and strong digestion. When a baby is delivered via c-section, he or she doesn't get exposed to these beneficial bacteria from mother. Instead, their first exposure to extrauterine bugs comes from the bacteria in the surgery room. The hospital's collection of microbes is quite different, and less optimal than mother's innate habitat of bugs. Scientists suggest that for better or worse, this initial impact of microbial colonization in the newborn could affect their health for the rest of their lives.

Easy Going

> Life won't always go as you have planned or envisioned. Learn to be flexible – bending and shifting with the winds of life. Relax into the flow and go with it!

Whenever and however you end up giving birth, make sure that wherever you are, you feel safe and secure. Prepare the environment as best you can, even if it is at the hospital. Adorn the room with flowers, diffuse essential oils, light candles, and play soft music. All in all, make sure that the environment is warm, soothing and peaceful. In India, we even massage the mother with warm sesame oil before she delivers. We also do a warm oil enema so that her delivery pains are lessoned. Whatever you need to do, just make sure that you are able to be grounded and centered in the process of your labor. This way, you'll be more able to access the qualities of your *inner beauty* like: strength, courage and bravery to bring you smoothly through your delivery.

Motherhood: Postpartum

After baby is born, there begins a vulnerable and tender period of time in which *inner beauty* is easily menaced. The post-partum transition is a delicate situation that needs to be carefully navigated by all involved. Mother, father and baby are getting acquainted for the first time in their new lives and relationships together. Mom is drained and depleted from the birthing process and both parents are getting too little sleep because of the new demands of their infant. The accumulation of physical, emotional, psychological and financial stress during this time can lead some new mothers to fall into a state of depression. *Inner beauty* is deeply challenged during this transition. In fact, it is susceptible to collapsing altogether under the all pressure of so much drastic change all at once.

Mom needs all the support she can get during this transition. Family, friends and neighbors need to step up to the plate and pitch in. Neighbors can watch other children, friends can bring over food, and family members can do the dishes or hold the baby while Mom takes a quick rest. The ancient wisdom of Ayurveda tells us that Mom can even benefit from receiving daily, or at least weekly, full body warm oil massages to reduce her incidence of postpartum depression and renew the strength of her *inner beauty*. The warmth of the oil and comfort of the touch provides the grounding and reassurance that Mom needs. If Mom herself is nourished, then she'll have more reserve to give her baby healthy, loving touch (maybe even in the form of warm oil massage) as well. The connection exchanged through touch enhances the bonding between mother and child and abates the potential threat of depression.

All in all, as Mom learns to take care of herself during this challenging period, she learns to fortify the strength and endurance of her *inner beauty*. She will then automatically transmit positive messages of *inner beauty* like: unconditional love, forgiveness and patience, to her baby. So when pre and postnatal transitions are approached with mindfulness and care, the qualities of *inner beauty* in both the mother and child can be reinforced and renewed at every turn.

Menopause

Unlike the cherished years of child rearing and fertility, most women dread the years surrounding menopause. There is a tremendous stigma around this transition among women in America. They seem to view it as life's greatest fall from grace. It is perceived as a desent from a woman's prime - a fall into the "dormant" phase – out of beauty, and definately out of sex appeal. Menopause is seen as this heinous hurdle every woman must at some point cross over.

I have to say, these sentiments are not entirely unfounded. The symptoms that plague menopausal women in America are formidable. Sadly, western women seem to suffer much more than the women I've witnessed go through menopause in India. But how and why could this be? Menopause is just menopause, right? Why would one group of women experience it any differently than another? The answer is because of lifestyle. Women in the west are stressed.

They're balancing countless responsibilities often with very little spousal or communal moral support. This degree of stress affects their hormones in such a way that their menopause becomes more distressing than it need be. This taxes both their *inner* and *outer beauty* as they experience undesirable changes in both their mood and physical body.

Resilience

> Keep your mind focused on the Divine. This way you will build strength and clarity in your mind and heart. Then, whatever challenges comes your way, you will be able to navigate through them with grace and fortitude.

Women who experience painful menopausal symptoms are often living through the consequences of not taking care of themselves when they were younger. They may have pushed themselves hard when they menstruated, maybe they went back to work only a week after giving birth, or maybe they over-exercised or held on to an unhealthy relationship. In any case, menopause is often the time when a woman's past finally shows up to knock on her doorstep asking to be let in. This is the time when women in the west are most abruptly confronted with the need to finally slow down and allow for a change of pace in their lives so that they can reestablish a connection with their *inner beauty*. They're given no other option but to begin to rectify the debt they've accumulated in their former years and revaluate where their true priorities lie.

In many developing countries many women don't know the word for menopause. Sometimes that is because they may be illiterate, but other times it is simply because it really isn't talked about. Culturally, women in India do not openly discuss issues surrounding the physical body. They keep these things private. Now, on one hand this can be detrimental because a woman may not understand the changes that are happening in her body, but on the other hand, it can be surprisingly be advantageous. You see, the meaning that we give to something in our lives changes our perception about it, and in turn, our perception changes our experience. That is why it is so important to maintain a vigorous sense of *inner beauty*. We need a positive self-perception and an optimistic outlook on life to cope with this challenging transition. Unfortunately however, the meaning assigned to menopause in the west is close to a living hell! Thus, women move into their later years expecting menopause to be just that.

In India on the other hand, we see that the opposite is true. There is very little expectation surrounding menopause because the concept is generally non-existent among most women. As a result, there is no culturally endorsed idea that menopause is such a bad time in life. The benefit in this case is that Indian women don't spend their lifetimes envisioning menopause with dread! They don't expend all their energy in fear, anxiety and worry over the topic. What ends up happening is that they simply live through the changes and trust in their bodies to take care of the details.

Humor

> Don't forget to laugh! Take every opportunity you can to make light and enjoy in life - it's too short not to.

In a way, all of us as women in the west are reinforcing the idea for each other that menopause is awful. It is our cultural meme. Yes, western women have more difficult transitions around menopause, but that doesn't mean the issue needs to be blown out of proportion. There's a lot of hype built up around the experience that just might not actually be necessary. The more we put ourselves into a fizzy about the idea (stress out, freak-out and worry), the more we set ourselves up for realizing our expectations.

Our beliefs set the stage for our experiences, so it is up to us to start seeing menopause as an opportunity for healing instead of a death sentence. We need to reorient our perception around menopause so that it reflects the qualities of *inner beauty*: confidence, assuredness, kindness, gentleness, non-judgment and patience. If we do this, then we might finally be able to make some positive changes in our life that will support us in living happily and healthily into our later years of life. So let us welcome this transition with open arms, expecting it to be none other than an opportunity to develop our *inner beauty*.

Conclusion

Overall, if you live congruently with the force of Nature, then you'll more easily be able to poise your mind in the light of your *inner beauty*. As you do this, the transitions in your life will become a source of celebration and joy instead of a point of stress, burden and embarrassment. The payoff for all your hard work is that you'll be able to transform every one of the challenges you face during these transitions, into sacred gems that will decorate the brilliance of your *inner beauty*. Enjoy!

Inner Beauty

Chapter 3

OUTER BEAUTY

The Outward Expression of Inner Beauty

Does Absolute Beauty Exist?

By now you've come to understand that real beauty is more than what just meets the eye - it is a reflection of the magnitude of your inner strength and virtue. We also know that it is truly in "the eye of the beholder" – it is a subjective experience determined by the state of an individual's mind. In other words, all the permutations of beauty in our lives ultimately come from within. Therefore, this begs the question as to whether or not any general standards of beauty actually exist. There must be some external, tangible attributes that people universally accept as beautiful.

Doctor Stephen Marquardt, an oral and facial surgeon, set out to define beauty in the absolute. He collected and analyzed data cross-culturally and found what he thinks to be the common denominator for universal beauty. He claims that beauty exists between the symmetry and harmony of the x and y axis of the face. He says that if beautiful, these various measurements of facial features reveal mathematical patterns that match the famous "golden rule," or the number phi (pronounced like the pie that you eat on Thanksgiving). Phi, also known as Fibonacci's number, is a ratio of 1.618:1 and likely a concept you were introduced to in 3rd grade math class. We see this ratio expressed in the geometrical configurations of nature time and time again. It can be found in the proportions of a sunflower, the spirals on a sea snail's shell, the spacing of leaves on a rose bush or arguably, in the facial features of a human being. Marquardt argues that when nature is in alignment with phi, then irrefutable beauty results.

While it could be true that our mind's eye is delighted by mathematically succinct dimensions, this is not the sole determining factor for beauty. Although a man or woman could be born with a facial structure that features the perfect ratio of phi, he or she may still be unattractive. For example, imagine a woman with a mathematically correct face, but her skin is blemished and dull, she has sunken eyes, pale lips, flaking nails, dry and thinning hair, and her muscles are wasting away. When she walks into the room she slouches. Her aura is negative and sickly. You feel awful in her presence. Would you still find this woman to be beautiful?

The truth is, beauty cannot be standardized. There is no absolute formula for beauty because it encompasses more than what can be calculated. Superficial, Barbie-like equations do not take into account the health and happiness of our minds, bodies and hearts.

Even if we accept that beauty is indeed more than just our genetic makeup, it doesn't mean that we can't make a healthy effort to enhance our God-give features. No matter how close or how far you stand from the "perfect phi face," you can still highlight the natural, external beauty you have been given. It is vitally important that we sense that our *inner beauty* can be projected into our *outer beauty*. While we may be full of harmony from within and even deeply appreciate our innate worth as a woman, we still have to make sure our skin isn't breaking out! We have to have some way of figuring out how to make our *inner beauty* show outwardly. We need a practical, how-to guide on self-care for external beauty. That's what this chapter is all about – learning how to take care of our own unique physicality, or *outer beauty,* so that it becomes a radiant reflection of our *inner beauty.*

The Desire for Beauty

So who on earth doesn't want to be externally beautiful? It is nothing to be ashamed of. This is a natural desire. The only risk we face in pursuing this is becoming overly focused on the *outer* measurement of beauty and forgetting about its truest expression in the form of *inner* value. If we focus on the external expression of our beauty being:

(1) a reflection of our *inner beauty*

(2) a mirror for the health of our physiology, then we're on the right track!

Humans have always found a way to adore themselves with beautiful artifacts, most often to appeal to a potential mate or to signify some sort of status. Early civilizations made jewelry out of bones, seeds, barks, stones, shells and feathers. They made skirts from leaves, and used natural pigment to paint different designs on their bodies. Some cultures even practiced body modification, piercing their ears and other areas as an expression of beauty. You see, beautifying ourselves is not a new concept. It has been practiced cross culturally throughout antiquity.

Our current world in the 21st century is no different. The desire to accent our inborn beauty with expensive jewelry, designer clothes, elaborate tattoos, body piercings, fancy sunglasses and nail polish, all come from a social and biological urge to be seen as attractive. It is not wrong to indulge in any of these things – we just have to do it with consciousness and awareness.

The caveat to pursuing external embellishment is that it not be used in a way which creates a false sense of self-worth. Look deeply into yourself to make sure that you don't desire that new purse because you are trying to cover up a sense of loneliness, despair or lack of self-confidence. We must make sure that our external endeavors towards beautification come from the right place. Any outer decorations we posses should compliment our external features *and* reflect our *inner beauty*. External beautification is not meant to cover up who you are; it is meant to accent your uniquely beautiful physical assets. Make up is not designed to hide your face, but rather to accentuate the beauty that is already there! Eye liner should magnify the sparkle in your eye and lip gloss should show off the natural rouge of your lips. Nothing can make up for true *outer beauty* resulting from healthy physiology and inner virtue. Not even top of the line cosmetics.

Do you recall the classic story of "Goldilocks and the Three Bears?" Goldilocks did not want her porridge too hot or too cold, she wanted it just right. The same idea applies to working with our ascetic senses. In Sanskrit, the ancient language of India, the word *lavanya* and *madhurya* both mean beauty. But the root of the word *lavanya* means salt and the root of the word *madhurya* means sweet.

So what do salty and sweet have to do with Goldilocks or beauty? Well, just as Goldilocks wanted the temperature of her porridge to be at *just right*, we too would never want a dish of ours to be overly salted or under salted; overly sweet or under sweet. If there's too much salt it can be hard to swallow. If there's too little, then the food tastes bland. If there's too much sweet in a dish, it is bad for your health and can taste like too much. If there's too little sweet on your plate, you can be left unsatisfied. We need just the perfect amount of salt and sweet to bring out the natural flavors of the food but not overwhelm them.

Salt and sweet are opposites, and they need to be in just the right quantities in order for something to taste good. That's why these terms are historically used to describe beauty. Beauty is about balance. Overdoing it with makeup, jewelry or other outward displays of beauty can make us look "over the top." And if we do not care about our outward appearance at all, we might come off as unkempt. What is needed is *just the right* amount of effort to allow our true beauty to be fully expressed.

Conclusion

No matter what point we're starting from in our venture towards achieving external beauty – whether you're a five time plastic surgery veteran or haven't worn a ounce of makeup in your life – this chapter will take you on a journey to learn how to care for you body naturally, from head to toe. Please join me in discovering your *outer beauty* in a whole new way!

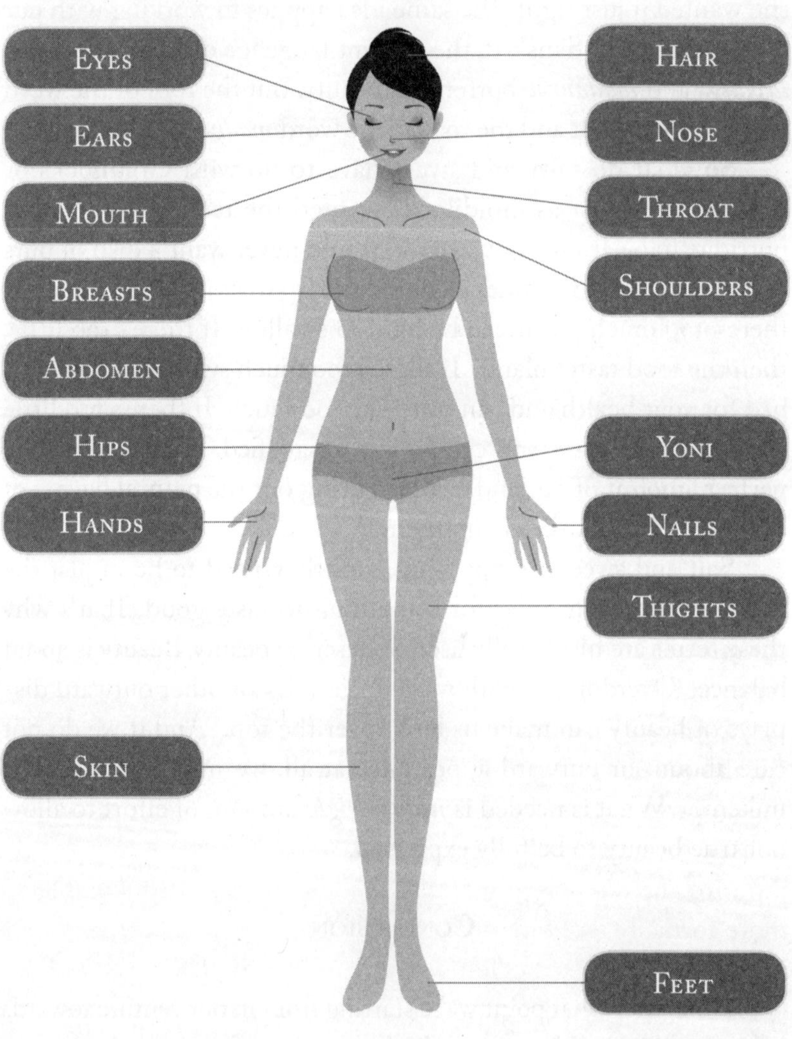

Outer Beauty and Ayurveda

Nature & Outer Beauty

The essence of our *outer beauty* is expressed through vibrant and healthy physiology. If our bodies aren't healthy, they won't *look* healthy, and health is what exemplifies external beauty. So before you try to stuff an extra lip gloss into your purse, you might first think about getting healthy. That is step #1 to achieving *outer beauty*.

I don't mean to tell you that if you want to get healthy you need to go out and find a good doctor. While that may sometimes be necessary, I aim to show you how you can understand the unique qualities of your own particular body *yourself*. I want you to be able to maximize your external beauty and physical health every day – not just after you've visited the doctor. I want to introduce to you a whole new perspective on what your individual mind and body need in order to be balanced and beautiful.

You'll discover that health is not a "one size fits all" program. What you need to thrive might be the worst thing ever for the health of your neighbor, and visa versa! If you want to be the healthiest version of yourself, then you need to understand the individuality of your own body. There is no one single recipe for wellness. Just as we are all beautiful in our own way, each of our physiology is unique.

Prior to this juncture, I've alluded several times to the ancient, holistic medicine of India, called Ayurveda. Now that we're entering into the discussion of *outer beauty*, I'm excited to be able to more formally and intently introduce you to this medicine that I love so much. It is pertinent to our subject of *outer beauty* because it teaches us how to harmonize our bodies with our own unique nature so that we can become our healthiest and thus, most beautiful. In other words, learning the basics of this science and how it applies to you, will help you skillfully navigate the ins and outs of your unique expression of external beauty. Ayurveda will teach you how to work with the Nature of your body so that you can get the changes that you're looking for naturally. Nothing is as effective as that. You see, when you are in harmony with Nature and understand how it works in your body, then you'll get results that last. You'll have more radiant skin, thicker hair, stronger nails, luscious lips, dazzling eyes, and more, because we are working *with* Nature to care for your physiology.

But first, before we begin, I'd just like to reinstate the idea that the desire to take care of our physical bodies and *outer beauty* has to come from a rooted foundation of *inner beauty* and self-love. If not, it will be difficult for us to actualize the physical self-care that is needed to manifest our *outer beauty*. So remembering that, let's dive into "Ayurveda 101!"

Ayurveda 101

What is the meaning of Ayurveda?

Ayurveda is a term made up of the *Sanskrit* words *"ayu"* and *"veda."* "Ayu" means life and "veda" means knowledge or science. Hence, the word Ayurveda means 'knowledge of life' or 'the science of life.' Fundamentally, Ayurveda is a science that prescribes medicinal treatments for the body, mind and spirit. The ancient scriptures that expound Ayurvedic principals originated in India 5-6 thousand years ago. It is one of the most ancient medical sciences of the world.

What are the basic princibles?

Ayurveda says that the universe is made up of five elements: air, fire, water, water and ether. These elements are the building blocks for the universe as a whole and all of its creation; including us - humankind. The five elements are distinguished by characteristic qualities that set them apart from one another.

Element	Qualities
Ether	Subtle, soft, clear, smooth, expanding
Air	Rough, dry, light, cold, mobile
Fire	Hot, sharp
Water	Flowing, wet, dull, soft, cloudy
Earth	Gross, heavy, static, hard, dens

Ayurveda conveniently compiles the qualities of these elements into three groups. These groups acts as one singular bio-psycho-spiritual forces of nature that we refer to as *doshas*. Each of the *doshas* possesses the qualities of two out of the five elements. The three *doshas* are referred to as: (1) *Vata*, (2) *Pitta* and (3) *Kapha*. The first, *Vata*, is a combination of space and air. It is responsible for every movement in the body - impulses, circulation, respiration, and elimination. The second, *Pitta dosha*, is a combination of fire and water and takes care of all transformation in the body. It governs heat, metabolism, temperature, and all metabolic chemical reactions. The last of the three, *Kapha dosha*, is a combination of water and earth. It is responsible for growth, protection, lubrication and sustenance. Together, these three doshas are simply ways of referring to the elements that exist within our bodies and the qualities that they impart on our psychological and physiological functioning.

Dosha	Elemental Composition	Description of Qualities	Physiological Impact
Vata	Ether + Air	Light, dry, cold, rough, subtle and mobile	Action, transportation and movement
Pitta	Fire + Water	Light, hot, sharp, oily, mobile, liquid	Transformation, conversion and digestion
Kapha	Water + Earth	Heavy, cold, moist, dull, soft, sticky and static	Construction, lubrication and nourishment

Your Nature is Your Beauty

As you can see, there are three primary ways in which Nature expresses itself in the body and mind. These three bioenergetic forces (or *dosha*s) can be represented by the three elements inherent in Nature – *Vata* (ether + air), *Pitta* (fire + water) and *Kapha* (water + earth). Most often, each of us is dominant in psychological or physiological characteristics of either one or two out of the three constitutions. Therefore, it is now our job is to discover which out of these three *dosha*s is most representative of us, and then apply our newfound knowledge to benefit our *outer beauty.*

Here are some examples, say that you find out that you have predominately air type, or *Vata* skin. In that case, you might need to apply extra moisturizer because excess air creates dryness and roughness. Alternativly, if you find you have more fire, or *Pitta* in your hair, then you may have to use natural remedies to cope with the early graying or thinning that is caused by excess heat. Knowing the elemental constituents of our physiology helps us prevent potential problems and recover from current imbalances. We learn to work alongside Nature, using Her intelligence to restore, rejuvenate and punctuate our natural *outer beauty.*

The constitutional body-type quiz that you're about to take will look at numerous different aspects of your physiology. You'll get a sense for overall which element(s) dominate the entirety of your makeup. Each of us has a unique combination of the elements or *dosha*s, that express themselves in totally individualized ways. The quiz you are about to take will give you a broad sense for which element(s) best describe you on the whole. Often times people score as being primarily dominant in one single *dosha*. However, sometimes people tie between two *dosha*s, and even more rarely, they'll score equally among all three. In former case of two *dosha*s tying for first place, both of the elements are co-dominant in the body. If this happens to describe you, then through this chapter and beyond, please refer to the descriptions designated for both of the *doshas* that characterize you. In the latter, unusual case that all three elements share near to equal responsibility in your body, then the best thing you can do is read through all the recommendations listed in this book and experiment with which ones feel best in your body.

Finally, it is important to note that having the perfect balance in your body does not mean attaining equal ratios of *Vata*, *Pitta* and *Kapha* qualities. Rather, it means living in harmony with the way that nature exists in you! The perfect score on this quiz is the score that is truly representative of you.

Find out your Dosha Type Body Constitution

Check the choices that are the closest match to your tendencies throughout your lifetime. Be honest!

	Vata	Pitta	Kapha
Body size	☐ Thin	☐ Medium	☐ Large
Weight	☐ Light	☐ Medium	☐ Heavy
Skin	☐ Dry, cold, rough	☐ Oily, flushed, warm	☐ Soft, smooth, pale
Complexion	☐ Dark, dull	☐ Red, glowing	☐ Pale, white
Face	☐ Oval	☐ Triangular	☐ Round
Eyes	☐ Small, dry, nervous	☐ Medium, sharp, bright	☐ Big, calm, loving
Hands	☐ Small, dry, cold	☐ Medium, moist	☐ Thick, firm

Outer Beauty

	Vata	Pitta	Kapha
Fingers	☐ Thin, long	☐ Medium, pointed	☐ Large, stocky
Joints	☐ Small, cracking	☐ Medium, moist	☐ Large, lubricated
Voice	☐ Weak, hoarse	☐ Strong tone	☐ Deep, good tone
Speech	☐ Talkative, rapid	☐ Clear, sharp	☐ Quiet, slow
Sleep	☐ Irregular	☐ Regular	☐ Deep
Activities	☐ Hyperactive	☐ Moderate	☐ Sedentary
Appetite	☐ Irregular	☐ Strong	☐ Slow, steady
Elimination	☐ Constipated	☐ Regular	☐ Sluggish
Emotions	☐ Anxious, worried	☐ Irritable, determined	☐ Calm, attachment
Memory	☐ Variable	☐ Selective	☐ Detailed
Mind	☐ Restless	☐ Impatient	☐ Calm
Hobbies	☐ Art, dance, travel	☐ Politics, sports	☐ Reading, gardening
Health Problems	☐ Anxiety, depression	☐ Fevers, heartburn, skin issues	☐ Congestion, allergies
Preferred Weather	☐ Warm, moist	☐ Cool, temperate	☐ Warm, dry
Total:			

Sensory Perception & Ayurveda

Now that you've come to understand the basics of Ayurveda and how you fit into the greater scheme of Nature, let's take a look at some more advanced Ayurvedic theory surrounding beauty. I'd like to share with you what Ayurveda has to say about the care of sensory organs and how their health contributes to our *outer beauty*. To begin with, Ayurveda connects each sensory organ and function with an associated element.

Correlation Between 5 Elements And Sensory Organs

Elements	Sense Organ	Tanmatra	Motor Organ
Ether	Ear	Sound	Vocal Cords
Air	Skin	Touch	Hands
Fire	Eyes	Sight	Feed
Water	Tongue	Taste	Urogenital System
Earth	Nose	Smell	Anus

Along that same vein, in Ayurvedic medicine, the face is partitioned into three sections from the forehead down to the chin. It is divided this way because each area corresponds with either the qualities of air *(Vata)*, fire *(Pitta)* or water *(Kapha)* respectively. Then, within each of these three distinct sections, there resides various sensory organ(s). Naturally, these organs reflect the qualities of the *dosha* that presides over the particular area where they are positioned on the face.

Take the example of the eyes. As you can see from the diagram below, the eyes are located in the area of the fire element. This means that they are sharp and hot in nature. Because Ayurveda tells us this, we know to treat the eyes with soothing and cooling foods and herbs. One of Ayurveda's main principals is to *counter a quality in Nature that is in excess, with its opposite.* Therefore, given that the Nature of the eyes is hot, they must be complimented with something cooling to maintain balance.

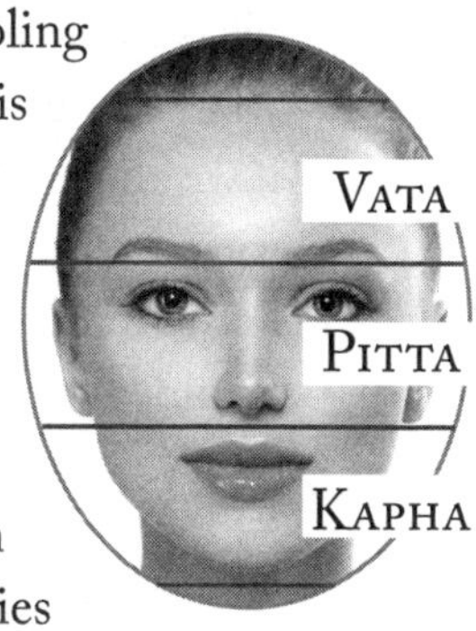

As you make your way through the rest of this chapter, you may want to refer back to this diagram as a guideline for figuring out which kinds of therapies (hot, cold, warm, moist, or drying) would be most beneficial and protective to each of your sensory organs. As you consider this, the key is to remember that *opposites balance.*

FEEDING OUR SENSES

Ayurveda makes a point to tell us that our diet doesn't just include the food that we eat. Instead, it says that we consume with all of our five senses. Good "food" for the eyes is to see the sunset, full moon, ocean or green hills. Conversely, watching horror films is an example of bad "food" for the eyes. In the same way, healthy consumption for the nose is to smell exquisite incense; *not* to take out the trash! Our ears love to hear soothing instrumental music. It relaxes our mind and changes our brain waves for the better. Heavy metal and rock music on the other hand, is *not* healing to our sense of hearing! For our skin, organic oils provide the best kind of nutrition. Much unlinke the synthetic chemicals lurking in most lotions on the shelves today, natural oils like sesame or coconut are good food for our skin. Additionally, our skin also enjoys healthy, nourishing food (litterally) in the form of fresh fruits and vegtables.

The nutrition that we offer our senses comes in the form of either positive or negative sensory experiences. If we want to optimize our *outer beauty*, then we need to surround our senses with pleasurable and harmonizing stimuli. When we do this, our eyes will be bright and our sense of hearing, taste, and smell, sharp. But if we abuse our senses by assaulting them with offensive input, then their acuity will be deadened. This is the link that Ayurveda makes between the energetic "food" for our senses and the resulting health or illness of our sensory organs.

Beauty as a Sixth Sense

All of our five senses are centered around one very important place - our face! In fact, we have more space devoted to interpreting facial signals in our brain than almost anything else. Coincidentally, beauty is in a large part, the expressions that we bare on our faces. If our eyes are narrowed, our brow furrowed and our lips curled inward, we understand that is the expression of anger. We do not expect loving, kind words to come from a person with this kind of face and we will thus respond to him or her with repulsion or fear. On the other hand, if our mouth curls up on the sides, our eyes are soft and engaged and we appear to be relaxed, others will be far more likely to approach us.

When we look at someone we use all our five senses to gage where that person is at and how we should best respond. Whether or not we find someone to be beautiful, is therefore dependent upon the feedback of our senses. If we generally find the object in front of us to be appealing to our senses, then we will call that thing beautiful. If we find it to be repulsive however, then we will call it ugly and unappealing. In this way, the sensation of beauty is like a sixth sense – it is the end product of the aggregate interpretation of all of our sensory information.

Therefore, we must take good care of each of our sensory organs. On an subtle, energetic level we can care for our senses by harmonizing our mind and spirit. On a gross physical level, we can care for our senses by using the natural tools and remedies given to us by Ayurveda. In the coming pages, we'll go through the care of each of our sensory organs as well as numerous other body parts pertinent to the topic of *outer beauty.* We'll do this by detailing specific guidelines set forth by Ayurveda for how to care for these vital and expressive aspects of our *inner* and *outer beauty.*

Outer Beauty: SKIN

Can you imagine having perfect skin? Your face would be free of blemishes and tight without wrinkles. It would be smooth, lustrous, elastic, soft, rosy in the right places, and otherwise evenly colored. You would feel as though you were vibrantly glowing from the inside, out. In Ayurvedic medicine we describe these people's skin as *prabha*, or having an aura and radiance like the full moon. Ayurveda would also say that your full, glowing skin would also be an indication of strong *ojas*, or the subtle essence of vitality in the body.

But what if the opposite was true? What if your skin actually left something to be desired? Ayurveda calls this *chaya,* meaning dull or pale. Most of us have had a run in with dullness or dryness from time to time before in our lives. Hardly any of us can claim to have gone a moment without a bit of puffy, wrinkled, sagging, discolored, or pale skin.

The fact of the matter is that although we all began our lives with perfect skin, not many of us can boast of the same, flawless texture by the time we are thirty. That's because most of us take our skin (which happens to be the largest organ of our body) very much for granted. We're almost certain to have inflicted some kind of damage to our skin in our younger years, whether we intended to or not, and now that we're older, we are suffering the consequences. But fear not; there is hope!

Inner Balance & Skin Care

Try thinking of the skin is the barometer of your health. It takes what's going on in your insides and expresses it outwardly. This is because it is an integrated part of your bodily system – it lives and breathes in conjunction with the rest of our organs. That is why if you want to take care of your skin, you have to learn to take care of yourself as a whole. Put another way, if you want to do well by your skin, than you have to make sure your physical body is clean on the outside with the help of proper skin care, and on the inside, with adequate diet, lifestyle and emotional well-being. You see, everything that is burdening our system, whether it be a heavy emotion or exposure to toxic chemicals, must be somehow be expelled through the body. The skin happens to be one of the quickest and surest ways to release metabolic build-up or emotional turmoil.

Think about it: day-to-day psychological stress, anger, irritation, frustration or suppressed grief can show up on your skin in the form of drawn and tired bags or lines. And, equally as possible, toxins accumulated from a poor diet and lack of exercise, could manifest as acne or a blotchy and pale complexion. In the end, the best thing we can do for our skin is minimize the amount of toxins (whether they be emotional or physical) that they body needs to push out.

Below you'll see I've charted some basic guidelines for foods and activities that both prohibit and promote beautiful skin. Follow the recommendations of what things to avoid and which things to embrace, and you'll be setting the stage for yourself to have beautiful skin once again!

Skin Friendly Lifestyle and Diet

Avoid	Favor
Food that is too hot and spicy	Whole grains, Rainbow Colored Vegetables & Fruits
Excessive consumption of fish	Mild flavors (not too sweet, salty or sour)
Sour fruits, Ice cream, Junk food	Sweet, juicy fruits
Excess salt	Cooked green veggies

Avoid	Favor
Alcohol, Smoking, Stress	Adequate protein
Excessive thinking and worrying	Relaxation and stress management
Lack of exercise	Regular exercise
Fewer than one bowel movement per day	Daily bowel movements
Excessive exposure to the sun (more than 20 minutes per day)	Less than 20 minutes per day in the sun
Dehydration	Adequate hydration

Don't forget that just because you have to take out certain foods in your diet in order to get your skin looking better, it doesn't mean that the food on your plate can't still be absolutely delicious. Try seasoning your home cooked meals with this delicious spice mixture designed to tantalize your taste buds *and* heal your skin!

Skin Friendly Homemade Spice Blend

✻ 5 tsp. coriander powder ✻ 4 tsp. fennel powder
✻ 3 tsp. turmeric powder ✻ 1 tsp. cinnamon powder
✻ 1/2 tsp. black pepper powder.

Mix all these spices together and keep the mixture in a glass jar. You can use this delicious blend to sprinkle on top of your food, on a salad, or use it as you cook or bake. Each of these spices are medicinal. They synergistically work together to cleanse your lymph, blood and fat tissues. Out of all of these spices, turmeric is your skin's greatest ally! It is is not only a potent antioxidant and anti-inflammatory, but it also gives luster and glow to the skin.

So now that you know all the basics, I think you're ready for me to share with you the details of my 10 best tips for skin care. You can think of the following as "The 10 Commandments" for flawless, radiant and healthy skin. Live by these points religiously, and you'll be bringing out the best in your skin every day! No amount of money spent on even the most top of the line skin care products could ever hope to achieve what these laws of a natural lifestyle can do.

The 10 Commandments of Beautiful Skin

1 RESPECT THE RHYTHMS OF THE SEASONS

According to Ayurveda, working *with* Nature rather than *against* Her, is the first law of well-being. The health of your skin is no exception to this.

For your skin:	
Winter	is the ideal season to provide deep nourishment
Spring	is the perfect opportunity to do a detoxification
Summer	is the time when you need to protect, protect!

Also, use common sense to synchronize your diet to be in tune with the seasons. An example of this would be eliminating hot, spicy foods during the hot weather season as this will increase the chances of skin breakouts.

2 DO NOT CONSUME SYNTHETIC PRODUCTS

Basically, if you can't eat it, don't put it on your skin. There are lots of choices in natural, botanical-based skin and beauty care products to experiment with. Once you've experienced the softer, subtler, more natural textures and fragrances, you won't be drawn to use anything artificial or chemical-based any more.

3 MAKE YOUR DIET RICH WITH PHYTO-NUTRIENTS

Pay attention to your diet. Feed your skin from the inside out. Eat cooked leafy greens, plenty of fresh seasonal veggies, and lots of sweet juicy fruits. These things are rich in natural antioxidants and help protect the skin from damage by free radicals and reactive oxygen-based chemicals that are widely linked to disease and aging.

4 EAT MINDFULLY & STOKE YOUR METABOLISM

The first thing to do is to develop healthy eating habits. Eating mindfully is very important for the health and appearance of your skin. You see, in order for your body to use everything you eat, it has to first digest and assimilate the nutrients. It can't do that very easily if you're eating standing up, on your way to work or while watching TV!

If we want our skin to be as nourished as possible, we have to make sure we are metabolizing every last bit of our nutrition and then regularly eliminating the rest! We can help our bodies do this by simply paying attention to our food when we're eating it so that our metabolism will be alert and ready to digest what we eat. Even something as simple as a little bit of fresh ginger and lime juice before a meal can help cue our "digestive fire," or metabolism, to start working. But be careful to avoid things like ice-cold beverages or too many carbonated drinks as these things will do the opposite. They will put a damper on the flame of our inner digestive fire. Finally, the last thing to remember is to eat only when you are hungry. Eating when you're not hungry means your digestive fire is not turned on, and as a result, toxins will accumulate. Instead, focus on your food at mealtimes and take a few minutes to sit quietly after a meal.

5 PRACTICE AYURVEDIC OIL MASSAGE DAILY

You're going to love this! Try doing a full-body, warm oil, self massage an integral part of your daily routine. When you discover the range of benefits a warm oil massage will deliver to your overall health, and especially your skin, you'll never think of massage as just an occasional luxury again! It increases circulation, helps the body flush out toxins and tones the skin, keeping it looking soft, smooth and supple. A full-body massage can be done before your morning bath or shower, or an hour or two before you go to bed (wait a couple of hours after a full meal though). See chapter 155 for instructions on how to do Ayurvedic Warm Oil Massage.

6 GET QUALITY REST

Beauty sleep is a real thing! Make sure you are getting both the quantity and quality of rejuvenating sleep that your body requires to function at optimal levels. It is pretty much impossible to turn back the negative effects of ongoing sleep deprivation – when it starts showing up in lackluster skin and pouches under the eyes, it might be too late. Your skin is like a mirror, it reflects everything that's happening inside your body and mind. When you've had enough rest, your high energy levels and general well-being can be found in your glowing skin and clear, bright eyes.

7 MANAGE YOUR STRESS

Stress is a silent killer, a modern plague and a hidden threat. Stress has many ways it shows up in the body and none of them are pretty. A stressful lifestyle is breeding ground for damaging free radicals to flourish and undermine your health and appearance. Try incorporating moderate exercise, yoga postures, meditation techniques and breathing exercises, all to help you combat the negative effects of stress. Use strategies that feel soothing to you – aromatherapy, music, laughter, the company of good friends, and a positive outlook. All these things can help balance your mind and emotions. Find what works for you.

8 DEVELOP A DAILY SKIN CARE REGIMEN *(AND STICK TO IT)*

Being regular with a basic program of skin care is key to getting consistently beautiful skin. Performing the four basic steps of cleansing, toning, moisturizing and nourishing twice daily – before you start your day and again when you go to bed – will keep your skin clean and healthy. Again, try to use natural products as much as possible. Skin care products that are rich in botanical nutrients can provide long term support for your skin. Ayurvedic herbs are especially rich in phytochemicals that deliver proven benefits. Some even have anti-dandruff, deodorizing and anti-aging properties. Lastly, avoid harsh soaps that will strip the innate moisture and balance from your skin. Instead, choose soaps that will be effective in toning and cleansing but that are still gentle.

9 TRY MAKING YOUR OWN SKIN CARE AID

We recognize that not everyone has the time or the temperament to make up custom skin or bath aids from scratch every day. But you've got to try it at least once! I promise you'll have fun and your skin will be grateful! There are so many options too. You can blend your own essential oils into a heavier base oil for an aromatic massages, mix up fruit to make a facial, or simply create a fragrant sachet of herbs and spices to scent your bath water with. You can also experiment with various floral waters by spraying them onto your skin as a toner. The subtle aroma will linger pleasantly around you and you can feel good about what you've put onto your skin. For more bright ideas, see our homemade skin care recipe section on page 181.

10 DEFINE YOUR OWN CONCEPT OF BEAUTY

Your outer image is a reflection of your mindset. A positive attitude about yourself will help project an aura of confidence and radiance that will enhance your appearance. After you've done all you can to develop healthy and regular diet and lifestyle habits, and pampered your skin with nourishing, natural skin care aids, then sit back and feel good about the way you look – healthy, radiant and enchantingly beautiful.

Outer Balance and Skin Care: The BASICS

Most of the tips we've discussed so far work on the skin from the inside, out. So now that you've nailed down how to play your "inner game," then you can start looking at how to care for your skin from the outside too. Like any tissue in your body, the skin needs tender loving care in order to both function optimally and look beautifully.

Throughout time different traditions have done everything under the sun to improve the condition of their skin - they've rubbed, scrubbed, greased, brushed, toned and steamed, to try and get the results they're looking for! But believe it or not, there are ultimately only four, very simple things that are needed to care for your skin. If you're able to do these four things, then you can rest assured that you'll be protecting your skin from the ill effects of the environment as well as the skin's natural process of cell degeneration and decay. These 4 Golden Steps of skin care are quite simply:

The 4 Golden Steps

Cleanse * Nourish * Moisturize * Tone

From these basics, you may need to expand and individualize your regimen based on the unique needs of your skin. It might be necessary to add in a mask, herbal stream, some exfoliation or a face pack from time to time. Fundamentally, the 4 Golden Steps should be what you stick to on a regular basis.

So what do these 4 Golden Steps really entail? Check it out.

Cleanse:

As it sounds, cleansing is meant to remove debris from the external environment that have gathered on the skin. It also helps get rid of impurities that are exiting the body via the pours of the skin. Keep in mind that cleansers should not strip the acidity away from the skin. As counter intuitive as this may sound, the natural acid is part of what keeps the skin looking clear and healthy.

Nourish:

Our skin needs nutrition just like we do. Nourishing our skin takes place at a deeper level than just moisturizing. Feeding our skin cells with vital nutrition provides a longer lasting and more substantial change for our skin, but the results are usually not immediate.

Moisturize:

This fulfills the skin's needs for hydration. It softens and protects the skin. Moisturizers affect the outermost skin layer to temporarily create a buffer between you and the harsh environment, protecting your skin from the cold, wind, sun and heat.

Tone:

Usually in the form of some kind of an astringent spray, toners are used to tighten up the skin's pores. The reason we do this is to "close the doors," to the influx of environmental pollutants like dust, dirt and toxins. This way our pours don't just soak up everything that comes their way!

Now it's time to get clear on our cosmetic vocabulary. When was the last time you really contemplated the differences between lotions, creams, toners, oils and moisturizers? Most of us just lump all of these things together in our minds, but really, they each have very different functions for the skin and should be rightfully distinguished from one another. So let's get this clear once and for all.

LOTION	The thinnest of the three moisturizers, lotions are a blend of liquid and oil (with liquid as a higher ratio than oil). They quickly absorb into the skin.
CREAM	Creams have a medium thickness and are soft, much like butter. They have a higher percentage of oil than lotions. They are more deeply moisturizing than simply lotions alone, but they often take a longer time to absorb.
OIL	Just as they sound, oils are pure fat with no added liquid. They provide hydrating and nutrients to the deep layer of the skin.
SERUM	This is a high concentration solution. It can penetrate far into your skin layers and deliver nutrients deeply because it consists of nanoparticals.

In Ayurvedic cosmetology we favor the use of oils over any other type of moisturizer. This is because Ayurvedic theory says that the skin is a byproduct of the fat tissue. We need to nourish the body with the right kinds of fats if we want our skin to be healthy. Furthermore, good quality oil also benefits the health of our joints, brain and the special skin proteins called collagen and elastin.

On the subject of fat, it is unfortunate that nowadays external beauty is associated with images of skin-and-bones women who are malnourished and lacking the oily nourishment that is a part of fat tissue. By the time these women are 40 or 50 years old, they'll be dried up and wrinkly! That's because *fat is a necessary component for beautiful skin and for health overall.*

Each body type has a healthy proportion of fat, muscle and bone tissue that is unique to their constitution. What is your nature and physiological relationship with healthy fat?

VATA (AIR) TYPES	PITTA (FIRE) TYPES	KAPHA (WATER) TYPES
will naturally be thinner and drier, so they'll need even more fat and oil both internally and externally to stay balanced.	will have more of a medium build with a moderate amount of innate oil.	are innately more voluptuous with plentiful oil. Not much additional oil is needed in the diet.

Please remember that beauty isn't exclusively attached to one type of body weight! Physical *outer beauty* is the special way in which we each inhabit our own constitutions in the most balanced and wholesome way possible.

Now that you've got your basic vocabulary down, it's time to get familiar with the basic "Do's and Don'ts" of skin care. These can act as the backdrop to everything new and exciting that you'll be incorporating into your natural skin care regimen.

DO
Nourish and moisturize your skin daily with oils appropriate for your skin type.
Use a mild herbal cleanser and lukewarm water.
Use natural skin care without preservatives or additives
Wash your skin twice a day, morning and evening with room temperature water.
Facial exercise once daily.

DON'T
Use very oily creams. They clog pores and cause puffiness.
Use soaps or harsh detergents on the face.
Use chemical make-up removers (instead, use cotton dipped in plain vegetable oil to remove eye make-up).
Use very hot or very cold water to wash your face as either will break capillaries.
Get excessive exposure to sun, salt-water, wind, cold weather and snow.
Wear face make-up when you go to sleep, no matter how tired you are!

If you combine the 4 Golden Steps of: cleansing, nourishing moistening and toning, along with the basic Do's and Don'ts, then you will fulfill all of your fundamental needs for external skin care. But before we get too excited, it's still important to learn exactly why the 4 Golden Steps and basic Do's and Don'ts work like they do. To fully understand, we'll have to dive into a little bit of the anatomy and physiology of this amazing organ that covers every inch of our body and which is so fundamental to our external beauty – the skin.

Outer Care: Anatomy and Physiology of the Skin

Naturally, the skin is full of life and vitality. Our skin has a tremendous power to restore, repair and replenish itself. The cells that make up our skin are constantly undergoing a process called mitosis, or cell division. They rapidly divide so that they can keep refueling the fortress (known as our skin) which wraps around our whole body. The skin acts as the first and primary self-defense mechanism that we have. It protects us from the elements and other potential threats like pathogenic bacteria or viruses. It can do this because it consists of three consecutive layers: the epidermis, the dermis, and the subcutaneous tissue.

Epidermis

The epidermis is the outermost, relatively thin and superficial layer of skin cells. It is is actually a bunch of dead cells. These cells are continuously sloughed off, as fresh cells rise up from below. Luckily, this makes our skin always new to some extent.

Dermis

This is a base layer of tissue that is much thicker and stronger. The dermis is a connective tissue framework that is full of blood and lymph vessels, nerves, glands, hair cells and whole variety of other biological cells. Ever heard of collagen treatments for wrinkles and scares? Well, collagen is a protein that resides in the dermis and is plentiful in healthy skin. As we age however, we produce less and less of it. Unhealthy skin comes from the decline in basic skin functions such as new cell growth, collagen production, blood circulation, secretion of ground substance (or a gel-like material that supports the health of cells), as well as immune and enzyme activity. An imbalance at the dermal layer contributes to the drab complexion and lack of glow or color that we see sometimes on the skin. It is essential that our skin products to optimize functioning at this layer so that we can get the young and radiant complexion we're looking for!

Subcutaneous Fat

Finally, underneath the upper two layers of skin is a whole lot of good quality fat tissue! This layer keeps us insulated from the cold and provides lubrication to our skin, but it can also create problems like cellulite. To resolve problems of cellulite, please see section on Exfoliating Scrub (Udvartana) on page 185

If you use proper skin care products, then you will get the following seven physiological benefits.

The Seven Benefits of Proper Skin Care	
1	Exfoliation to remove dead skin cells.
2	Epidermal stimulation for new cell growth.
3	Anti-oxidant properties for cellular rejuvenation and repair.
4	Improved capillary blood flow.
5	Immune-stimulation.
6	Penetrating moisture and nutrients to replenish all layers of skin tissue.
7	Natural glow and luster to the skin

Next, if you are an Ayurvedic lover, you may be interested in taking a deeper look at the chart below. Check out the anatomy and physiology of the skin from an Ayurvedic perspective and you'll see how it corresponds, according to my understanding, to our western understanding of the skin and disease.

East to West
Skin Layers

Layer of Skin {Western}	Layer of Skin {Eastern}	Corresponding Ayruvedic Tissue
(Epidermis) Stratum corneum	Avabhasini	Rasa - plasma
Stratum lucidum Stratum basale	Lohita	Rakta - blood vessels / red blood cells
Stratum Granulosum	Shweta	Mamsa- muscles Meda - fatty tissue (nurtures the upper and lower three layers)
Dermis (Papillary and Reticular layer)	Tamra	Meda - fatty tissue (nurtures the upper and lower three layers)
Dermis	Vedini	Asthi- nerve endings
Hypodermis	Rohini	Majja-deeper blood vessels and lymph vessels
Hypodermis	Mansadhara	Shukra

East to West
Physiological Functions of Skin

Layer of Skin {Western}	Ayurvedic Function	Possible Imbalances
(Epidermis) Stratum corneum	Aura, Color, Luster, Hydration	Dry skin, Wrinkles
Stratum lucidum Stratum basale	Shiny, Rosy Color	Moles /Hypo and Hyper pigmentations

LAYER OF SKIN {WESTERN}	AYURVEDIC FUNCTION	POSSIBLE IMBALANCES
Stratum Granulosum	Firmness, Suppleness	Loose skin, lack of tone, Sagging skin
Dermis (Papillary and Reticular layer)	Nourishment, Collagen, Elastin	Erysipelas, Vitiligo, Skin Infections
Dermis	Sensation of pain	Nerve pain, Shingles
Hypodermis	Healing, Regeneration, Reduction of inflammation, Maintenance of body temperature	Swollen Glands, Tumors, Scars
Hypodermis	Immune System, Anti-aging, Attractive ness	Blood Impurities Skin cancers

THE SKIN-BRAIN CONNECTION & AYURVEDIC WARM OIL MASSAGE

For a long time in the Intensive Care Units in hospitals it was the standard practice to place premature babies into incubators where they received little or no human-human contact. Many of these babies developed a condition known as "failure to thrive." They were unable to gain weight and over time often failed to grow in height. It wasn't until years later that scientists and doctors put two-and-two together and finally realized that the cause of this problem was due to a lack of physical touch.

The power that touch has to heal and nourish comes from its deep and primordial connection to our central nervous system (CNS). The link between the CNS and the skin is inexorable. Their tie goes as far back as the first stages of development in utero. Both the skin and the nervous system are derived from one of three fundamental embryonic germ layers tissues – the ectoderm. In other words, the skin and the nervous system are different branches coming off of the same tree.

Today there are countless studies that substantiate the connection between the skin and brain. Much research has documented the calming effects of touch by measuring the decline of stress fighting hormones such as cortisol. Still other studies show an increase in immune function, and a decrease in anxiety and inflammatory markers with Swedish massage.

What we see is that touch has a profoundly soothing and relaxing affect on the nervous system. In Ayurveda, *Vata* controls the nervous system and is responsible for the perception of touch. Therefore, the best way for us to positively impact our frazzled nervous system (or to sooth aggravated *Vata)* is to receive soothing, loving touch.

For centuries, Ayurveda has used a practice called *abhyanga* (pronounced *'aub-he-un-ga'*) or warm oil massage. *Abhyanga* is one of Ayurveda's time-tested models for actively communicating a message of peace, calm and security to an overworked or frail nervous system.

Abhyanga is a full body, head to toe, massage with warm herbal oil. You can receive *abhyanga* by a trained professional or it can be done daily at home by yourself. Practicing *abhyanga* on a daily or weekly basis is especially beneficial for air type or *Vata* constitutions. Since they are already more prone to fear, anxiety and worry, the grounding and soothing effects of *abhyanga* are particularly needed. *Pitta* and *Kapha* types can also benefit from *abhyanga,* especially if they are feeling stressed or burnt out, but they may need to use different oils and also take into account the seasonal fluctuations.

Constitutional Indications For Base Massage Oils

Dosha	Dominant Element	Ideal Oil	Best Season for Use
Vata	Air	Sesame (cold pressed)	Year round
Pitta	Fire	Coconut	Summer
Kapha	Water	Sesame	Fall, Winter

For Ayurveda lovers, you can use Ayurvedic herbal oils according to their body consitution.
You can find these oils at www.ayurvedichealing.net.

- Skin Tone Oil for nourishing Vata
- Detox Oil for cleansing Kapha and Pitta

Constitutional Indications For Essential Oils

Additionally, if you'd like to add a touch of aromatherapy to your oils (or in your baths), here's some options based on *dosha*. Aromatherapy is the use of the extracts of aromatic plant for therapeutic benefit.

Dosha	Qualities of Aroma Needed	Best Essential Oils	Benefits
Vata	Calming, pacifying	Basil, Orange, Geranium, Clove, Rose	Promotes sleep. Stabilizes metabolism. Reduces restlessness and anxiety.
Pitta	Cooling, sweet	Sandalwood, Mint, Rose, Jasmine	Reduces irritability, excess heat, anger and jealousy.
Kapha	Stimulating, spicy	Juniper, Ginger, Eucalyptus, Camphor, Clove, Saffron	Reduces blockages, fat, water retention. Stimulates metabolism.

How To Perform Abhyanga

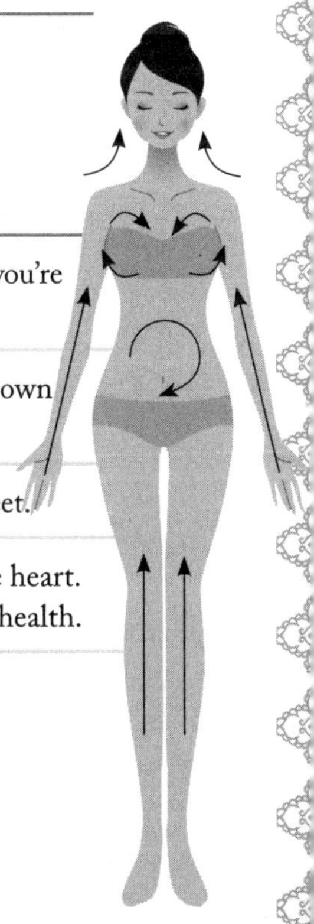

- Bathe a glass jar of oil in hot water to gentle heat the oil you're about to apply.
- Situate yourself in a warm room without a draft and lay down an old towel that you can get oil on without worry.
- Begin your massage with your head first, and then your feet.
- In general, make your massage strokes upward toward the heart. This will help lymphatic drainage which is important for health.

- Around the navel and along the joints, massage in a circular, clockwise direction.
- Allow the oil to sit and soak into your skin for about 20 minutes.
- Shower off the oil in a warm shower or bath. Careful not to slip!
- That's it! You're done. Now you can bask in just how good it feels to have soft and hydrated skin without needing to apply lotion after your shower.

The Skin as a Digestive Organ

Have you ever wondered what happens to everything you put onto your skin? Believe it or not, in a way it is actually "eaten." The skin, much like the mouth, does its own consuming of everything that you put onto it. You see, our skin is like both a sponge and a stomach. It soaks up and digests everything that we put on it. Think of it this way –if you wouldn't put it in your mouth, don't put in on your skin – because either way, it will be "eaten."

In Ayurvedic medicine we have identified a force of nature that is responsible for processing what our skin comes into contact with. In this understanding, we say that the element of fire or the *Pitta dosha* (specifically the *agni*, or metabolism of the *sub-dosha bhrajaka Pitta*), takes substances from the skin and transforms them into nutrition for the skin. If this process is going well, then the skin will absorb all that is beneficial and eliminates the rest. If the skin-digestion is not working well however, then our pours may become blocked with impurities and our skin won't be able to breathe. This is why sweating is so important – it opens up our pores and allows our skin to release any toxins that could have accumulated from either the faulty digestive capacity of *Pitta* in the skin or an over exposure to harmful substances.

The skin also serves as a detoxification pathway. There are three main ways that the body detoxifies: (1) through urine, (2) feces, and (3) sweat. Out of all of these waste excreting organs, the skin is the largest. Problems like acne, rashes or eczema occur when the skin is attempting to expel metabolic toxins from the blood.

But how did those toxins get into the blood stream in the first place? Well, that's where the liver comes in. The liver is the organ that detoxifies all of our blood. In Ayurvedic terms, it cleanses *all* that we take in through each and every one of our senses. It is responsible for keeping what is needed to nourish the body and for breaking down anything that is not. When unneeded substances are properly broken down, they can more easily be eliminated. That's why if the liver is functioning optimally then there should be a very minimal presence of toxins in the blood. If the liver is bogged down by poor diet, cigarettes, alcohol, prescription drugs, synthetic hormones, or even the chemicals in your skin care, then it isn't able to do its job as well. When there is too much of a burden on the liver, then toxins accumulate and impurities begin to circulate through the blood.

Excess Toxic Load →

Liver Function (↓) Toxins in Blood (↑) Skin Problems (↑)

The blood and the skin are mirrors of each other. Whatever is in the blood shows on the skin and visa versa. If the liver is strong and blood is clean and free of toxins, then the skin will shine with luster and health. If the liver is managing a diet and lifestyle with a substantial toxic load however, its ability to cleanse will be compromised and consequently, impurities in the blood will accumulate. When this happens, wastes will be carried to the skin where they will be forced to exit the body in the form of acne, rosacea, psoriasis, eczema, warts or vitiligo depending on various factors.

Healthy Skin = Healthy Liver + Healthy Blood + Healthy Lymph

To help achieve the proper circulation of blood and lymphatic tissue, consider doing a sauna, steam bath or drinking **Lympth Tea** (see resrouces section). This will allow you to sweat the toxins out of your body. Steam dilates blood vessels and opens channels so that impurities can easily move out. As you sweat out toxins, you will feel lighter, almost as though you've lost weight and your metabolism will improve. Additionally, saunas also relax the muscles and relieve stiffness and rehydrates dry skin. If you want to magnify the detoxification process then consider using my signature **Detox Oil** (see page 191). Massage this medicinal oil in an upward direction before you enter the sauna.

Overall, the take home message here is that *if you want to heal your skin you have to first look at the health of your liver and blood.* Depending on your situation, you may even need to follow a supervised detoxification regimen that will take the pressure off your liver and purify your blood. There is no topical skin cream, no matter how amazing, that can even hope to resolve a skin problem whose root begin in the liver.

Outer Care: Cosmetics

Most of us aren't aware that this stomach-sponge organ called the skin has been inadvertently consuming toxins for as long as we've lived! Unless we've been making our own beauty care products at home, living in a bubble, or paying *a lot* of attention to ingredient lists, then we've been absorbing approximately 130 different chemicals in a day!

Yes, the FDA, and of course the cosmetic companies they

endorse, have deemed some of these substances safe in small quantities. But consider how these things add up over a lifetime. Take for your favorite hairspray for instance. It is likely filled with substances called phthalates. Phthalates are a class of chemicals often found in artificial fragrances and plastics. They are well established hormone disrupters. Phthalates have been indicated in birth defects, infertility and cancer. If you use this hair spray daily, over time, the level of these harmful substances will undoubtedly accumulate in your tissues.

Phthalates are just one of the 10,500 synthetic chemicals that are produced for body care products today. The scary fact is that according to the Environmental Working Group, 90% of these cosmetic ingredients have not even been evaluated for safety by the Cosmetic Ingredient Review, the FDA, or any other organization devoted to public health! In Europe on the other hand, 1,110 personal care products have been *banned from the market* due to concerns about the nature of their side effects. Sadly, in the United States, *only 10* of these chemicals have been prohibited.

Those of us living in the USA have to be evermore alert and cautious when purchasing any beauty care products off of the self at our typical drug store. It is up to us to educate ourselves enough to police the products on the shelf and determine whether or not they are suitable for our use.

Now, grab your containers of skin care products and check them against a reliable information source like the Environmental Working Group or ewg.org.

WHY DO SO MANY SKIN CARE PRODUCTS USE THESE POTENTIALLY HAZARDOUS INGREDIENTS?

SIMPLE ANSWER: BECAUSE THEY'RE CHEAP, READILY AVAILABLE, AND EASY TO DILUTE.

Who could have guessed that the silky lotion you've been using for all these years could be turning your hormones upside down or even taxing the function of your liver? How would you ever have known that the lipstick you wear likely contains numerous heavy metals?

It might be hard for you to think about going through your cupboards and letting go of that special product you've used for decades; but fear not! There are other, better options at your disposal. The good news is you can stop paying hundreds of dollars on that name brand anti-wrinkle cream (filled with harmful, toxic chemicals) because Nature has provided you with all that is needed to fix the problem. Plus, natural substitutes are almost always cheaper and sometimes even more effective than their over-the-counter imitations.

As you've probably already gathered by now, I always go by the philosophy that *Mother Nature Knows Best*. If we disregard what Nature has to offer and instead consume (through our skin) standard commercial beauty products, then we disrespect our bodies and expose ourselves to harmful toxins. Isn't it better to just stick with time-tested, "God-made" (natural) substances instead of risk the often times unknown side effects of the"Man-made" (synthetic) products? After all, Nature does indeed know best.

If you still want to look your best but desire to ditch all the phony, highly marketed products out there, then this is the chapter for you. I'll be sharing with you all of my best tips for *outer beauty* home remedies that really work! All the recipes you'll find in this book are 100% natural and practical solutions for healthy, radiant, smooth and lustrous skin.

Simple but powerful, these formulas are time honored by India's traditional, five thousand year old system of medicine, Ayurveda. They impart the ancient secrets of flawless skin and contain nothing but the best of Nature's ingredients. And the good news is you don't have to wait to start jumping into exploring natural home remedies.

In fact, you can probably get started right now! I'm about to share with you some simple home remedies for beautiful skin that you can likely pull right out of your cupboards. There's no need to go out and purchase fancy herbs and other ingredients when your kitchen most likely is already equip with the basics!

Kitchen Solutions for Beautiful Skin

Lime Juice

One of the most important aids in promoting health and beautiful skin is the use of lime juice. Take the juice of one lime and 1-2 tsp. of whole milk, plus 2-3 pinches of cinnamon. Blend together and apply to face, arms and legs. This application should be left on for five minutes and then showered off. It will help you get rid of pimples and keep your skin young, beautiful and lustrous.

Orange Juice

Orange juice is extraordinarily valuable to enhance a glowing complexion. Take 1-2 tps. of O.J. and apply it liberally over the face. After 2-3 minutes, wash it off. Fun, right?

Watermelon Juice

The juice of watermelon is useful in the removal of blemishes on the skin. Simply grate and squeez a small piece of watermelon and then apply it to your face and neck for about 15 minutes. Then, wash it off with hot water and follow with a splash of cool water.

Tomato Juice

Tomato pulp can be applied liberally on the face. Leave it on for ½ hour and then rinse with warm water. If this is repeated daily, you'll find you have good complexion and those nasty little pimples go away in no time!

Lentil Paste

Take 2 tsp. of lentil flour and add a little water to make a thin paste. Apply this mixture as a mask. Wait for five mintues and then wash it off. This will enhance luster and glow.

Almond Paste

Soak almonds overnight in water. In the morning, dispel the leftover water and almond peels. Put the almonds into a blender. Blend up the almonds with a little fresh cream and rose buds. Apply this regularly and you'll prevent the early appearance of wrinkles, black heads, dryness, and pimples and you'll be sure to keep your skin fresh and clear!

Potato Cure

Wash one raw potato, slice it into round pieces and place them all over your face. Keep this on for 15 minutes and wash your face with water. This is good for oily skin. It will also make your skin soft.

Cucumber Pack

Grate 2-3 tsp. of cucumber and add to 1 tsp. of milk. Apply all over face and wash it off after 15 minutes. This mixture will absorb excessive heat and reduce acne.

Oatmeal Paste

Take 2-3 tsp. of oatmeal powder and mix it with 1/2 tsp. of sesame oil and 1/2 tsp. of lemon juice. Make a thick paste out of these three ingredients. Apply the mixture to your face and then wash it off after 10-15 minutes. You'll see that after you complete this you skin is softer and more lustrous.

Inner & Outer Skin Care: Ayurveda's Three Skin Types

Once upon a time there lived a dedicated and astute physician and philosopher named Galen. He was a Greek man and the very first person to create medicinal creams meant for beauty. "But why on earth would a doctor be interested in beauty products?" you might be asking yourself. The answer is: health. Since *outer beauty* is ultimately a reflection of a healthy inner physiology, then it would absolutely be a physician's duty to consider the overall expression of health, beauty and vitality in his patient. Furthermore, since no two people are ever exactly alike, the physician has to know his patient well enough to create a custom formula that will address their specific skin's needs and deficiencies.

In an effort to meet this need for personalized herbal cosmetics, Galen carried out various experiments in the field we now call herbal cosmetology. One day he discovered that vegetable oil, water and a little bee's wax could be mixed to make an excellent cold cream. Little did he know that his simple three part mixture would become an important base for herbal cosmetics for centuries to come.

Now that he had his base, all Galen needed to do was personalize. While he may have had his own unique method of doing this,

I am going to share with you the technique that comes from the medicine that I've studied – Ayurveda. According to Ayurvedic medicine, skin types, like body types, or constitutions, can be grouped into three categories based on the qualities of the various elements of Nature. As you may recall, they are most simply: *Vata* (air), *Pitta* (fire) and *Kapha* (water).

Each skin type displays unique characteristics. Air types are prone to dryness, fire types to more redness and water, to more oiliness. Every one of us has some of the qualities of air, fire and water, but usually one type predominates. You may find a difference between your consitutuional type and your skin type. If this happens, it is not a cause for worry. It just means that there is an element or *dosha* within you that is slightly aggrovated.

When in balance all skin types radiate beauty and health. However, each type also tends towards its own particular weaknesses. When imbalanced, these weaknesses manifest in a variety of skin problems. If you'd like to see what your skin type is, and therefore what imbalances you are prone towards and how to take care of them, then take a moment to fill out this survey.

Skin Questionnaire

To determine your Skin Type, please fill out this questionnaire. Select all answers that apply. Answer according to how your skin has been throughout your life - not according to any recent imbalances that have shown up.

Physical Traits	A	B	C
Skin	☐ Dry, thin, Lack of tone or luster	☐ Soft, Fair, Very sensitive, Medium Thick	☐ Thick, Soft, oily, Shiny

Outer Beauty

	☐ Rough, cold, small pores	☐ Oily, Sweaty, Warm, Medium Pores	☐ Oily, Cold, Enlarged pores
	☐ Chapping and cracking, Premature wrinkles	☐ Redness, freckles, Moles, Acne, photosensitivity	☐ Itching, Prone for Fungal Infection
	☐ Dry rashes, corn	☐ Acne, Redness, Inflammation	☐ Large pustules, Acne
	☐ Dry Eczema	☐ Blackheads, Wet Eczema	☐ Cystic formations
Temperature	☐ Cold	☐ Warm	☐ Cool
Color	☐ Darker olive	☐ Reddish	☐ Pale
Finger Nails	☐ Thin/ cracking	☐ Pink/soft/ medium	☐ Thick/wide/ white
Weather that bothers you	☐ Cold and dry	☐ Hot and sunny	☐ Cold and damp
Lips	☐ Cracking, thin, dry	☐ Medium or soft	☐ Large or smooth
Total			

Mostly "A" answers -

Your skin is predominantly Air, Vata

Mostly "B" answers

Your skin is predominantly Fire, Pitta

Mostly "C" answers

Your skin is predominantly Water, Kapha

It is helpful to find out which skin type you are so that you can work *with* Nature to make sure that your skin looks and feels its best. When we know which element most predominates in the organ of our skin, then we are able to properly personalize our herbal cosmetics accordingly. With individualized skin care that matches our skin type, we are equip to correct any existing imbalances and/or to prevent future disturbances from manifesting.

In the following section, I've outlined each of the three different skin types and all their unique strengths and weakness. Be sure to read in detail the description that best corresponds to your quiz score. For each elemental skin type I've included instructions to: (1) cleanse (2) nourish (3) moisturize and (4) tone with simple, all natural, home-made skin care solutions.

Vata: Air Type Skin

Description

The person with air type skin has dry, thin and finely pored skin. It is also quite delicate and cool to the touch. When balanced, it glows with a sweet lightness and a refinement that is elegant and attractive. When imbalanced, it is prone to excessive dryness and may become rough and flaky.

Potential Problems

The greatest beauty challenge for air type skin is that it is predisposed to symptoms of early aging. If you have this kind of skin then you may tend to develop wrinkles earlier than most due to your tendency towards dryness and thinness. Plus, if your digestion is not in balance, then your skin can begin to look dull and grayish, even in your 20's and 30's. In addition, your skin may have a tendency for disorders like dry eczema. Mental stress such as worry, fear and lack of sleep, also have a deleterious effect on air type skin and leave it looking tired and lifeless.

Recommendations for Care

With a little knowledge you can preserve and protect the delicate beauty of your air type skin. Since your skin doesn't contain much moisture, preventing it from drying out is of paramount importance for you. You can avoid excessive dryness by eating a diet with foods that are warm,well cooked and moist from the addition of fat like ghee or olive oil. The best tastes to favor in your diet are: sour, salty and sweet (naturally sweet foods like fruits and grains; not refined sugar)! Each of these tastes has a soothing effect on the nervous system of a person with air type skin and will help prevent dryness.

Likewise, stay away from dry foods like crackers or cold foods taken right out of the fridge. Instead of drinking ice water, try having at least 8 glasses of warm water throughout the day. Plus, eat plenty of sweet juicy fruits. These things will keep your cells deeply hydrated and the effect will surely show up on your skin.

Next, I know it may sound strange, but going to bed early (before 10pm) is a very soothing lifestyle practice for people who have the air skin type. Additionally, avoid cleansing products that dry the skin (like alcohol-based cleansers) and perform Ayurvedic warm oil massage to your whole body in the morning before you shower (see page 155). Full body oil massage or *abhyanga* will not only be amazingly soothing for you, but it will also be hydrating and extra protective for your skin. You skin is naturally sensitive so having an additional layer of moisture embedded into it before you begin your day will certainly help calm your mind and shield your skin from environmental stressors like the cold, rough wind for instance.

Air Type Skin

- Make sleeping and eating habits regular
- Eat warm, well cooked foods with plenty of good fats
- Practice Ayurvedic warm oil massage
- Stay hydrated

Case Study: Air Imbalance

A lovely 34 year young woman named "Sally" from the Philippines, came to see me complaining of dry patches of eczema around her elbows, constipation, mood swings and irregular menstruation. As Sally recounted her history to me, it became very clear that from the time she was 10 years old and moved to the USA, she had been dealing with emotional, financial and physical hardship. As a result, her whole body was dry – a telltale sign of *Vata* vitiation.

To remedy this excessive dryness, we immediately began a treatment plan that included oleation both internally and externally. Internally, she included more good fats into her diet and I gave her demulcent herbs that would support and nourish her nervous system and hormonal balance. Externally, she practiced *abhyanga* and used an herbal oil that would hydrate and heal her skin. We also spoke about forgiving her past so that she could release the tension it had been holding onto for so long. Finally, after about four to five months on this regimen, she felt far less stressed and came into the office looking more upbeat and confident than I had ever seen her before. Her menses became regular, her libido was stronger, her bowl movements were regular and she had no more dry patches on her elbows. At large, the treatment of her excess *Vata* allowed her to feel more grounded, relaxed and soothed overall, which allowed her skin to rejuvenate and recover.

Skin Care Regimen f or Vata/ Dry SKIN

CLEANSE

Ingredients	Instructions
1 tsp almond powder ½ tsp whole milk or coconut milk	Mix almond powder with milk. Make a thin paste. Apply a thin layer of paste to your face. Gently massage – do not rub or scrub. Wash off with warm water before it begins to dry.

NOURISH

Ingredients	Instructions
1 tsp almond oil 1-2 drops lavender or chamomile oil 5-6 drops water	Mix ingredients Gently massage onto face and neck. Leave on. You may include a *marma* point massage if you wish. See page 177 for instructions.

MOISTURIZE

Ingredients	Instructions
1 tsp powdered milk ½ tsp honey ½ tsp olive oil or avocado oil	Mix ingredients well. Gently massage onto face. Keep on for 10-15 minutes. Wash with warm water

TONE

Ingredients	Instructions
Organic chamomile oil	Mix 1 part oil with 1 part water. Put into cosmetic spray bottle. Spritz onto face.

Pitta: Fire Type Skin

Description

If you have a predominately fire type nature in your skin, then you have skin that is fair, soft, warm and of medium thickness. When balanced, your skin has a beautiful, slightly rosy or golden glow, as if illuminated from within. Your complexion tends towards pink or reddish and often, you'll have a copious amount of freckles or moles.

Potential Problems

Among the many beauty challenges for the person with fire type skin is the tendency to develop rashes, rosacea, acne, liver spots (small, patchy, dark discolorations often found on the hands) or pigmentation disorders. Additionally, because of the large proportion of the fire element in your constitution, your skin does not tolerate heat or sun very well. You are probably photosensitive are likely to accumulate sun damage over the years. Fire type skin is also aggravated by emotional stress, and in particular, suppressed anger, frustration or resentment.

Recommendations for Care

First and foremost, avoid excessive sunlight, tanning treatments and highly heating therapies like saunas or whole body steams. Stay away from hot, spicy foods and favor astringent, bitter and sweet foods (again naturally sweet – this isn't your ticket to go out and eat doughnuts!) Favor sweet juicy fruits, especially melons and pears, cooked greens and rose petal preserves are especially good as well. Drink plenty of room temperature water. This will help wash impurities from your sensitive fire type skin and keep it from over -heating. Finally, be sure to get your emotional stress under control through plenty of outdoor exercise, meditation and yoga.

In terms of environment, it's important to reduce external and internal exposure to synthetic chemicals. Avoid skin products that are abrasive, heating or which contain artificial colors or preservatives. Make sure that whatever you use, it is hypoallergenic.

Fire Type Skin

- Protect yourself from the sun
- Choose hypoallergenic, all natural, gentle skin care
- Avoid hot spicy, oily or fired foods
- Eat cooling foods like mint, cilantro, and coconut

Case Study: Fire Imbalance

I knew my new client "Rita" had a *Pitta* aggravation because she was palpably angry. Her frustration around her upbringing and the strain that she witnessed between her parents left her feeling fiery, bitter and resentful. These emotions augmented the already strong fire that was present in her constitution. As a result, Rita had symptoms of excess heat that showed up as acne and redness on her skin, and chronic headaches.

I knew if we wanted to pacify the aggravated fire, then we would have to cool her off and nourish her. I put her on a cooling, alkalizing, and anti-inflammatory diet alongside with cleansing herbs that would push out the excess accumulated heat. Then, to soften her anger and freshen up her perspective, I asked her to incorporate group yoga, meditation and walks in the forest or swimming in the ocean, into her daily routine. After about 4-5 months on this regimen, her anger had substantially reduced, her acne had cleared up and her headaches were gone.

Skin Care Regimen for SENSITIVE & OILY SKIN

CLEANSE

Ingredients	Instructions
1 tsp lentil flour ½ tsp Neem or Triphala powder 1-2 tsp Water	Mix flour and herbs with water to make a thin paste. Apply paste to face. Wash off with cool water before it dries.

NOURISH

Ingredients	Instructions
1 tsp olive or coconut oil 1-2 drops of lemon, orange or sandalwood essential oil 5-6 drops of water	Mix ingredients. Massage gently onto face and neck and leave on.

MOISTURIZE

Ingredients	Instructions
1 tsp jojoba oil 1-2 drops geranium essential oil	Mix ingredients. Gently massage face and neck with mixture and leave on

TONE

Ingredients	Instructions
Organic peppermint oil	Mix 1 part oil with 1 part water . Put into cosmetic spray bottle. Spritz onto face.

Kapha: Water Type Skin

Description

Water type skin is thick, oily, soft and cool to the touch. If you have this skin type your complexion is a glowing porcelain whitish color, like the moon. Water skin types have a more generous amount of collagen and connective tissue and because of this are fortunate to develop wrinkles much later in life compared to their fire and air counterparts.

Potential Problems

If your Water type skin becomes imbalanced, it can show up as enlarged pores, excessively oily skin, moist types of eczema, blackheads, acne or pimples and water retention. Water skin is also more prone to fungal infections.

Recommendations for Care

Skin that is predominately of the water-like qualities is more prone to clogging and needs more cleansing than other skin types. Therefore, be careful to avoid greasy, clogging creams. Likewise avoid heavy, hard to digest foods like fried foods, fatty meats, cheeses and rich desserts. Eat lighter, easier to digest, astringent, bitter and pungent (well-spiced) foods as they'll balance your tendency towards dampness. This will help your your sluggish digestion and metabolism.

In terms of lifestyle, take warm baths often and use gentle cleansers to open the skin pores. Avoid stagnation by getting regular exercise which will increase circulation and help to purify the skin through the sweating process. Additionally, if you find you are having fewer than one bowel movement in a day, then it is important to address the problem, as elimination is another way to expel toxins that would otherwise have to come out through the skin. Lastly, for your skin care products, choose oil reducing, cleansing and exfoliation products. If you need a moisturizer make sure it is light, not heavy.

Water Type Skin
Exercise regularly
Eliminate regularly
Exfoliate
Eat food that is light and well spiced
Avoid heavy foods like cheeses, sugars and fatty meats

Case Study: Water Imbalance

A beautiful woman named "Laura" came into my office at 32 years young complaining of water retention, irregular menses, weight gain, hair loss and ovarian cysts. Her skin was puffy and swollen and she was sometimes tired and depressed. The cool, heavy, and moist qualities of the element of water were weighing her down and we needed to lift her up. Laura started to counter the cool quality by doing hot yoga, the static quality by increasing her exercise and doing regular lymphatic oil massage, and the moist quality by adding hot, drying spices into her diet. Next, she began taking some Ayurvedic herbs to balance her hormones and emotions. Then, to increase her glucose sensitivity, Laura took out all grain, sugar, cheese and all restaurant food from her diet and instead incorporated more cooked bitter greens. Finally, to give added support for her hair, Laura used natural Ayurvedic topical hair oil on her scalp every night before bed. After eight to nine months on this program, Laura's thyroid levels had normalized, she started to loose weight and she noticed some new hair growth. Her menses had normalized and much to her relief, her skin was no longer swollen either.

SKIN CARE REGIMEN FOR THICK & OILY SKIN

CLEANSE

INGREDIENTS	INSTRUCTIONS
½ tsp honey ½ tsp lemon juice	Mix together and apply on face. Wash off.

NOURISH

INGREDIENTS	INSTRUCTIONS
½ tsp. sesame oil 1-2 drops of lemongrass essential oil 3-4 drops of water	Mix ingredients. Apply to face and neck. Leave on.

MOISTURIZE

INGREDIENTS	INSTRUCTIONS
1/2 tsp. sunflower oil 1-2 drops rosemary or bergamot essential oil	Mix ingredients Gently massage onto face and neck and leave on.

TONE

INGREDIENTS	INSTRUCTIONS
Organic sage oil	Mix 1 part oil with 1 part water. Put into cosmetic spray bottle. Spritz onto face.

This is an extra, add-on skin care secrete that you'll love! No matter what your skin type is, you can benefit from this short but powerful practice called *marma* point massage. *Marma* points are vital points that are the seats of life or *prana*. They are vortex centers for the subtle energetic pathways in our bodies and they can benefit the health of any constitution. To incorporate these points into your routine, simply press gently on the sites shown in the corresponding figure for 2-3 seconds, and then release. Activating these points will not only rejuvenate the vitality of your skin, but your whole body as well! Try it out!

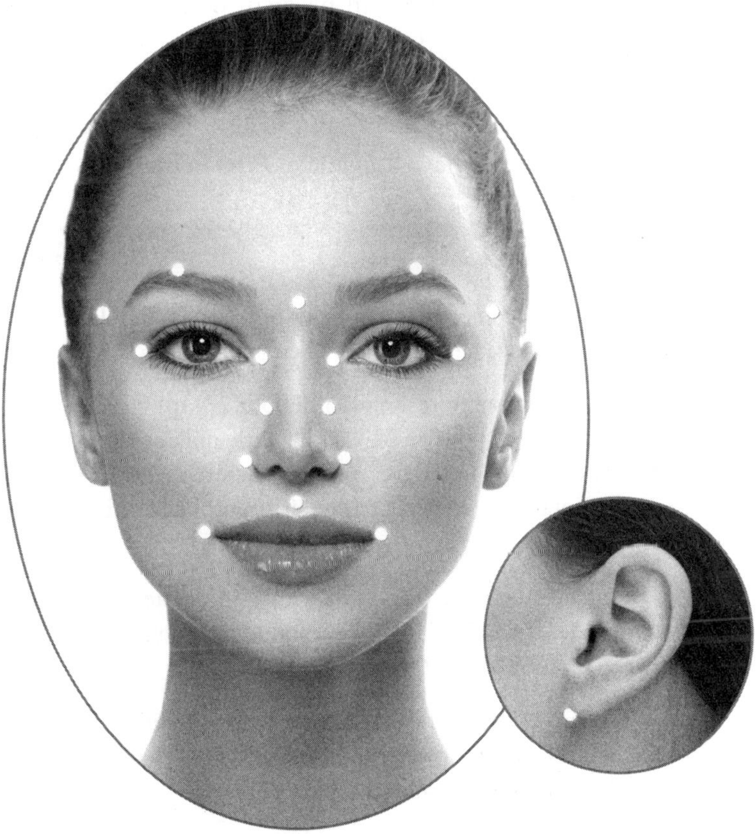

Common Skin Problems & Natural Solutions

ACNE & PIMPLES

When all three energies of the body (*Vata*, *Pitta* and *Kapha*) are aggravated then we see things like acne, pimples, and blackheads come up. The *Pitta dosha* or fire element however, is the most susceptible to producing acne.

The element of fire can be disturbed by things that are very common to our everyday lives like the intake of: alcohol, tea, coffee, spicy oily or fired foods. Additionally, regular occurrences like stress, tension, pollution, and chemicals can also aggravate *Pitta.* If we want to control acne, we have to manage *Pitta* in our lives and our bodies.

NATURAL SOLUTION

- Drink ¼ cup of aloe vera pulp (not if pregnant). Do this one time per day in the morning on an empty stomach.
- Make a paste from 1 tsp. lentil flour, 1/4 tps. turmeric and 1/4 tsp. nutmeg powder. Mix with a little milk or water to make a paste. Apply to the face and rinse before it gets dry. Your skin will maintain a yellow hue temporarily but the benefits are worth the sacrifice!
- Grind cumin seeds and mix with a little water until a paste is made. Then apply to the face and leave it on for 15 minutes and wash off with cool water.
- Take 1-2 stems of cilantro leaves and mix with 4-5 mint leaves and a little bit of water in blender. Make a thin paste. Apply and keep it on for 10 minutes; then wash off.

NATURAL SOLUTION

- Cook 4-5 tsp. of oatmeal with water. Let it cool and then apply it over the face for about 10-15 minutes. Wash off with water.

PIGMENTATION

According to Ayurveda, an imbalance in the subdosha of *Bhrajaka Pitta* (aforementioned in the discussion of the skin as a digestive organ) is what causes problems with the pigmentation of the skin. *Bhrajaka Pitta* governs the production of melanin in the skin and if disturbed can cause discoloration. Excessive exposure to the sun, irregular eating and sleeping habits, as well as the consumption of food and drink that are heating, all contribute to the malfunction of *bhrajaka.*

NATURAL SOLUTIONS

- Grind five almonds to make about 2stp of powder. Mix this powder with a few drops of lemon juice and water to make a paste. Apply this paste to the face and neck (or wherever pigmentation problems occur). Leave on for about fifteen minutes, then rinse.
- Apply ripe mashed papaya juice, or mashed papaya meat to the affected areas for 10-15 minutes and then wash off with water.

ECZEMA AND PSORIASIS

Both of these skin imbalances are similar and are characterized by dry, itchy, red and oozing sores or patches on the skin. This is caused by an excess of foods that are too hot, sour or rough in nature and it is exasperated by stress, tension and anger as well as harsh chemicals. According to Ayurveda, these are caused by aggravating *Vata* (air) and *Pitta* (fire) through unbalanced diet and/or lifestyle.

Natural Solution

- Follow a simple, bland diet
- Manage anger and stress
- Take ¼ cup aloe vera juice on an empty stomach in the morning
- Cleanse the liver, to purify the blood and resolve skin problems with herbs like: Triphala, Turmeric, Anata, Manjishta, Guduchi and Neem.

Rosacea

Prominent redness on the T-zone - the nose, forehead, and cheeks - as well as the presence of acne-like bumps or papules, thickened skin, sensitive skin with broken blood vessels and excessive flushing, makes for the condition known as rosacea. This excessive redness and irritation is caused by too many spicy, sour or fermented foods as well as alcohol, smoking, caffeine, stress, irritability and anger. Additionally, it is aggravated by a sluggish digestion and weak metabolism.

Natural Solution

- Follow a cooling, *Pitta* pacifying diet
- Manage anger and stress
- Remove alcohol and caffeine
- Incorporate soothing, nourishing and cooling Ayurvedic herbs like: Sandalwood, Rose, Jasmine, Hibiscus, Shatavari, or Indian Sasparilla.

Premature Aging

This is due to the aggravation of *Vata*. The air element naturally increases with age, but the early onset of aging indicates excessive amounts of *Vata*. Aging causes dryness and wrinkling of the skin. Factors like excessive thinking, stress, tension, overworking, strain, irregular sleeping and eating habits or cold and dry foods, all catalyze aging. Additionally, things like artificial flavors, colors, preservatives and chemicals hasten aging by increasing the toxic burden on the body.

Natural Solution

- Beat one egg white and spread a thin film on your face. Rinse off after 15-20 minutes. This mask will tighten the skin and reduce wrinkles.
- Massage the face with ghee or almond or coconut oil and leave on.
- Apply a mixture of 1 tsp. aloe vera gel with ½ tsp. of almond oil. Rinse off after about 15- 20 minutes.
- Strain yogurt with a fine cheesecloth so that you extract 1 tbs of whey. Mix this with ½ tsp of honey and apply to the face and neck. Wash off after about 10-15 minutes. It will help to reduce wrinkles and keep the skin fresh and smooth.

Natural Homemade Skin Care

Herbal Cleansers

Herbal Cleansers are one option to fulfill the cleansing portion of 4 Golden Steps in your healthy skin regimen. Plus, being 100% natural, they also have the added benefit of nourishing your skin while you cleanse.

VATA

CREAMY ALMOND CLEANSER	NUTMEG CLEANSER
Mix 1 tsp. almond powder with ½ tsp milk powder and 1 tsp of lemon juice or orange juice. Use as a cleanser.	Mix the powder ½ tsp. of nutmeg with a enough water or milk to make a paste. Apply and watch how nutmeg cleanses your skin, reduces acne and improves luster.

PITTA

COOLING CLEANSER	ROSE CLEANSER
Freshly Gratecucumber, squeeze juice and simply apply	Mix ½ tsp. of rose water with 1/2 tsp. of almond oil. Apply this mixture to the neck, face and around the eye area. Leave it on for 5 minutes. Wash off with warm water. This mixture thoroughly cleanses and soothes. It is astringent, anti-inflammatory, antiseptic and has a lovely scent.

KAPHA

NEEM CLEANSER
Take 2-3 drops of Neem oil and mix well with 1 tsp of water. Apply for 5 minutes and then wash off with warm water. This mixture is especially beneficial for oily or sensitive skin, so it can be used for fire-type skin as well. The herb in this formula is highly effect as a deep cleaning cleanser for oily, acne-prone or sensitive skin. It assists in removing dehydrated layers the skin and helps to soothe itchiness or irritation.

ALOE VERA EXTRACT

Apply aloe vera gel all over face and leave it on for 5 minutes. Wash off with warm water.

Aloe vera extract has been used to help heal burns, and treat everything from eczema, sores, acne, insect bites and more! It is an antiseptic, highly lubricant and will penetrate deep into the skin to provide a deep and through cleansing. It can also be used for fire-type skin.

NATURAL SKIN CARE RECIPES FOR ALL SKIN TYPES

Apart from the 4 Golden Steps, if you would like to try the following recepies from time to time, have at it!

FACE CREAM

INGREDIENTS	INSTRUCTIONS
½ tsp honey ½ tsp milk powder ½ tsp olive oil.	Mix honey with milk powder and olive oil. Gently massage onto face and neck and leave on.

FACE PACK

Face packs are simply a combination of herbal powders mixed with water or milk to make a thin paste. All these herbs help nourish and cleanse your skin.

INGREDIENTS	INSTRUCTIONS
1 tsp. Manjistha powder ½ tsp. Turmeric powder 2 tsp. Ananta or Indian Sarsparilla 5 tsp. Lentil flour 1 tsp. Lodhra	Mix ingredients with a little bit of milk or water, so as to make a thin paste. Apply and leave on for 10 minutes, then rinse.

MASK

Face masks with fruit brighten the skin because fruit is a good source of enzymes and vitamin C. These masks also remove dead skin cells, leaving your skin smoother than ever before. Typically, these are best used once every two weeks.

VATA (AIR) TYPES	PITTA (FIRE) TYPES	KAPHA (WATER) TYPES
Mash the fruit of banana or avocado. Simply apply this to the face and leave on for 10 minutes. Wash with warm water.	Mash the fruits of pears or apricots. Add 1-2 tsp. of Kaolin or Fuller's Water. Mix and apply to the skin for 10 minutes, then rinse.	Use the fruits of strawberry or papaya and mash them together with 1-2 tsp. of oat bran. Apply and leave on for 10 minutes. Wash off.

Universal Mask (*Vata-Pitta-Kapha Friendly*)	
Option 1	Simply applying Greek yogurt makes a fabulous mask. Leave on for ten minutes and then rinse off. The lactic acid produced from the healthy microbes breaks down dead skin cells and the natural probiotics reduce the appearance of blemishes. Plus, this mask will hydrate your skin so that its youthful appearance is restored!
Option 2	Take 2-3 tsp. of green clay and mix with ½ tsp of rose water. Make a thin paste and wash off before it gets dry.

Exfoliating Scrub (Udvartana)

This is an optional addition to the 4 Golden Steps if indicated for you. You might want to incorporate this option if you have excessively oily skin or feel you have a build-up of old, dry skin that has been hanging on for too long!

Exfoliation is a process which entails the removal of the outermost superficial, surface layer of the skin that is made up of old, dead skin cells. This microderm abrasion technique leaves your skin surprisingly radiant and smooth!

Udvartana is also a wonderful way to detoxify the lymph, which helps to resolve the source issue of many skin problems. Plus, in moving the lymphatic tissue, it works wonders for cellulite too!

Base Option 1:

Ingredients	Instructions
4 tbs. orange peel powder 2 tbs. oatmeal powder 2 tbs. wheat germ powder	Mix ingredients together and keep in an air tight glass container. Use as you would soap in the shower. This is good for all skin types.

Base Option 2:

Ingredients	Instructions
1 cup wheat bran ½ cup oat bran 4 tsp Indian Sasparilla powder 2 tsp dry basil powder ½ cup mung bean flour	Mix ingredients together and keep in an air tight glass container. Use as you would soap in the shower.
To customize for *Vata*	Mix 1 tsp of the dry mixture from base option 1 or 2, with 2 tsp. of sesame oil. Use as you would soap in the shower.
To customize for *Pitta*	Mix 1 tsp of the dry mixture from base options 1 or 2, with1 tsp of sesame oil and ½ tsp of lemon juice. Use as you would soap in the shower.
To customize for *Kapha*	Use base options 1 or 2 .Use on full body like you would soap.

Steam

This is one of the extended steps you can choose to do for your skin care routine. It can be done after cleansing or exfoliation, depending on your skin type and condition. After steaming, use a moisturizer or moisturizing mask to replenish the hydration of the skin.

Steam promotes vasodilatation and therefore increases blood circulation and opens the pores. This helps to eliminate toxins and debris from the deeper layers of the skin.

It is indicated for general skin congestion characterized

by puffiness and swelling, as well as for dry or cystic acne.

Option 1

Ingredients	Instructions
Water	Simply boil water in a pot and position your head over the steam. Then drape a towel over your head and keep covered for 5-7 minutes.

Option 2

Ingredients	Instructions
Water with Fresh Herbs *Vata: Basil or Lavender* *Pitta: Mint or Hibiscus or Jasmine* *Kapha: Sage, Rosemary, Lemon Grass or Eucalyptus*	Boil water with a handful of fresh herbs and perform the steam as indicated in option 1.

Option 3

Ingredients	Instructions
Water and Essential Oil *Vata: Geranium or Lavender* *Pitta: Jasmine or Orange or Mint* *Kapha: Sage or Tea Tree*	Boil water and add 2-3 drops of essential oil and perform the steam as indicated in option 1.

Glowing Skin Juice

The food that you eat affects your skin, and this delicious juice recipe is wonderfully nutritious! Your skin will thank you.

Ingredients	Instructions
2-3 carrots 5-6 cilantro stems 1 cup of kale leaves ¼ cup of mint ½ of a lemon 1 inch of ginger root.	Take these ingredients and juice them. Drink and enjoy!

The Skin and The Sun

The sun gives us energy and strength. Its bright energy uplifts our body, mind and spirit. It is a major contributor to our overall health and wellbeing. We must be mindful however, that too much of a good thing doesn't make it better! While moderate amounts of sun exposure are health-promoting, excessive time spent in the sun can be harmful. Especially for the already fiery, *Pitta* types.

Let's learn a little bit about how the sun affects our skin.

UVA rays

These are sun beams that are most prominent in the morning and late afternoon times. Surprisingly, these rays are more harmful than even the mid-day sun. They penetrate deeply and rapidly through the skin so their impact is substantial. Most sunscreens do not protect against this type of radiation.

UVB rays

These rays are highest at mid-day. Luckily, they only reach the superficial layers of the skin, so they are less harmful than morning or evening UVA radiation. The downside however, is that they can burn the skin if we're unprotected. But if we get just the right amount, UVB rays will give us exactly what we need to manufacture vitamin D3.

So what is just the right amount of sun exposure anyway? The answer is: about ten minutes per day in the mid-day sun. If you have to be in the sun for more than ten minutes, you may consider applying some sunscreen to protect your skin from the hot and sometimes drying qualities of the heat. Excess sun can cause wrinkles, damage delicate skin and over the long term, possibly provoke cancer.

As contradictory as it may sound, you should not use conventional sunscreen to protect yourself from rays. It is the unfortunate fact that most sunscreens these days are loaded with chemicals, some of which are ironically carcinogenic.

While it seems that all is lost, there is as always, a natural solution. I've put together some practical tips so that you can avoid harmful radiation and toxic sunscreens.

Check with the EWG

Before you apply your sunscreen it is a good idea to reference the Environmental Working Group's guide for the safety of ingredients. There website is: www.ewg.org.

Wear Protective Clothing

In the heat, wear light, breathable, natural fiber and white colored clothing. Be sure to sport your favorite hats and sunglasses as well!

Put on Natural Sunscreen

Apply vegetable oils as sunscreen. Yes, that's right - oils just like the ones in your cupboard that you cook with. Believe it or not, carrot seed oil, wheat germ oil, raspberry seed oil, coconut oil, peanut oil, sesame oil, avocado oil and more, all have UV filters. They contain natural tocopherol, carotenoids and essential fatty acids, each of which are nourishing and protective to the skin. In other words, these oils have natural, in-born sun protection factor or SPF! Please see recipe section so you can make your very own, 100% natural, nourishing and protective sunscreen.

Make Your Own Natural Sunscreen

The emollient properties of the oils in this recipe do wonders to protect against the inevitable dryness that comes with time spent in the outdoors. In addition, they buffer UV radiation naturally. Finally, a sunscreen that does more good than it does harm!

Ingredients	Instructions
1/2 cup avocado oil ¼ cup olive oil 1 tsp. carrot seed oil 1 tsp. red Raspberry seed oil 1tsp. sesame oil ½ tsp. essential oil of your choice (Peppermint, Lavender or Orange) *If you'd like you can add zinc oxide and increase the SPF value.*	Mix all the ingredients in a glass jar and keep it in a cool place. Apply like regular sunscreen.

Premade Remedies

If you don't have time to make your own skin care products, you can visit my website at www.ayurvedichealing.net to purchase the oils that I mix myself by hand. They are my signature formulas that I use regularly in my clinic and always get good, consistent results.

Skin Tone Oil

For all skin types who want to firm and tone their skin.
Promotes vibrant, healthy and glowing skin.

Ingredients	Instructions
Almond, neem, apricot kernel, avocado, and sesame oil. Rosewood and geranium essential oil.	Use the pads of your fingertips to massage **Skin Tone Oil** gently onto your face 2 x per day – preferably morning and evening, before bed.

Detox Massage Oil

For all skin types who want to move toxins out of fatty tissue.
Helps with lymphatic drainage and healthy circulation

Ingredients	Instructions
Organic sesame oil, organic lavender, cinnamon, bergamot and lemon oil.	Gently massage a small amount of **Detox Massage Oil** on your body before taking a warm shower, bathing or doing rigorous exercise.

Herbal Supplements

Vital Skin

To cleanse, nourish and rejuvenate the skin. For all skin types.

Ingredients
Guduchi Extract, Amalaki Extract, Turmeric Extract, Ananthamool, Manjistha, Neem Extract

Vital Blood

Helps to eliminate toxins by supporting the liver to cleanse the lymph and blood.

Ingredients
Amalaki, Haritaki, Bibhitaki, Turmeric, Gudduchi, Manjistha, Kutki and Neem

Vital Liver

Protects and purifys the liver.

Ingredients
Bhumiamalaki, Andrographis, Ginger, Indian Long Pepper, Gudduchi, Kutki, Bhringraj, Milk thistle.

VITAL WOMAN

Supports the female reproductive system and balances hormones.

INGREDIENTS
Shatavari, Ashwagandha, Musta, Dashamoola, Ashoka, Shilajit, Indian Long Pepper, Licorice.

DETOX HERBAL TEA

Promotes gentle detoxification by purifying the blood. Improves circulation and cleanses and rejuvenates the skin.

INGREDIENTS
Organic lemongrass, Organic peppermint leaves, Organic holy basil leaf, Organic echinacea root, Organic dandelion root, Organic astragalus root and Organic ginger root.

LYMPH TEA

Lymph herbal tea contains a unique blend of Ayurvedic herbs and spices that promote lymphatic movement and healthy immunity. This formula will clear lymphatic stagnation, maintain breast health, reduce heat and inflammation, decrease swelling and puffiness, enhance circulation and reduce cellulite.

INGREDIENTS
Organic cumin seeds, Organic peppermint leaves, Organic holy basil leaf, Organic coriander seeds, Organic fennel seeds, Organic ginger root, Organic turmeric and Organic fenugreek seeds.

Outer Beauty: HAIR

The Mane Attraction

Your hair is likely the first thing that someone notices when they look at you. A hair style can make a statement, for better or for worse, even from great distances. Have you ever caught yourself doing a head turn because someone from across the street was sporting an outrageous hair-do? Have you ever found yourself at a party staring in envy from across the room at someone's silky smooth locks? It's likely that you've accidentally experienced both of these hair-induced follies. But don't worry; it is natural to be fascinated by hair. Hair is so intriguing because it speaks volumes about the person whose head it is on! Some people keep their hair long, some people very short. Some people dye their hair bright colors, some people let the natural changes in color take their course. Some choose to style their hair in a traditional, classic fashion and others like flaunt a more edgy look. Some people's hair looks lustrous and thick and other's looks drab, thin and frail. All these variables give us a first impression about the kind of person we're dealing with. Although we may not want to "judge a book by its cover," so to speak, it is difficult to avoid doing so when it comes to hair. Most of the time people do their hair in such a way that reflects who they are or who they want to be. Again, we see that our *outer beauty*, whether consciously or not, reflects the inner state of our mind, not to mention the health of our physiology as well.

Healthy Body ~Healthy Hair

In the system of Ayurvedic medicine, the hair is seen an

extension of the powerful energy that flows along the channel of the spine. Our hair is intimately tied to this life force energy that is refered to as *prana* (also known as *qi* in the Chinese medical system).

Ayurvedic medicine also says that our hair is representative of the quality of our bones. It is considered, along with the nails, to be a type of by-product of osseous (bone) tissue. For example, we often see hair loss in overweight individuals because of faulty fat metabolism. When fat metabolism is compromised, impurities accumulate and deprive the bone tissue of its needed nutrition. So if you want to take care of your hair, you must take care of your bones too.

If we want to learn how to take care of our hair from the inside, out then we first need to get all the basics down. We need to understand how the hair is structured and what it does to function.

To begin with, hair is made up of a strong and durable protein called keratin. Each and every one of these strands of hair is housed within a long shaft called a follicle. The teenie-tiny hair fits into its follicle just like your arm fits through a long, tight sleeve. The job of the follicle is to anchor the hair deep within the fatty layer of the skin so that it can sit there securely on your head.

At the very bottom of the hair follicle sits a relatively giant bulbous structure of living cells. This sac of cells is plainly referred to as "the bulb" and it is the birthplace for all new hair cells. This is the only part of your hair that is living. Once your hair has breached the boarder of your scalp and is on top of your head, it is no longer alive (hint: that's why when you get your hair cut it doesn't hurt). The bulbous end of your hair follicle is buried deep inside your skin so that it can be protected and surrounded by a bunch of nourishing blood vessels. The blood vessels innervate the bulb so that they can deliver important hormones, bring in nutrients and remove wastes from the site.

The events that occur in the hair bulb under the skin determine the cycles and rates of your hair's growth, as well its oily secretions and the change in the color as you age. While hair color is genetically determined, the rate of decay in the pigmentation of the melanin cells can depend on many factors including diet and lifestyle. Most people's hair grows at a rate of about one-half inch per month, but it of course varies because Nature likes to keep things interesting. As with anything in Nature, the rate of hair growth is based on body type, season, and of course, age.

Ayurvedic Hair Types

According to Ayurvedic medicine, Nature is everywhere and exists in everything. The qualities of the elements influence everything from the transitions in our lives, to the food we eat and the skin type we have. Ayurvedic wisdom divides the hair into three types according to the qualities of the elements. To reveiw: air *(Vata dosha)*, fire *(Pitta dosha)* and water *(Kapha dosha)*. Read the descriptions below and take the quiz to see what type of hair you have.

Hair Type Questionnaire

To determine your hair type, please fill out this questionnaire. If within any category you find that you have traits that fall under more than one category, select all that apply. If something does not apply to you, please do not answer and simply skip to the next question.

A	B	C
☐ Dry & Rough	☐ Oily	☐ Shiny
☐ Dull in color	☐ Lighter in color	☐ Darker in color

☐ Curly	☐ Straight and thin	☐ Thick
☐ Dandruff on scalp	☐ Warm, sweaty scalp	☐ Oily and scaly scalp
☐ Split Ends	☐ Tendency of early graying and thinning	☐ Grows easily
Total	Total	Total

Mostly (a) responses

Your hair is dominant in the Air element or Vata

Mostly (b) responses

Your hair is dominant in the Fire element or Pitta

Mostly (c) responses

Your hair is dominant in the Water element or Kapha

Vata - Air Type Hair

Description

People with hair that expresses the air element usually have dark, coarse, wiry, frizzy and dry hair. Their hair is easily tangled and has the tendency to become dull and splay out into split ends. Out of all the other types, the person with air type hair is most susceptible to developing dandruff, dry eczema, and a dry scalp.

Recommendations for care

Ground Out	
Diet For Internal Oleation	Consume whole grains, nuts, seeds, olive oil, coconut oil, ghee and avocado.
For External Oleation	Do *abhyanga*, or Ayurvedic full body warm oil massage once per week. Do Ayurvedic scalp massage. Gently, in a circular motion, massage Bhringrha or Bramhi oil to the scalp before going to bed at night. If you can't easily get those Ayurvedic medicated oils then simply take 2 ounces of sesame oil, add 10 drops of lavender, add 5 drops of bergamont oil and all mix together in a big jar. Take 1 tsp. of this oil for your at home scalp massage. This is a wonderfully soothing homemade oil for scalp massage. The next morning, wash off the oil in warm water with organic shampoo. Not only will this assist in relieving dryness, but it will also aid in deeper sleep (which can be a challenge for a *Vata* type person).

Pitta - Fire Type Hair

Description:

If you predominantly have the element of fire in your hair then it is generally of a lighter color like brown, blond or red. Hair that expresses fire is usually light, fine and silky however these types also face the problems of premature graying and baldness.

Recommendations for Care

Cool Down	
Diet	Make sure to avoid foods that are too spicy or oily. Also stay away from sour or fermented foods, including alcohol. Instead favor green leafy vegetables, fresh fruits, coconut water and fresh herbs like mint or cilantro.
Cooling Scalp Massage	Mix 2 ounces of coconut oil with 10 drops of peppermint essential oil and 5 drops of orange essential oil. Apply at night and leave in to wash the next morning.

Kapha - Water Type Hair

Description:

If your hair is dominant in the element of water then it will be generally dark in color, thick, wavy and oily in texture and heavy in weight. This hair is generally very healthy and lustrous however it is prone to excess oil and heaviness.

Recommendation for Care

Lighten up	
Diet	Reduce the heaviness in your life and in your hair by avoiding sweet, sour, salty and oily foods. Instead, add more heating spices like mustard seed to support your metabolism so that you can cut through some of that excess oil.
Stimulating Scalp Massage:	Combine 2 ounces of sesame oil with 10 drops of basil essential oil and 5 drops of sage essential oil. Massage scalp and leave on for 20 minutes, then rinse.

Inner Care for the Hair

Nutrition

The reason that diet is included in our conversation about hair is because hair, like any other cell of the body, is nourished by the food that we consume, breakdown and then absorb. Both our metabolic strength and the quality of the food that we take in combine to create a nutrient rich environment for the cells of our hair to bathe in.

Protein, Fat & Calcium

As far as hair is concerned, the more protein, good quality fat and calcium the better! If you're not well nourished, your hair won't be either. So if you're looking for good sources of healthy fat, protein and calcium then include: organic, pasture raised milk and meat, buttermilk, cheese, ghee, eggs and butter. It is also beneficial to incorporate whole grains, nuts and seeds, as well as seasonal vegetables and sprouts. Finally in terms of specific nutrients, it is important to maximize sulfur, Vitamin C, all the B Vitamins and Omega 3 Fatty Acids too.

Cooling

Along with a nutrient and protein rich diet, the *quality* of the foods you consume should also be cooling in nature since the hair is not supported by heat. Slip a slice of cucumber into your water or sip on the nectar of a coconut fruit. Use spices like coriander and fennel to flavor your foods and keep up with your freshly cooked bitter greens. On the flip side, make sure to avoid hot, spicy, and fried foods as well as excess yogurt, coffee, alcohol, tea, tomatoes or citrus. All of these things are heating and can aggravate hair loss or graying. Of course, lastly, stay away from fast foods, refined flours and other processed foods containing artificial colors and flavors.

These foods will increase your load of toxins and compromise your metabolic health, both of which translate to less healthy hair.

The Healthy Hair Nutrition Checklist

Food	Micronutrients	Benefits
☐ Oats	Potassium, magnesium, phosphorous, zinc	Promotes hair grwoth
☐ Eggs	Good source of keratin: protein in hair.	Strengthens hair and brings luster.
☐ Fish	Omega 3 Fatty acids: especially in cold water fish like salmon or sardines.	Moisturizing to scalp.
☐ Spirulina	Good source of keratin: protein in hair.	Strengthens hair.
☐ Hazelnuts	Folate, vitamin B, antioxidant rich, and anti-inflammatory.	Protective to scalp.
☐ Pumpkin Seeds	Zinc.	Enhances growth of hair follicle.
☐ Brown rice	Silica and iron.	Enhances luster and improves health of scalp.
☐ Sweet Potatoes	Beta carotene and vitamin A.	For dull and dry hair.

Lifestyle & Herbs

For good hair health it is important to keep blood circulating to the scalp. Regular scalp massages and sweating (from a sauna or exercise) help to bring in nutrients and remove wastes from the hair cells. Additionally, Ayurveda has some wonderful herbs that work to improve blood flow, stimulate hair follicle growth and remove dead cells from the epidermis.

For hair growth:	Licorice, Brahmi, Bhringraj, Amalaki, Mandukaparni, Fenugreek
For graying:	Bhringraj, Nirgundi, Hibiscus

Outer Care for the Hair

Ayurvedic Scalp Massage

The head is arguably the most important part of the body to care for. Luckily, Ayurveda has the perfect solution for daily care of the head and scalp and it's called *shiro-abhyanga,* or head massage. The benefits of doing this practice are innumerable. According to one of the ancient texts of Ayurveda, the Charaka Samhita, regular oil massage of the scalp does the following:

It is at once detoxifying and deeply nourishing

It stimulates circulation, nourishes the roots of the hair, makes the mind more alert and the mood more stable, promotes solid sleep, enhances memory and keeps away the negative effects of stress.

It is used to treat baldness, premature graying, dandruff, hair loss,insomnia, headache, memory loss, high blood pressure, anxiety and nervous disorders such as paralysis, Parkinson's or Bell's Palsy.

As you can see, this simple activity can have far reaching effects not only on the health of your hair but also on your nervous system as a whole. What's more, is that you can augment the positive effects of Ayurvedic scalp massage by adding specific essential oils or infusing herbs into your base oil. I recommend that you perform self-oil massage on your scalp at least one to two times per week.

How to Do Ayurvedic Scalp Massage

- Before bed, massage coconut oil liberally throughout your scalp in gentle, clockwise circular motions without using your nails. (It is important you slightly warm the oil that you'll be using before applying it).
- Do not be afraid to get a little oil on your ears, forehead, neck and temples too, as you'll find that it will be extra calming to your nervous system.
- Then, leave in on at least 20 minutes for it to soak in before showering it off with warm (not hot) water and organic shampoo. Alternatively, you can leave it on overnight and wash off the next morning.

Don't Fry Your Brain

Because our hair is such a big and visible component of our appearance, and because it is a mirror to our body's inner vitality, it can be very distressing when something starts to go wrong in this arena. According to Ayurveda, excessive heat or fire element in the body is primarily responsible for hair problems. Therefore, it is our job to keep the scalp as cool as possible and to protect it from the sun and other sources of heat. Given that, on a daily basis it is important not to wash your hair in hot, scalding water. As relaxing as this may feel to you, it is not best. Instead favor water that has been cooled to a nice lukewarm temperature. The head and brain need to be kept cool so as not to overheat or "fry your brain." Try thinking of it this way: imagine your brain as a solid, hardened ball of ghee or clarified butter. If your butter-brain, so to speak, gets too hot, then it will melt! In other words, if your head is exposed to too much heat then you're setting yourself up for damage both to your hair and your sensory perception.

Common Hair Problems & Natural Solutions

If your aim is to treat your hair for a specific condition then below you can match your personal aim with the natural treatment that will suit you best. Many of the ingredients are simple kitchen herbs, but if there is something listed below in a recipe that you can't find at your local natural foods store, check out my recommended resources section in the back of the book page 300.

Hair Loss

Perhaps the single most horrifying of experience surrounding hair is when it starts to fall out in bunches. While some hair loss is natural, normal, and to be expected, problems start happening when the rate of hair loses is higher than the rate of its regeneration. This is the point at which you'll start to notice a thinning, receding hair line or patches of baldness. There are numerous reasons why this could be happening and the most important thing is that you discover the unique cause of your own hair loss. It is worthy to note that although we are aware that genetics plays a role in male baldness, the reasons for hair loss listed below are specific to women.

Causes of Hair Loss	
Alopecia Areata	Present in both males and females, this condition is identified by the rapid loss of hair in patches. The likely culprit in this disorder is autoimmunity, or the body fighting against its own tissue.
Temporary Illness	You may find that after being sick for a little while that large clumps of your hair fall out. This is normal and only temporary. Your body simply had to direct its resources to fighting the illness rather than sustaining your hair growth.
Age	As we get older our cells go through a natrual degeneration process and our hair cells become weaker.
Radiation or Chemotherapy:	Unfortunately a common side effect of cancer treatment is hair loss due to the harsh chemicals that strip the body of its reserves and leave no energy for the process of hair growth.
Hormonal	In times like childbirth, menopause, post-partum or in hormonal dysregulation like hypothyroidism, hair loss can occur .

CAUSES OF HAIR LOSS	
Diet	Not getting enough, or the right kind of nutrition can cause the hair to fall out (see the portion on nutrition for hair).
Stress, Worry, Lack of Sleep	Taxing to the body at large, these things cause our hair to become weak and it can fall out.
Prescription medication	The unfortunate side effect of many drugs such as birth-control pills or anti-depressants, is that they can cause the hair to fall out.
Environmental Exposure	Too much dust, water or other environmental pollutants can cause the hair to come out.
Chemicals	Many hair products although touted to be beneficial for your hair, often contain dangerous chemicals, some of which can cause hair loss.

NATURAL SOLUTIONS FOR HAIR LOSS	
Option 1	Make a paste with 3-4 tsp. *Triphala* powder and a bit of water. Apply to your scalp and leave it on for 10 minutes; then rinse with warm water. No need to use shampoo after this rinse. This can be used as a stimulus for hair growth and it can prevent future hair loss.
Option 2	After shampooing, apply a mixture of 2 tsp. olive or sesame oil and 1tsp. fresh ginger root juice. Apply this mixture to your scalp and rinse your hair properly with water.

DANDRUFF

This condition can be caused by either dry or oily skin. In the case of dry skin, there is itching, white flacks, eczema or psoriasis.

In the case of dandruff caused by oily skin, the presence of white flakes will still be there but the cause is seborrhic dermatitis.

NATURAL SOLUTIONS FOR DANDRUFF	
Option 1	Apply apple cider vinegar and massage to your scalp. Keep on for 10 minutes and then rinse.
Option 2	Boil 1 tsp. of the herb *Triphala* in 5 cups of water for 10 minutes. Strain with a cheese cloth, let cool and then rinse your hair with the concoction.
Option 3	Mix 1 tsp. of the herb *Amalaki* in powder form, with 2 tsp. of dry orange or lemon peel, 1-2 tsp. of Fenugreek seeds and 2 cups of water. Boil all of this together for 5-7 minutes. Strain and then wash your hair with the medicated water. You may condition afterwards if you desire. This can be done 1 x per week.

DULLNESS

(LACK OF SHINE OR LUSTER)

Dullness is connected to dryness and an aggravation of the air element, or *Vata*.

NATURAL SOLUTIONS FOR DULLNESS	
Option 1	Add a few leaves of Hibiscus to some hot water and brew it like a tea. Then, take the juice of a lime and squeeze it into the sieved mixture. Apply this to the hair before shampooing.
Option 2	Rinse your hair with1 cup water + 1 tsp. lemon juice or 1 tsp. vinegar. *For oily hair only.

NATURAL SOLUTIONS FOR DULLNESS	
Option 3	Peal the skin off of a orange and then boil in 2 cups of water for 10 minutes. Strain the mixture. Wash your hair as you would, and then after shampooing, use this concoction as your last rinse. *For soft and silky hair. Will also reduce dandruff.

SPLIT ENDS

Split ends are caused by exposure to heat and sun. Habitually using a hair dryer, or harsh chemical hair products are usually the main culprits at work.

NATURAL SOLUTIONS FOR SPLIT ENDS	
Option 1	Massage almond or avocado oil on the scalp before going to bed at night. In the morning, wash your hair with mild shampoo.
Option 2	Trim your hair.
Option 3	Include in your diet foods that are rich in proteins, vitamin B and keratin. Examples of these foods are: whole grains, nuts, seeds, eggs and fish.

EARLY GRAYING

Graying hair in old age is normal, but graying in one's 20's or 30's is premature. According to Ayurveda the primary cause of early graying is excessive heat in the head. Excess heat irritates the scalp causing folliculitis and results in both early graying and balding. This can happen as a result of the inordinate consumption of sour, salty, fermented, oily / deep friend food or alcohol, and it can also be exacerbated by stress irritability and anger.

Natural Solutions for Early Graying	
Option 1	Eat *Pitta* pacifying foods: cooling, juicy fruits like coconut and lots of green leafy veggies!
Option 2	Massage your head with coconut oil 2 x week.
Option 3	Apply *nasya*, or Ayurvedic nose drops with medicated *bramhi oil.* (see section on the nose, page 229, for more details).
Option 4	Give yourself a massage with coconut oil or ghee 2 x week. (see section on feet, page 250 for more details and why this is effective).
Option 5	Wash your hair with a cooling herbal shampoo that contains mint or *amalaki*.

Homemade Hair Care

There are plenty of wonderful, simple, and all natural solutions that you can easily whip up today in your own kitchen! All you'll need are a few handy herbs, some natural soap as a base, and your favorite essential oils. The following recipes will provide you with the perfect combination of nutrients that your hair has been begging for all along. Plus, the good news is that they're all suitable for any hair type but can be customized to your liking at will.

Natural Shampoos

Natural shampoos will help keep the follicles of your hair clean, unclogged and open so that you can maintain proper hygiene and detoxification.

Ingredients	Instructions
1 tbsp. Triphala powder 8 oz water 2 oz liquid olive soap 10 drops lavender essential oil 	Bring herbs and water to a boil and then simmer for 10 minutes. Take pot off the stove and let the mixture cool. Finally, strain the liquid and discard the herbs. Keep the "tea" that has been infused with the herbs. Add a little natural soap and the essential oil to your liquid herbal tea. Voi la! This should yield of 8-10 ounces of shampoo that you can use for 15 days if kept in the refrigerator.

Ingredients	Instructions
1 cup *Shikakai powder 1/2 cup Bramhi powder 1 cup Amalaki powder 1 cup Orange peel 1/4 cup Fenugreek seeds 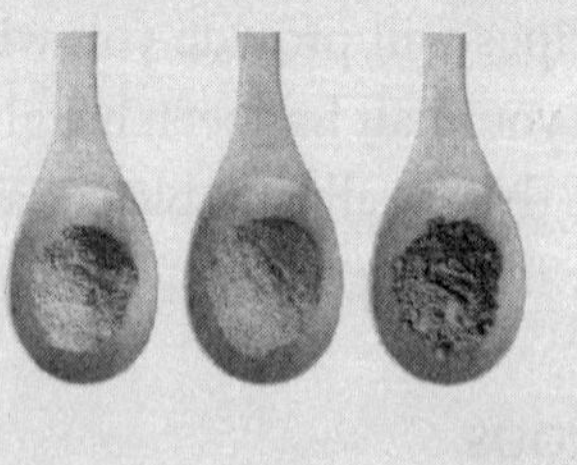	Mix the above ingredients together and store in a glass bottle. To begin making your shampoo, take 2 tsp of your pre-made mixture and add 2 cups of water in a small pot. Boil this concoction for 7-8 minutes. Strain the liquid and discard the herbs. Use once per week to cleanse the hair.

Natural Conditioners

After washing, the hair tends to dry out. That's why it's a good idea to apply moisturizing herbs and oil directly onto the hair after shampooing.

Ingredients	Instructions
Olive oil or almond oil	It can't get any simpler than this! Just use either one of these oils in place of your regular conditioner.

Ingredients	Instructions
1/4 cup aloe vera gel ½ juice of lemon 2-3- drops essential oils of your choice. (I find rosemary or mint to be lovely).	Mix ingredients and apply to shampooed hair. Leave on for 2-3 minutes, then rinse.

Purifying And Stimulating Hair / Scalp Rinse

The soothing and cleansing effect of the vinegar as well as other herbs and essential oils improves blood circulation to the hair follicle.

Ingredients

2 tbs coarsely ground mint leaves
1 tbs coarsely ground rosemary leaves
4-5 drops of essential oils of your choice
(I prefer lemongrass)
2 cups of apple cider vinegar

Instructions

- After you've coarsely chopped all your herbs, then use a glass jar to pour the apple cider vinegar over the herbs so that they are submerged. Stir the mixture and then cover with a lid. At room temperature, let this mixture sit for two weeks.
- At the end of two weeks, use a fine strainer to separate the herbs from the vinegar. Discard the herbs and keep the infused vinegar in a dark bottle in the refrigerator where you can store the mixture for 2-4 months. This will yield around 15-20 treatments.
- To apply, take 1-2 tablespoons of the infused vinegar and add it to 1 cup of warm water. Use this on your scalp after you've completed your regular shampoo and conditioning. Do not rinse it out with water. Simply let it stay on your hair and dry naturally after your shower. You can do this once per week for maintenance.

Eyes

The Subtle Beauty of the Eye

There is something about the eyes that draws us in more than any other sensory organ. We are fascinated with them. Their expression intrigues us and their sparkle delights us. Looking deeply at them we can detect discreet subtleties in the intention, emotion and character of any human being or animal before us. When gazing into another's eyes, we feel as though we receive the essence of their pure consciousness or spirit. It is therefore quite fitting that they should be so often referred to as the "windows of the soul."

Our eyes have two different ways of seeing – physically and energetically. According to Ayurveda, the subtle aspect of our eye theoretically possesses our memories, perception of reality and potential for what I like to call "divine sight." Secondly, and more familiarly, there is the physical organ of the eye which takes care of the biological processes of vision.

Compared to the mundane but highly important duties of the physical eye, the subtle or energetic eye fosters the deeper and more esoteric aspects of our vision. It is endowed with the intuitive power and intrinsic clairvoyance that we all have the potential to develop. The idea of the subtle eye stretches our concept of *seeing* from being simply a biological phenomena involving photoreceptor cells, to a function of spiritual insight and wisdom.

If we want to access the potential for wisdom that exists within our subtle eye, then we have to clear negative memories and attitudes that may be shrouding the clarity of our inner awareness. We can do this by acknowledging the hang-ups we have in our minds. Tools like meditation, affirmations and visualizations can help us set down the burdens of our gloomy perceptions, in favor of attaining a deeper, clearer sight at the locust of our subtle eye. Additionally, we can choose to avoid exposing our eyes to violent films or honor movies that not only incite a stress response in the body but also pollute the purity of the subtle eye. You see, the subtle and gross eye work together. The sensory information that our physical eye receives is stored in our memory and interpreted by our subtle eye. This is why the stimulus our eye receives should be wholesome and unadulterated.

Finally, we can understand the virtues of the subtle eye as a reflection of our own *inner beauty*. As the sight of our subtle eye is fine-tuned, so is the quality of our *inner beauty*. The more clearly we see the world, the more accurately we perceive ourselves; and when we access the truth about ourselves, we recover the workings of our *inner beauty*. The subtle eye therefore, reinforces the cultivation of *inner beauty* which eventually, inspires the earnest care for the outer, physical organ of the eye.

Since the eyes are not only a vital physical organ but also the "gateway to the soul," we want to ensure that their physical manifestation is indeed a reflection of the *inner beauty* we possess. Many people attempt to beautify their eyes with cosmetic eye surgeries like blepharoplasty, eye lid plastic surgery, eye brow lifts and eye lash transplants, but ultimately nothing can ever take the place of healthy eyes that shine with beauty from the inside out. As an exercise for your subtle eye, try asking this question:

"How Can I Cultivate a Positive Outlook and Visualize Only Good Things?"

The Physical Beauty of the Eye

Now, as we all know, the physical outer aspect of the eye is hugely important as well! We so heavily rely on the smooth and painless operation of our eyesight every day. Without it we would be lost. The health of our biological eye can easily be taken for granted but the truth is that if we neglect caring for this amazing organ, we will surely regret it. It is crucial to ensure the proper care of our eyes, even in our early years, so that we can prevent problems in the future. As with all aspects of our lives, it is up to us to take care of our *inner* and *outer beauty* so that they both reflect the light of our spirits and good will.

In Ayurvedic terms, the eye is governed by the fire element or *Pitta dosha*, and therefore requires the overall balance of heat in the body. Review the following information about the eyes and hopefully you'll get some good ideas about how you can maintain the healthy functioning of your physical eye throughout your life.

Eye Health

According to Ayurvedic medicine, the overuse, under use or abuse of any sensory organ can all contribute to disease in their own way. For the eyes specifically, Ayurveda identifies several main contributors that reinforce the development of eye disorders: constipation, impurities in the blood, and excessive heat. Other common causes are as follows:

General Causes of Eye Imbalances	
Central Nervous System Imbalance:	Several well-defined neurodegenerative conditions that affect the brain and spinal cord have manifestations in the eye and ocular symptoms often precede conventional diagnosis of such CNS disorders.
Metabolic Dysfunction:	Diabetes, Mitochondrial DNA mutation, Mitochondrial protein malfunction and oxidative stress can lead to retinopathy, visual deficits and eventually blindness.
Continual Staring at Close Objects for Prolonged Periods:	Eye strain from computers, tablets, smart phones, or minute articles (like in the case of work done by astronomers or scientists).
Working Night Shifts:	Forcing the eyes to be open when they should naturally be closed and only exposed to darkness.
Traumatic Injury:	Accidental injury to the eye.
Excessively Heating Lifestyle:	Consuming sour, salty or fermented foods and/or engaging in frequent intercourse or regular saunas which promote increased sweating. Also, working in kitchens, smoking cigarettes and having poor eye hygiene.
Environmental Distress:	Smoking, dust, pollen, sun, wind, low humidity, high altitudes

SOLUTIONS FOR EYE IMBALANCES

Ayurveda has some wonderful remedies for eye disturbances. It recommends using the healing power of Nature to nourish the eyes through simple but profound restorative activities. Most of these are totally free and available to all of us.

GENERAL SOLUTIONS FOR EYE IMBALANCES	
Nature Gazing	Look at the sunrise, sunsets and full moons.
Breathing Exercises	Practice *pranayama*, or intentional breathing exercises. Good options are *nadi-shodana* or *kabalbhati*.
Therapeutic Bodywork	Get Ayurvedic treatments designed to support eye health. Good options are: *Pad dhara, Shirobasti, Shirolepam, Nasya, or Netrabasti.*
Nature Walking	Walk barefoot on the grass and/or sand.
Foot Massage	Reflexology shows that the feet mirror the eyes. Traditionally massaging the feet with a kanse metal bowl is healing to the eyes.
Eye Drops	Use Ayurvedic herbal eye drops.
Eye Exercises	Try frequently palming or blinking. If using a screen, set a clock for brief breaks at intervals of 20 minutes. At those junctures, look out a window 20 feet away (the distance at which the eye muscles can relax). Fix your sight on some greenery in a natural setting and then blink for 20 seconds.

General Solutions for Eye Imbalances	
Herbs	Use Ayurvedic herbs that are specific for the eyes: Triphala, Saffron, Garlic, Cayenne, Ginkgo Biloba, Licorice, Green tea and/or herbal medicated ghee (like Triphala, Licorice, or Bramhi).
Diet	Eat a nutrient rich diet filled with whole grains and fresh, colorful vegetables and fruits along with good fats like avocado, coconut oil, ghee, and cold pressed olive oil.

Ayurveda divides the symptoms of eye disorders into three main categories based on the *doshas*. Below you'll find descriptions of the problems and solutions for eye imbalances related to *Vata* (air), *Pitta* (fire) and *Kapha* (water) respectively. You'll also discover simple, homemade remedies so you can nurse your eyes back to health with cost effective and 100% natural recipes.

Vata (Air)
Imbalance in the Eyes

Causes	• Excessive exercise, sweating • Excess dry, cold, bitter foods • Excess detoxification • Grief, worry, tension • Excess use of screens (tv, computer) • Chronic constipation
Symptoms	• Dry and scratchy eyes • Stinging, sandy sensation • Sensitivity to light • Problems with tear production • Eyelid turns inward • Eyelid sags away from the eyeball • Disruption of blinking mechanism • Strain from computer, driving or reading • Dark circles under the eyes
Solutions	• Lubrication: Topical herbal eye drops • Yoga: Lion pose (simhasana) • Posture: Sitting straight with the feet on the floor to reduce back stress. Also, incorporate a cushion for the lower back and get regular neck and shoulder massages. • Eye exercises • Frequent blinking

PITTA (FIRE)
IMBALANCE IN THE EYES

Causes	Anger, Jealousy, Irritability Stress Alcohol, Spicy- Salty foods, Smoking Hyperacidity High Blood pressure Hot weather, Sauna
Symptoms	Redness/blood shot Burning sensation Headaches Inflammation Irritability Sensitive to light
Solutions	Cooling eye packs with rose water Cucumber slices Cold tea bags Castor oil—1-2 drops on index finger tip and apply like an eye liner in each eye before going to bed Massage your feet with ghee or castor oil before going to bed, then wear old socks

KAPHA (WATER) IMBALANCE IN THE EYES

Causes	Poor Appetite, Slow Digestion-Metabolism Water retention Overweight Hormonal Imbalance Lack of sleep Sodium intake, alcohol Allergy (food, pet, pollen, carpet, paint)
Symptoms	Discomfort, Itching Heaviness, puffiness Blurry vision Eye discharge, mucous deposits/slimy discharge Pain: headaches, nausea Drooping eyelids
Solutions	Eye exercises Palming, blinking Warm eye packs Steam inhalation Nose drops Eye drops Neti pot

Ears

The Subtle Beauty of the Ear

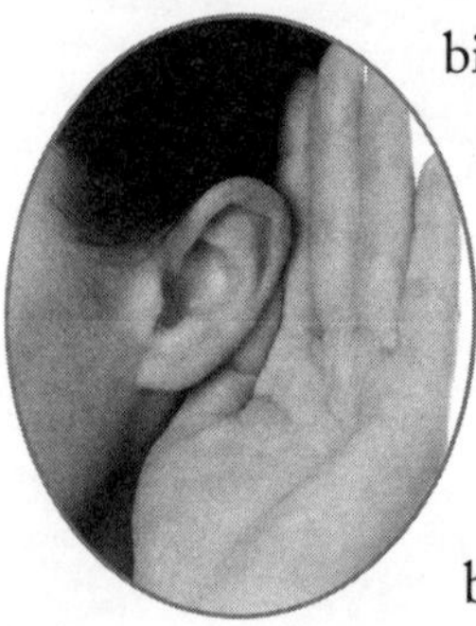

As with the eyes, the ears also have both a subtle and biological component to their function. The subtle nature of the ear takes sound and translates it into a meaning or sensation that reverberates throughout the body. Therefore, when we hear good things, the light of the subtle ear shines as it fills our body with positive vibrations. When we surround our ears with pleasant tones like the voice of our loved ones, the song of the birds, a babbling brook, or Mozart's masterpieces, then we nourish the health of our subtle ear.

A great example of a practical application of this phenomenon is music therapy. It is a relatively new field that has taken advantage of the healing power of sound to induce a state of peace, calm and harmony in people who are coping with intense stress. Another illustration of the value of the subtle ear is called *"Karna Vedham."* It is a Hindu ceremony for the piercing of the ears of a young child from twelve days to one year old. It is a rite of passage that is believed to poise the child's ears to hear only sacred sounds. The consumption of these sounds through the sensory organ of the ear are said to be deeply and mystically cleansing and nourishing to the child's soul.

As healing as sounds can be, they can also be harmful if they're coming from the wrong source or being heard at the wrong decibel. If we consume overly loud and offensive noises, then there will be an adverse effect on our nervous systems. For instance, some construction workers may hear the noise of a jack hammer for eight hours a day. Similarly, workers on airport runways are constantly exposed to the noise of planes landing and taking off. In another way, hearing someone speak negatively about you or a loved one can also harm the wellbeing of the figurative subtle ear. So as we seek to care for the external beauty of our physical ears, we must first take into account the state of our subtle ear and expose ourselves to only sweet, comforting and uplifting sounds.

"Bhadram karnebhi shrunuyam devaha".
"Let my ears hear only good words"

Additionally, you can reflect upon the following question to promote the purity of your subtle, energetic ear:

"How Can I Train My Ears to Listen to the Rhythm and Vibration of the Universe?"

The Physical Beauty of the Ear

According to Ayurveda, the ear is one of the sites where *Vata* or the air element, likes to reside in the body. Because *Vata* is already so cold, dry and rough, in order to stay balanced, the ears attempt to antidote these qualities with their opposites - things that are warm, smooth and moist. In fact, many surfers who spend hours every day in the cold water with the cool breeze blowing straight into their ears develop something known as "surfer's ear." Surfer's ear occurs when the ear bone proliferates and expands over the passageway of the ear. It does this in an attempt to construct a shield from the frequent exposure to cold wind.

Solution to Ear Imbalances

Karna Pooran

Karna pooran is an Ayurvedic technique used to remedy ear imbalances. It is a process by which one applies either warm sesame oil or medicated herbal oil into the ear canal. This warm lubrication counters the cold, dry and rough nature of the ear and hence alleviates innumerable auditory problems.

Karna pooran is traditionally used in Ayurvedic medicine as part of one's typical daily routine. It is considered to be preventive medicine so as to avoid the accumulation of *Vata*, or excess air in the ear. The daily practice of this treatment is especially important for people who are dominantly *Vata* in constitution. The indications for *karna pooran* are:

(1) when the weather is cold and windy

(2) when traveling - especially by plane

(3) when performing any outdoor activity in which there is substantial movement or wind like: biking, jogging, hiking, sailing or skiing.

It is crucial to protect the delicate features of our precious ears so that we do not risk exposing them to the threat of potential imbalance.

Ear Imbalances

Loss of balance, Ear ache, Ear infection , Headaches, Swimmer's ear, Ringing (tinnitus) , Wax build up, Hearing loss

Benefits of Karna Pooran

- Strengthens the auditory system

Benefits of Karna Pooran

- Reduces dryness or itching in ears
- Prevents ear infections
- Reduces ringing
- Reduces tension in neck and jaw to diminish TMJ
- Relieves headache
- Assists in reducing Vertigo
- Reduces congestion from wax or yeast overgrowth

How to use Karna Poorn

Do this practice before going to bed.

- Use herbal oil prescribed by an Ayurvedic Practitioner or simply use organic, non toasted sesame oil.
- Put the oil of your choice into a glass bottle. Submerge the bottle into hot water for 5 minutes to make it warm. (Make sure the oil is not too hot to the touch before administering).
- Place 3-4 drops of oil in each ear.
- Insert a small bit of cotton into each ear to hold the oil there for a few minutes.

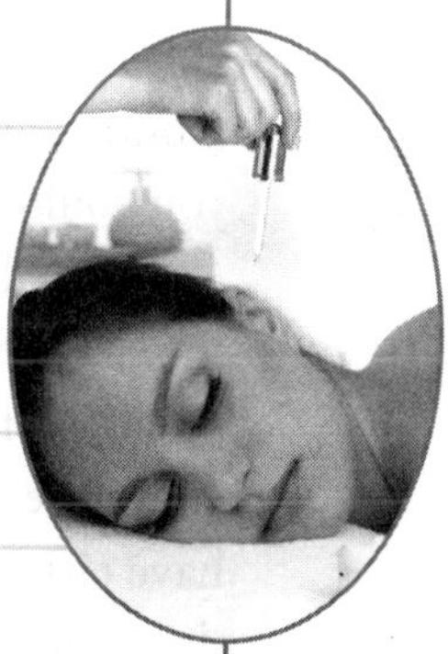

Nose

THE SUBTLE BEAUTY OF THE NOSE

Similar to the eyes and ears, the nose too, is a sensory organ which functions from both a subtle and a tangible, biological level. The subtle nose receives the sensory information of smell, so when we engulf ourselves with wonderful scents, we nourish the health of our nose. According to Ayurveda the nose is the doorway to *prana*, or the life force. It is the gateway to our brain. Whatever we put into our nose, travels to our brain.

Think about a time when you came home and someone had cooked a delicious meal for you. The whole house smelled of sweet spices and freshly cooked food. As you came in the door, you probably felt comforted, satisfied and welcomed just because you came into a warm home filled with a glorious smell! Then, as you were waiting to serve up your dish, you likely became hungry. The smell of the food stimulated your appetite and a whole cascade of digestive hormones were released in response to the smells around you. As a result, your body was ready to digest your food and you could sit down and enjoy your meal without any indigestion.

Equally as wondrous are the scents of essential oils. Distilling the essence of medicinal plants and applying them to your body is the practice of aromatherapy. The aromas of these herbs enter through your nose and effect the functioning of your cranial nerves. They can have either a stimulatory or calming effect on your nervous system depending on the combination of herbs that are in your oil blend. They are a very potent yet subtle and gentle way of administering the healing constituents of medicinal plants.

The power of smell has far-reaching effects in our lives. It influences molecules as small as our hormones and evokes memories as intimate as our first kiss or our mother rocking us to sleep. One whiff of your grandmother's perfume and you're suddenly transported back in time into her living room as a child. But as with any sensory organ, the impact smell can have can either be positive or negative depending on the nature of the stimuli. Long term exposure to rancid, putrid or other foul smells can be shocking to the nervous system and offensive to the wellness of our sensory experience. If you want to ensure the proper care of your sense of smell then ask yourself:

> "How can I Best Expose Myself to Delightful, Pleasurable and Healing Scents?"

The Physical Beauty of the Nose

"Nose jobs" as they're called, are huge in the USA. The nose sits right there, smack dab in the middle of your face. You could say that all the rest of your features are essentially positioned around it! It is no wonder that people today go to great lengths, including painful plastic surgeries to beautify their noses. However, the ancient Ayurvedic text of Sushruta Samhita (Chikitsa Sthana, chapter 19), suggests that nose piercings were widely prevalent in ancient times as well. It was believed that piercing the nose near a particular nodule on the nostril lessened the pain of the monthly menstrual cycle. Nowadays, nose piercings are simply a fashion trend, but back then they had a purpose and meaning outside of just external adornment. Even today, when a Hindu bride wears a nose ring it is symbolic of her commitment to provide her future family with good smells like freshly cut flowers, a home cooked meal, or the burning of sacred sandalwood incense. Again, we see how our external ornamentation is truly designed to be a reflection of our *inner beauty* rather than a filler for our lack of self confidence.

Natural Solutions for the Nose

According to Ayurveda, it is important to keep the nasal passages lubricated in an effort to prevent serious infections as well as the common cold. To remedy the vulnerability of the nose to dryness, debris, and bacteria, Ayurveda uses something called *Nasya. Nasya* is the administration of warm (possibly medicated) sesame oil into the nasal passage.

Nose Imbalances
Sinusitis, Nose bleeds, Nasal polyps, Stuffy nose, Running nose, Nasal congestion, Diminished smell

Benefits of Nasya
Prevents infections
Cleanses nasal passage
Releases tension headaches
Improves quality of voice
Bestows mental clarity
Prevents insomnia
Reduces anger and irritability

How to Perform Naysa:

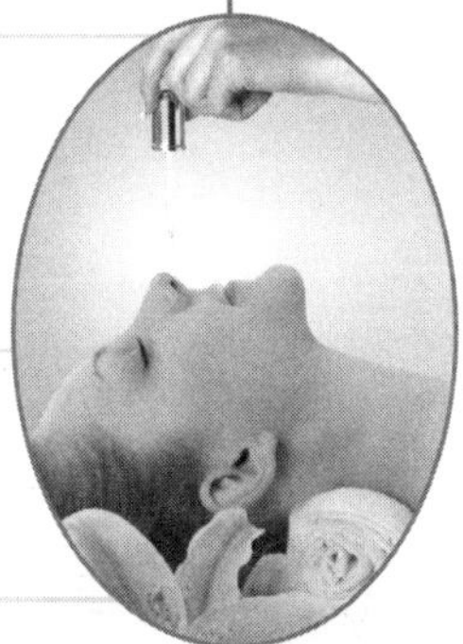

- Wait until you have an empty stomach. First thing in the morning or before bed at night is best.
- See steps for heating and obtaining oil under *Karana purna* (oil treatment for the ears). *Please note that for frequent bleeding of the nose, it is best to use warm ghee instead of sesame oil.
- Once oil is properly heated in a dropper, lay with your back on the couch and your head tilted at a 90 degree angle so that your chin is as far back as it will reach.
- Slowly administer 1-3 drops in each nostril and wait, staying in the same position, for a few minutes.

Mouth

"Satyam Bruyat Priyam Bruyat"
Always speak sweetly and honestly

External beauty of the mouth

"Healthy mouth, Healthy you!"

When we talk about the mouth we are referring to the tongue, gums, lips and teeth. Good oral hygiene and can improve our overall health and confidence. Conversely, bad breath, crooked teeth, and bleeding gums can adversely affect self-esteem and be a sign of poor health. That's why it's very important to thoroughly take care of this area of our bodies.

Collectively, the organs in the mouth are overflowing with nerve endings. The mouth is one of the most sensual parts of our bodies. As we kiss a lover, we use the intimacy of our mouths to express our deepest of feelings. Our mouths are also our center for taste - another highly pleasurable experience in life! We can all attest to the divine satisfaction of tasting a delicious dish freshly made just to our liking. The mouth is the first place where we take in and process our nourishment. But, watch out for the quality of nourishment you're giving yourself. Do you overload on carbs or sweets? If you crave sugars then you might need to look at the degree of emotional satisfaction in your life. Are you lacking love or affection in your world? If you're not in a partnership, then perhaps it has been a long time since you've been touched or kissed lovingly. If this is the case, then it is deeply important to do everything in your power to tune into your senses. Do self-massage, keep sweet aromas in the house (like rose, sandalwood, or jasmine for example), and listen to beautiful music or watch heart-warming movies. Engage your senses with pleasurable stimulus. All thesc things will help you feel nourished and will reduce your cravings for sweets.

Ask yourself:

> "How Can I better nourish my physical and emotional health?"

Someone once told me, "God has given us two eyes to see better, two ears to listen more, but only one mouth to speak *less*!" This humorous phrase has a lot of meaning. It is taxing on our energy and the energy of those around us if we talk too much! So to get a sense for the subtle, *inner beauty* of the mouth, you may want to contemplate the following question:

> "When and where do I exert too much energy in unnecessary talking?"

Potential Imbalances

Dry mouth, Chapped, Cracking and Dry lips, Thrush, Cold sores, Geographic tongue, Oral cancer, TMJ, Chipped teeth, Periodontitis, Gum disease, Cavities, Tooth ache.

Natural Solutions:

- To strengthen and nourish gums, prevent cavities and reduce oral pain or sensitivities, do Ayurvedic oil pulling or *kaval.*

Natural Solutions:

- To stimulate taste buds, clean the tongue and ignite metabolism, scrape your tongue with a copper scraper regularly in the morning before brushing your teeth.
- To remove plaque, use an herbal tooth paste with the herb *neem* as the main ingredient.
- For bleeding gums, gently massage the herb *triphala* into your gums.
- For a tooth ache, try applying clove oil on the painful area.
- For dry lips, apply ghee to moisten the lips.

"To be successful in life, do not lie. Do not decieve anyone. Do not hurt anyone. And be softspoken."

~ Pramila Thakar, born 1929 India ~

Throat

Yoga, a sister science to Ayurveda in the Vedantic tradition of India, says that the throat is one of the seven major subtle energy centers or *chakras*, in the body. The seven chakras are seen as "wheels of light" aligned along the spinal column. The fifth wheel is located at the throat and is called *vishuddha*. It is responsible for self-expression, creativity and communication.

In this way, the Vedas are referring to the subtle throat, or the energetic component of this physical part of our bodies. If this chakra is imbalanced, then it will be difficult for someone to express themselves. They may be shy or fearful, or may talk too much or too little. Speaking words of love, compassion and kindness beautifies the *inner beauty* of the throat from the inside, out. It is truly as Audrey Hepburn says, "For beautiful lips, speak only good words." If you want to get to augment the energy of your subtle throat, than ask yourself the question:

"How Can I Speak Sweet and Truthful Words?"

Potential Imbalances

Thyroid problems, Swollen lymph glands, Hoarse voice, Pharyngitis, Laryngitis, Unable to vocalize your intention, Speech problems like stuttering, Fear of speaking, Speaking too much, Sore throat, Wrinkles, Lying

Natural Solutions:

- Neck and shoulder massage to release tension and stress
- Massage throat in upward direction towards mandible to avoid wrinkles. Use sesame or **Skin Tone Oil** (see resources for more information).
- Drink warm water like herbal teas, or hot water infused with fresh ginger or min.t
- Gargle with 1 cup warm water, ¼ tsp turmeric powder and ½ tsp salt.
- Speak the truth.
- Sing or chant *mantras* (sacred sounds and prayers).

Shoulders

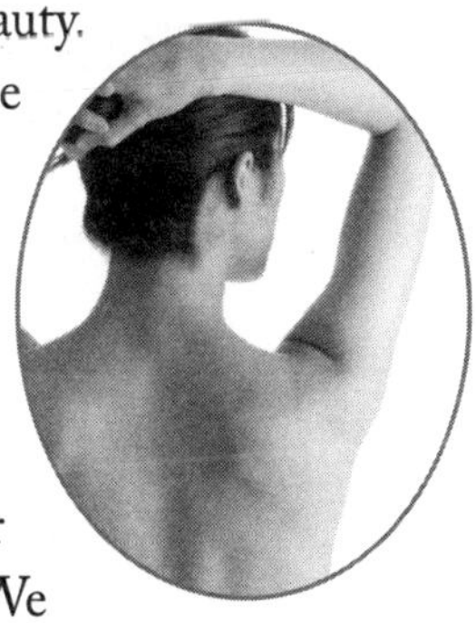

The shoulders play a significant role in our outer beauty. The collarbone is even sometimes referred to as "the beauty bone." It makes a woman tall and elegant. If you keep your shoulders back while sitting and walking, you feel confident and proud. Plus, automatically your spine and neck align and that relieves tension in your back. Many of us hold on to so much stress, especially in our neck and shoulders. With so much tension, our muscles become locked up, tight, knotted and painful. We need natural solutions that will bring us real relief and help us to maintain this integral part of our *outer beauty.*

Next, there is a reason we say, "You can cry on my shoulder." The shoulders are strong, firm and stable. They provide the perfect resting spot for a sad, weary friend. So if you want to get in touch with the *inner beauty* of your shoulders, then ask yourself the question:

> "How Can I Best Support
> Myself, My Family and My Friends?"

Potential Imbalances
Tension, Poor spinal alignment, Ache, Hunched back, Joint pain

Natural Solutions:

❦	Massage to your whole body with sesame oil (see Abhyanga page 155). This will help to reduce stiffness, stress, tension, nerve pain and fatigue.
❦	Do neck and shoulder exercises.
❦	Lift weights.
❦	Go on walks or play sports – get your blood flowing.
❦	Make a bath with 5-6 tsp. of Himalayan salt and soak for 20 minutes.
❦	Dance.

Hands

According to the Hindu and Yogic traditions, people greet each other with a *mudra* or hand gesture. The hands are placed against the chest in the prayer position and the word "*namaste*" is spoken. This term means "I honor the divine within you." It is a gesture of respect and a reminder of the divinity in all of creation.

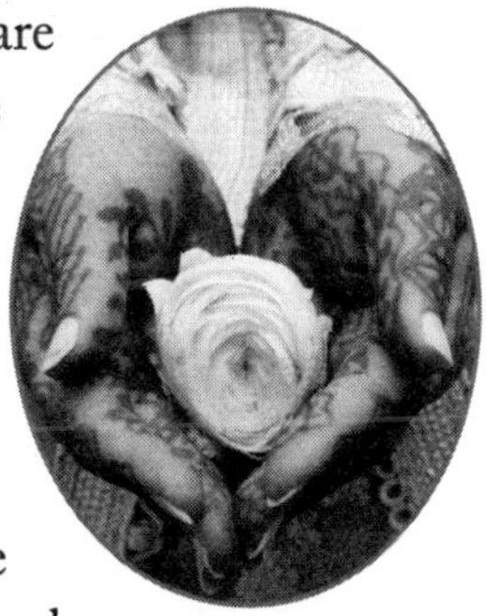

During special occasions in India, the art of *mehndi* or body art with henna is practiced. Henna is a non-permanent, natural dye that comes from the leaves of the henna plant. Traditionally the designs tattooed with henna are highly intricate and very feminine. They impart a somewhat mystical and goddess-like energy when placed upon the body. They are most notably propitious on the hands of the bride in a Hindu wedding ceremony. The hands, like the feet, easily pick up and release toxins so the application of henna is auspicious because it helps to rid the hands of any heating, inflammatory toxins.

Finally, our hands are also our greatest tools for healing. According to the ancient Ayurvedic scholar Sushruta, *"Hastam evam pradhan yantram!"* - meaning the hands posess potent healing power! This is the *inner beauty* present within the hands.

Ask yourself:

"How Can My Hands Bring More Healing Energy Into the World?"

Potential Imbalances

Carries germs, Dryness and cracking, Warts, Nerve pain, Wrist pain, Sweaty hands

Natural Solutions:

- It is important to wash your hands, but there is no need to use abrasive cleansers. Choose herbal soaps instead. They will be less harmful to your skin.
- A simple cleansing solution for your hands: cut ½ lemon and squeeze its juice into a bowl with ½ tsp. of Himalayan salt. Then mix these together. Apply this mixture in circular motions to the hands, rubbing for about 3-4 minutes. Wash off and see the improvement in the texture and circulation.
- Massage your hands with sesame or olive oil. Stretch and wiggle your fingers! Let the oil absorb fully to reduce dryness.
- For greasy hands use cornmeal or oatmeal to cleanse instead of harsh detergents.

Generous

Whenever you can, give. Offer of your time, money and heart for the good of others.

Nails

Everyone has uniquely different texture, shapes and colors to their nails. Generally, healthy nails are pink, soft, shiny and strong with regular growth. Here are the characteristic traits of nails depending upon the elements that are most dominate within them.

Vata nails have a tendency of brittle or easily breakable nails. They also often have dryness or ridges.

Pitta nails are rosy, soft and oily.

Kapha nails are larger in shape, strong and do not break easily.

As a general rule however, if the nails are robust and strong, it is considered to be a sign of good health (and certainly it is beautiful as well). If the nails are weak, rigid, spotty, discolored or brittle, then it could indicate that your bone tissue is weak. Like the hair, according to Ayurvedic medicine, the nails are a byproduct of bone tissue. Therefore, if the nails are unhealthy, it is important to consider the strength of the bones as well. That's why we need to pay attention to our nails. Keep your eye on them because they could be indicating a deeper health problem.

Potential Imbalances

Nail Clubbing, Nail Pitting, Indentations, Hangnails
Nail biting, Brittle nails, Fungus

Natural Solutions:

- Warm compress of fresh aloe vera gel for an infected finger. Cover with warm damp cloth.
- To prevent biting nails, apply aloe vera get or castor oil to the tips of your nails. This will discourage you from biting.
- Do not tear off hangnails. Cut the flap of skin with nail clippers or scissors. Then massage the area of the hangnails, along with your nails and cuticles, with a couple drops of castor oil before going to bed.
- Moisturize cuticles with castor oil daily.
- To strengthen nails try henna paste. Henna is conditioning and fortifying for the nails, although it will temporarily dye your nails orange or red.
- Use acetone based nail polish remover which contains essential oils that prevent the drying of the nails. Or, apply a little castor oil the nails after using nail polish.
- Limit professional manicures as the chemicals used are harsh and drying.

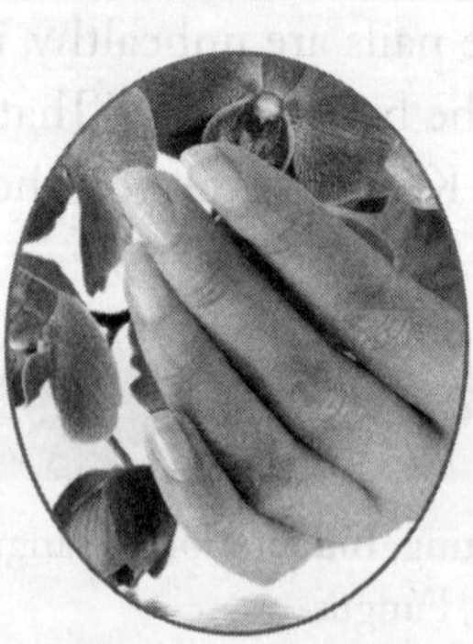

Breasts

The breasts of a woman are designed to offer nourishment, sustenance to every person that has ever been born. Every new baby has laid upon the bosom of a woman. The breasts are like an extension of the heart. Holding babies, children or other loved ones close to the chest marks a display of heartfelt affection. If you want to get more in touch with the subtle, energetic aspect of love within your breasts, then ask yourself this question:

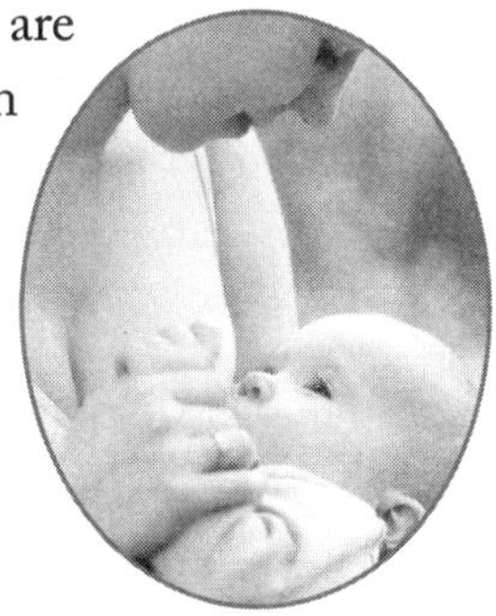

"How Can I Give More Love?"

*To anyone - my children, myself, my work, my family or even my pet.

On a physical level, the breasts are densely packed with lymphatic and adipose (fat) tissue. Because toxins like to accumulate in these types of tissues, the breasts are at risk of harboring impurities. The breasts need a way to drain the toxins that become lodged in their fat and lymphatic cells. See the list below for numerous ways to open the channels in the breasts so that undesirable build-up can take the fast train out!

Potential Imbalances
Breast Soreness, Fibrocystic Breasts, Invasive or Noninvasive Breast Cancer, Breast Lumps

Natural Solutions:
Dry brush massage.
Lymphatic drainage massage.
Exercise.
Avoid under wire bras.
Avoid antiperspirants.
Eat fresh, organic colorful vegetables and fruits and consume a high fiber, plant based diet low in saturated animal fat.
Reduce caffein.e
Drink **Lymph Tea** (to purchase visit: Ayurvedichealing.net)
Choose spices and herbs that support cleansing and nourishing: shatavari, dandelion, fenugreek, turmeric, cumin and fennel.
Remove smoking and consumption of hard liquor.
Watch your personal care products to make sure you are not applying lotions with toxic endocrine disrupters.

Abdomen

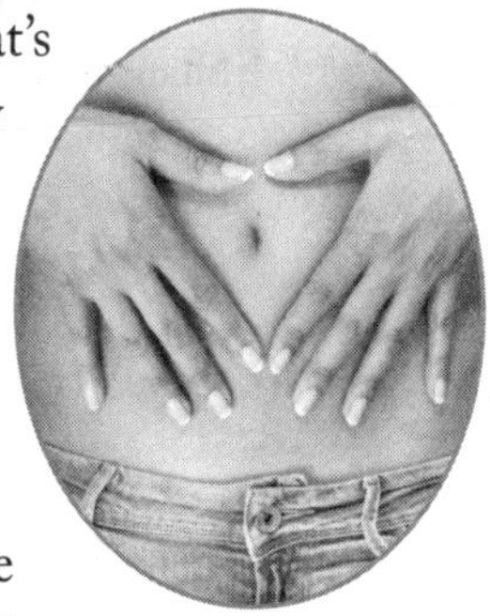

Everyone wants their belly to be flat and skinny. That's the truth! But in modern day culture we see many, many people holding excess fat around their abdomen. Not only is this undesirable from the standpoint of *outer beauty* but it also affects our health. Fat around the abdomen is more problematic than fat anywhere else in the body. It is associated with an excess of cortisol, a powerful stress hormone. Too much cortisol depletes the adrenals and compromises the endocrine system, creating other problems like hypothyroidism or irregular menstruation. Furthermore, if you have too much of this visceral fat, you are also vulnerable to other health problems like: obesity, high blood pressure, diabetes and certain cancers.

If we want our abdomen to stay fit and lean, then we have to ensure that our metabolisms are up to par. According to Ayurveda, anything undigested – whether it be a food or an emotion – creates a certain level of toxicity in our bodies. These toxins have an affinity for fat tissue and like to lodge themselves in the fat around our bellies and thighs. Unfortunately, they remain in the body for a long time and do not easily come out. That is why we need to keep a clean diet and make a concerted effort to detoxify (using Ayurveda's detox system called *panchakarma*) on a regular basis so that we can keep our metabolism strong and steer clear of toxins.

Ask yourself:

"How Can I 'Digest'
Both My Food and Life Experiences?"

Potential Imbalances

Indigestion, Gas, bloating, Metabolic Syndrome, Obesity, Diabetes, Inflammation of the stomach, pancreas, liver, and intestines; GERD/ acid reflux, Peptic ulcers , Constipation, Diarrhea, Nausea, Intestinal cramping or colic , Vomiting, Weight gain

Natural Solutions:

- Honor your appetite, digestion and the season at hand.
- Eat complex carbohydrates and a diet full of fiber (including soluble and insoluble fiber).
- Limit fatty foods.
- Limit carbonated, iced-cold and caffeinated drinks.
- Eat freshly prepared home made food as much as possible.
- Eat plenty of vegetables and fruits (nature has offered a lot of options).
- Hydrate yourself properly with good quality water.
- Exercise.
- Do abdominal crunches.

Hips

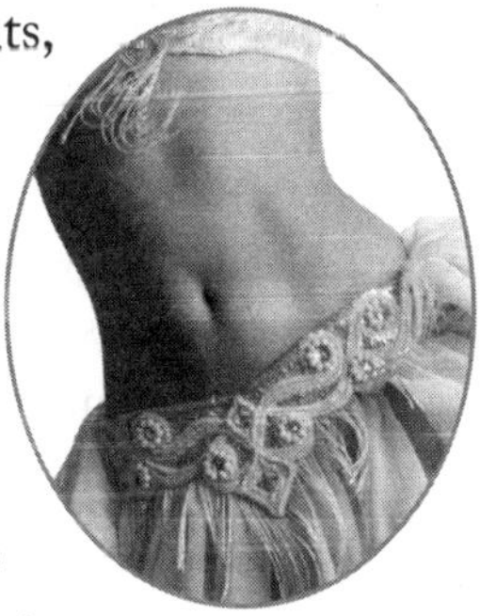

As one of the body's largest weight bearing joints, the hips make up the bones of our pelvis. They also encompass the muscles of the thighs and buttocks and provide the container for the reproductive organs, bladder, rectum and so on. The hips and all their associated muscles, nerves and blood vessels are what allow you to stand upright and walk. They give you the balance you need to move forward in life. So in order to give more energetic support to your pelvic girdle, and cultivate to the *inner beauty* of your hips, then ask yourself this question:

"How Can I Maintain Better Balance in My Life?"

Potential Imbalances

Fracture, Dislocation, Hip joint pain

Natural Solutions:

- Reduce inflammation with herbs like turmeric.
- Maintain a healthy weight.
- Support your lower back.
- Do sun salutations (or leg stretching and thoracic twists).
- Walk regularly.

Yoni

In the ancient language of Ayurveda called *Sanskrit*, we refer to a woman's vagina as her yoni (pronounced yo-nee). The Sanskrit root word for *yoni* is *'yuj'* which means to unite (the word *yoga* shares the same root). The *yoni* is the place where male and female energies converge. It is also the passageway through which mother and infant are united upon delivery.

At the *yoni*, a women experiences the cosmic cycle of creation and destruction. The *yoni* is the source of creation and re-creation - if a woman's egg is fertilized, there is creation; if it is not, there is destruction and the lining of the uterus is shed. The *yoni* is a beautiful, sacred and holy organ well deserving of respect and appreciation by ourselves and the world at large. Unique to women alone, it holds the energetic and physical capacity to give birth to the whole of human creation. Unfortunately however, women all too often associated their *yonis* with suffering from painful memories, venereal diseases or fear, insecurity, guilt, shame and doubt. Therefore, we all need to support ourselves and our fellow sisters in healing our relationship with our *yonis*. When we do this we can thrive as women and if we wish, confidently bring happy, healthy families into the world.

"How Can I Maintain the Purity and Sanctity of My Yoni?"

Potential Imbalances

Dryness, Pain with intercourse, Bacterial Vaginosis, Yeast infections Itching, Excessive sex, Sexual abuse, Sexually Transmitted Infections, Prolapse.

Natural Solutions:

- The mucosal lining of the vagina is filled with immune cells, so to prevent infection, keep this area clean.
- Perform gentle internal oil massage with **Skin Tone Oil** for dryness.
- Wear natural, breathable cotton clothes.
- Soak a tampon with sesame oil and insert it overnight. Remove the next morning. This can both prevent and treat some infections. (This is a common Ayurvedic therapy called *Yoni pichu*).
- Practice yogic postures that will bring strength to pelvic girdle: shoulder stand, *moolabandha*, squats.
- Practice intercourse in moderation and in a consensual, loving partnership.
- Make a sitbaths with *triphala* powder by adding 4-5 tsp. of this herb to your bath tub.
- Practicing *Yoni mudra* gives strength to this area.
- According to Ayurveda, the downward force of *Vata* and *Shakti* are responsible for this area. This is why receiving nourishing oil enemas are good for all reproductive tissue.
- Watch your personal care products to make sure you are not applying lotions with toxic hormone disrupters.

Thighs

From the perspective of *outer beauty* most women desire to tone and sculpt their thighs, buttocks and calves. This can often be difficult because there is a natural tendency for the body to accumulate fat in these areas. The thighs holds such a major bone (the femur) and numerous major muscles, that the body automatically wants to direct excess resources (a.k.a. fat) to them.

But before you go on to take a look at all the natural things you can do to remedy excess weight in the thighs, first consider the symbolic meaning of your thighs and how they relate to your *inner beauty*.

ASK YOURSELF:

"HOW CAN I MOVE WITH MORE GRACE THROUGH MY LIFE?"

POTENTIAL IMBALANCES
Fatty depositions, Cellulite, Swollen legs , Spider veins

NATURAL SOLUTIONS:

- High fiber diet.
- Proper exercise.
- Sweating through exercise or sauna.
- Yoga or Stretching.
- Walking.
- Dance.

Feet

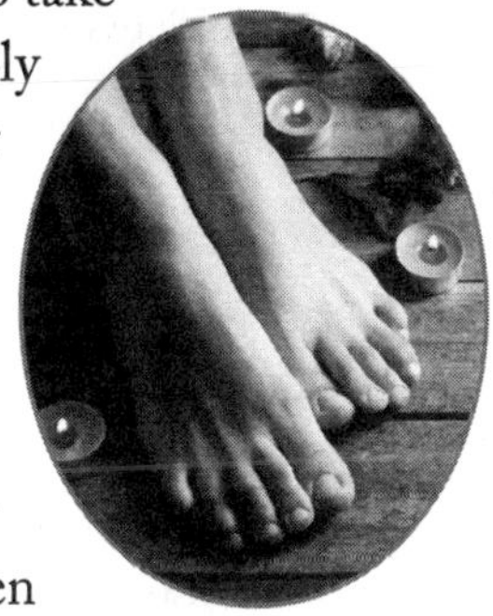

In many traditional cultures it is the custom to take your shoes off at the front door. While this certainly ensures that the carpet is not dirtied with mud or other debris collected on the bottom of your shoes, it also symbolizes a change in energy. As you enter the home, you are leaving the world behind you when you remove your shoes. Your action signifies your shift into a new environment that has a different, warmer and more intimate energy. In India this is done when entering a temple or any other sacred grounds. Sometimes people even take the time to wash their feet before coming into their home or place of worship. This is because the feet are gateways for the absorption and release of both good and bad energy. It would be appropriate then, to cleanse the feet of anything undesirable, whether physical or energetic, so as to enter a sacred space with clean and pure energy. So ask yourself:

"WHAT KINDS OF ENERGY DO I PICK UP?"

"WHAT TYPE OF ENERGY DO I WANT TO RECEIVE IN MY LIFE?"

Additionally, the state of the feet also corresponds to the health of the body as a whole. In reflexology, or *marma* in Ayurveda, the feet are seen as mirrors to each and every organ in the body. Pressing upon select points increases the flow of *prana*, or lifeforce, to the corresponding component of the body. Taking care of the feet is akin to taking care of the whole body, both physically and energetically.

POTENTIAL IMBALANCES

Plantar fasciitis, Arch pain / strain, Achilles tendonitis, Bunions, Athlete's foot

NATURAL SOLUTIONS: PADA ABHYANGA

Ayurvedic foot massage or *pada abhyanga*, can be done with caster oil or ghee before going to bed at night (be sure to put on old socks when you're done though, otherwise your sheets will be stained). Check out the diagram below so you can find special *marma* points (or reflexology locations) to press upon during your massage. In general, just make sure that the way you're massaging feels soothing and nourishing to you. You need not give a deep tissue foot massage in order to maximize the benefits of *pada abhyanga*.

BENEFITS OF PADA ABHYANGA:

- Relaxes achy and tired feet.
- Reduces excessive heat & inflammation.
- Helps to detoxify the internal organs.
- Helps to reduce eye strain and tiredness.
- Promote deeper sleep & relaxation.
- Helps in reduction of stress and anxiety.
- Increases *prana* and restores the flow of innate energy.
- Improves emotional irritability and anger.
- Calms and grounds the nervous system.

Benefits of Pada Abhyanga:

- Enhances circulation & improves joints mobility in legs.

Other Natural Solutions:

- Walk on the sand barefoot.
- Walk on green grass barefoot.
- Make a Himalayan salt bath for your feet. Add 5-6 tsp. of salt to a tub of warm water and soak for 10 minutes.
- To feel refreshed, simply wash your feet with cold water.
- To detoxify, soak your feet for 15 minutes in a bucket with 3-4 tsp. of baking soda. Then dry your feet and wear socks.
- Massage your feet with a Kanse metal bowl. This leads a different kind of sensation than foot massage with the hands.
- Give an exfoliate scrub to your feet. Mix 1 tbs. of Himalayan salt with 1 tbs. of olive oil and 4-5 drops of orange essential oil. Apply this mixture to your legs, feet and hands; then rinse off. You will find it is relaxing, refreshing and rejuvenating!

! TIP:

Even if you follow your homemade recipe to a 'T,' you may find you need to add just a tad more water to thin-out your paste, or maybe you want to put in a little more herb to thicken it up. I encourage you to experiment with slight variations until you master your own, unique creation! Don't be shy. It's okay to make mistakes at first - that's all part of the learning process.

Chapter 4

LASTING BEAUTY

Maintaining Beauty Through the Years

Lasting beauty is the epitome of beauty. It is an expression of beauty that someone embodies completely. When you are in the presence of someone who has *lasting beauty*, you can see that they are fully situated in themselves. They walk with grace, they know their body, they speak with kindness, their skin glows, their bodies are healthy and strong and their eyes sparkle. The joy and peace that surround these people comes from deep within them and radiates gently out into the world. It is clear that they are living their lives mindfully – tuned in to the beauty that exists all around them and within them. They are grateful for having the opportunity to experience a human life and hope to impact the world in the most positive way they can. Even if something challenging comes their way, they are steadfast in their character and their ethics, morals and values remain paramount. They are not swayed by the winds of change because they are tethered to the anchor of their own *inner beauty*. This kind of beauty, *lasting beauty*, endures across time and space; come what may. It has the strength of 1,000 warriors and the grace of 1,000 dancers. It is the ultimate and pure manifestation of beauty.

Although it may seem that possessing this kind of beauty is a farfetched goal, it really is not. *Lasting beauty* is mastery of beauty, yes; but it is not unattainable. If you're in graduate school to get a Master's degree in Economics, you don't expect to receive that degree overnight! It will take years of hard work, education and then post-graduate professional experience for you to truly master your subject. The same goes for self-mastery of beauty. Deciding that you want to be a manifestation of *lasting beauty* as it expresses uniquely through you, is an investment. Fortunately, unlike most higher education in our country, graduating with self-mastery of beauty does not take enormous financial resources. It does however, take a substantial investment in your Self, as well as two other rather monumental prerequisites - *inner beauty* and *outer beauty*.

As you may remember from earlier chapters, *lasting beauty* is the final product that results after a combination of *inner* and *outer beauty* have both been fully developed in a person. Of these two substrates, *inner beauty* is the most basic, primary ingredient that sets the stage for *lasting beauty* . Beyond that, *outer beauty* must be added into the equation as an external expression of *inner beauty.* Together *inner* and *outer beauty* synergestically combine to produce ageless, *lasting beauty.*

If you find yourself feeling overwhelmed in your efforts to achieve *lasting beauty*, then it never hurts for you to go back to the basics. Just focus on *inner beauty* and the rest will unfold naturally from there. If on the other hand, you already have a good handle on both your inner and *outer beauty*, then now it's time for you to move onto the next step. If you truly want to solidify *lasting beauty* in yourself and in your life, then you have to be ready to adopt a lifestyle that will support you in your aim. The *lasting beauty* lifestyle is one that is sustainable and life-giving on all levels. It is designed to simultaneously ensure the maintenance of both your inner and outer worlds so that they culminate to create a beauty that lasts. In the coming pages, we'll uncover the framework of the *lasting beauty* lifestyle and give you all the details you'll need to take your beauty to the next level.

The Landscapes of Lasting Beauty

Take a moment to imagine the picture of the most beautiful home you've ever seen or hope to one day see. Your visualization might conjure up a picture of the home you live in now, a home you visited long ago, or even just one that you dreamt of in your mind. Chances are that no matter what kind of home you're thinking of, it is bound to have pristine landscaping all around the premises. Likely it has a lush front yard and a verdant back yard, each with their own distinct plants, flowers, lawn, trees and bushes. Now, say for instance that in the front lawn there were two distinct areas; one in which the plants liked a lot of shade and the other in which they preferred more sun. The same goes for the backyard; one portion of the soil is good for planting tomatoes and the other is better for growing daisies. Believe it or not, the layout of this landscaping provides a perfect illustration for the layout of your life. Your front lawn can be likened to your outer public world and your backyard to your inner private world. Then the miniature micro climates of the front and back lawns, each with their own variety of plant life, can be considered as different facets of your inner and outer realities.

If you will, stay with me for a moment here in this analogy. To re-cap, we've got two landscapes: front and back, plus an additional two micro-environments within each of the greater macro landscapes. That makes a total of four micro-environments and two major landscapes. Each of these unique, miniature micro territories within the back yard and front yards render their own set of benefits and challenges to your home at large. If each area is well taken care of then the landscaping of the house will flourish and the home will surely become beautiful. If they are not tended to however, then the whole home is compromised in its appearance and health. In other words, when every part of the landscape, front and back, is well maintained then the geography of the home as a whole will exemplify what we like to call lasting, enduring beauty.

The Landscapes of *Lasting Beauty*

Inner Landscape {Backyard}	Outer Landscape {Front yard}
Psychological Environment	Social Environment
Physiological Environment	Climatological Environment

Now let's look at each of the micro environments within the context of their greater landscaping. To begin with, the inner landscape, or backyard, is made up of both the psychological and physiological aspects of our lives. The health of our minds and bodies comes from within and requires the most pro-active attention out of all of the four micro-environments.

The outer landscape or front yard, represents the external components of our life journey. Its micro-environments are symbolic of the social and climatological relationships we foster in our outer world. What I mean by "climatological relationship" is the dynamic we have with Nature and all Her seasons and cycles. And finally, what I am referring to when I say "social," is the network of friends, family and loved ones that we champion in our communities. These two aspects of our outer landscape combine to give it its characteristic outward affiliation.

Each and every one of these miniature environments within the two inner and outer landscapes of our reality, demands detailed love and attention if it is to thrive. It is all too easy for us to neglect any one of these areas in favor of "over-watering" so to speak, the other areas with which we are more comfortable and familiar. If we want to viably propagate the seedlings of ever-*lasting beauty*, then we must carefully tend to the total of the four environments alive within our inner and outer landscapes.

Inner Landscape: The Psychological Environment

The first and most delicate micro-climate within the greater internal landscape, or backyard as we know it, is our psychological reality. This area on the map is where all of our mental, emotional and spiritual health is centered. It is arguably the most temperamental and easily neglected aspect of both the back and front yards combined. That's because the health of our mind and spirit are not nearly as valued in modern culture today as they have been throughout history in traditional or indigenous cultures. In fact, the inner landscape as a whole tends to be ignored by the vast majority of people today. The reason why that happens is because the inner world it is not directly visible and the rewards of its harvest are subtle, personal changes that tend to go unrecognized by the outer world. Since there's nothing flashy or showy about that, there's a lot less motivation for us to actively maintain this area. As a result, weeds are sure to start growing and feelings of depression, anxiety, loneliness and anger start to sprout up from the untended earth.

The Psychological Environment

=

Metal, Emotional & Spiritual Wellbeing

Often times people today don't have role model for what psycho-spiritual well being should look like. They're left aimlessly searching to find their way through this amorphous and intimidating aspect of their existence. Unfortunately along their quest many get lost and it's sometimes hard to find their way back home. We need to have the right tools and a good solid map securely in our back pocket if we want to reclaim this vital territory of our inner landscape. We have to use everything we've got - shovels, hoses, sprinklers and fertilizers, to help us pull out the weeds and plant new seeds that will grow in their place. Therefore, I'd like to share three main tools with you; one that can be used for each of the three component of the psychological environment: mental, emotional and spiritual.

Mental Component

Stress Management

The modern world is wracked with this thing we refer to as "stress." Its ubiquitous presence has left us frazzled, tired, wired and sometimes without the strength to carry on. In fact, it is the underlying culprit in a plethora of mental as well as physical conditions we see today. On the mental side, it incites afflictions of anxiety, depression, insomnia, irritability, inability to focus, obsessive preoccupations, and mood swings. On the physical end, it is indicated in almost every modern chronic disease out there.

Stress literally steals from our physical reserve and undermines the stability of our emotions. It leaves its mark in our lives in the form of wrinkles, dry skin and early graying and a looming sense of malaise. It diminishes both our *inner* and *outer beauty,* and is thus a serious obstacle to the attainment of *lasting beauty. Lasting beauty* is a lifestyle in which stress can clearly not be a part.

When stress threatens to usurp our sense of coherence and happiness in life, we have to stick up for ourselves. We have to get our stress to a level in which we are managing it, not it managing us. If we want to take care of our inner landscape's psychological environment, then we have to start living in a way that will support our nervous systems instead of breaking it down. I know this doesn't just happen overnight, but I'm going to share some simple tips with you that you can start incorporating now. Then, slowly but surely get back into the driver's seat of your life.

What are your secrets for a long healthy life?

> "Leave it alone; let it do itself; God knows what to do to keep you alive and well…I don't try to make things grand but people say I have a knack for making things happen!"
>
> *~ Fruma Kit Endler, born 1920, Russia ~*

Manage Your Time

Plan ahead and don't let yourself get flustered in a race against the clock. Schedule in time for self-care just as if you would schedule in time for an important meeting. And last, don't schedule yourself to the max. Budget in transition time between events and leave breathing room for spontaneous life events, or unexpected quality time with loved ones.

Prioritize

Not everything needs to get done today. Let the unnecessary things slide and focus on what is most important to the moment at hand. Merely ensuring that your top priorities are taken care of will make you feel on top of your "To Do" list and far more at ease. Last, remember that stress management itself needs to be a *top priority* in your schedule if you truly want to maintain *lasting beauty* and strong mental health.

Identify the Trigger(s)

See if you can identify those things that really set off your stress response. Do your best to avoid those situations and ask for help from loved ones if you know you'll be encountering an unavoidable trigger in the near future.

Just say "no"

Remember the campaign *"Just Say 'No' to Drugs?"* For some, of us, getting "high" off of stress hormones like adrenaline and nor-epinepherine is not too dissimilar from other drug additions. *"Just Say 'No' to Stress"* needs to be the reinforcing motto of our lives so we don't start heading in the wrong direction! It's too easy to spread yourself too thin, so start practicing your "no" when someone requests you do something that may not be altogether necessary. Look at your schedule realistically, not idealistically. Then say "no" to those obligations which will not be manageable in a sustainable fashion. Know your limits and act with conviction to reinforce them.

> "Always follow your heart. Don't let anyone talk you into something that your inner voice (gut) says 'no."
>
> ~ *Ruth Runze, born 1929 Germany* ~

Emotional Component

Mindful Expression:

When we feel hurt, we all feel emotion surging through our bodies. In response, some of us withdraw from the world, others may get angry and still others cry themselves to sleep. While it is good for us to experience our emotions, we still need to be aware to not overly indulge in them. It's too easy to become stuck. We have to find a way for our feelings to move through us and then out so that we can move on with our lives.

The way we process and expel our emotions will vary from person to person, but whatever method you choose, be sure to make it constructive and non-harming. Expressing anger by punching somebody or communicating your pain by giving someone the silent treatment are both forms of violence. It's just that one is distinctly combative and the other passively aggressive. If you need some better ideas of how to release the powerful emotions that come up in your life in a way that is healing, peaceful and even strengthening, then check out the options below.

Support Groups

When people who share something in common come together in a group with the intention of supporting one another, there is a potent healing synergy that arises. Knowing that you are not alone in your experience of a strong emotion can be profoundly reassuring and validating. Being in the company of others who are enduring a similar challenge helps normalize your experience. You learn that it's okay to feel what you're feeling. Sometimes, simply the act of accepting the emotion can be all that is needed to let it go and move forward. So seek out a support group in your area that centers around the emotional challenge you're facing. I'm sure that you'll be pleasantly surprised to find there are many diverse types of support groups are out there!

Counseling

Finding someone who is a neutral, professionally trained counselor is a wonderful resource to help you sort through confusing, conflicting and befuddling emotions. Make sure that the professional you chose to work with empowers you to move through your emotions instead of enabling you to stay stuck.

Confidant

Our emotional health is largely dependent on having someone who really cares for us and will be there in times of need. When something distressing occurs in our lives, it's important to have a friend, spouse, partner or family member with whom we trust enough to be vulnerable. If we don't have this type of person in our lives, then we can set a specific intention to develop this type of healing, intimate relationship to rely on.

Physical Activity

Move it out! Get out of your head and into your body! Let your pent up emotions come out with every bead of sweat that drips from your brow. Leave your feelings on the basketball court, track field, or at the gym. Our bodies and minds are one singular continuum, so if you change the state of your body, you're likely going to be able to change the state of your mind and emotions as well.

Creativity

Potent emotions can be the perfect impetus for creative juices. Some people like to dance out their emotions, sing at the top of their lungs, throw paint onto a canvas or madly scribble their feelings out onto a piece of paper. Whatever method you choose, there is something deeply satisfying about seeing, hearing or feeling your emotions flow out of you in the form of art.

Spiritual Component

Think back to the two morning walks we took together at the very start of this book. Do remember just how different those two experiences were? In one, you were fully available in the present moment and it was as though everything you encountered was enlivened and animated. The sunrise, the clouds and the crispness of the air all felt like they were expressions of something Divine. And in fact, they were. That's because Beauty is most simply the Divine Truth of creation manifest outwardly. It is our tangible sensory experience of Oneness, Wholeness and Unity.

If we want to encourage the spiritual presence of Beauty in our lives then we have to train our senses to be subtly attuned to the present moment. As we practice this, the spirit of Beauty opens itself up to us more and more. We begin to recognize the miracle of life in all of its shapes and sizes. This is what it means to be awakened to the art of living, and thus, to the mastery of Beauty.

If you're interested in watering your spiritual garden, then you must find the way of doing so that most speaks to you. Whatever modality you pursue, make sure that it feels right, feeds your spirit and brings you back into the present moment. Listed below are several options for you to experiment with. See what works best for you to access your spiritual connection to Life and Beauty. With a little research, you can most likely find any of these options available to you in your local area. For some of the disciplines I've mentioned, I suggest making a concerted effort to find teachers whose perspective specifically resonates with your ideas and beliefs. Enjoy the journey!

MEDITATION

Meditation is a tool that is intended to quiet the ceaseless thoughts that overtake our mind and overshadow our connection with the Divine. When we practice meditation, we observe our thoughts without judgment and become a witness to the wonderings of our mind. With time, our busy mind becomes trained in a one pointed focus and distractions are not as overpowering as they once were. In deep meditation, brain waves change to offer us simultaneously deep relaxation in conjunction with sharp attentiveness. In this way, meditation allows us to arrive fully and attentively into the peace of the present moment so we can find the Beauty at hand.

"I don't close my eyes and go 'ommmm' but I meditate when I paint. Sometimes I paint in my head. And whenever I paint it's always very quiet."
~ *Sondra Jolles of New York, born 1928* ~

Yoga / Tai Chi / Qigong

Syncing breath with movement is a form of meditation. Ancient Indian and Chinese traditions have used these disciplines for centuries to bring about the harmony of energy and connection to Spirit. When we focus on our breath, our mind is quieted and our body's life force energy (*prana* in the Yogic tradition and *qi* in the Chinese tradition) can flow freely. The smooth flow of vital energy brings about healing of mind, body and spirit and a stronger connection to all that which is beautiful.

Breathing (Pranayama)

Whether or not you're interested in connecting with a Higher Power per se, you can still care for the spiritual component of your psyche. In the tradition of Yoga, a sister science to Ayurveda, surrendering ourselves to our breath is a very effective way of connecting with our energetic field. We can simply listen to its ebb and flow and garner a sense of collective communion with Life and Beauty that we might otherwise have missed going about our busy days.

Affirmation

What you believe is what you become. Use the affirmation, "I am young and beautiful." As you say this, know that it is true. Remember that you are alive and beautiful as you meet life smiling and unafraid. You are a woman who welcomes the challenges of life with resilience and spiritual strength. Affirm these things and over time, you will surely be transformed by this practice.

Visualization

The way you see yourself today is the person you will surely become tomorrow. Take advantage of the power of your mind to enhance your beauty and catapult you towards your dreams. Manifesting your intentions begins with positive envisioning. To start, I suggest keeping a framed photograph of yourself as a young child in your bedroom. Visualize yourself as that youthful, vibrant spirit you see in the photograph. Doing this you'll recapture your youth even as you age.

What do you consider to be an absolute must for success in life?

"You really have to love something to be successful. Concentrate on what you want to be and then you'll get there."

~ *Phyllis Katz, born 1918* ~

Conclusion: Happy Molecules

Maintaining the care of our inner landscape and specifically our psychological environment, is the first step in accessing *lasting beauty*. As we've learned before, true beauty starts from within and nothing is more important than the state of our mind for cultivating *inner beauty*. Establishing *inner beauty* will transform into *outer beauty* and finally, *lasting beauty*, so long as we abide by the principals of healthy living.

We can better understand the importance of the psychological environment when we look at what I call "happy molecules." By taking care of the mental, spiritual and emotional components of our mind, we inadvertently teach our body to produce an exponential amount of positive, life supporting biochemistry. In other words, when we manage our stress, process our emotions and have a connection to Spirit in our lives, then we fill our bodies with things called neropepetides (or protein based signal molecules). These so called "happy molecules" translate into feelings of contentment, satisfaction, fulfillment and overall happiness. The more of these "happy molecules" that are floating around our nervous systems, the happier our bodies will be on the whole. You see, our minds affect the state of our bodies so if we desire to live a life of inner, outer and *lasting beauty*, then we must first begin our journey with addressing the mind.

> " Liking, loving and respecting ones' self sends messages around the body and mind that promote well being and happiness, without which good health can be elusive. A healthy happy person interacts in a better way with the others and the world."
>
> ~ *Dhaj Sumner, born 1930 New Zealand* ~

Inner Landscape: The Physiological Environment

If we zoom into another part of the inner landscape, we find a very particular area which is unique to each individual – the physical body. Each of our bodies functions in a completely individualized way. No two people are exactly the same, so we cannot expect to offer each person the same guidelines on how to care for their physical body. Therefore, as we enter into the discussion of the physiological environment, I will divide my suggested recommendations into categories based on the three Ayurvedic body types: *Vata*, *Pitta* and water *Kapha*.

The Physiological Environment
=
Diet / Digestion, Exercise & Sleep
*Based on body type

Diet and Digestion

You can tell if someone has strong digestion because they also have strength of character, energetic stamina and beauty that is reflected in clear skin, bright eyes, shinning hair, strong nails and moist lips – they are the picture of *lasting beauty*. Ayurvedic medicine has been very clear on the utterly incomparable importance of proper digestion when compared with any other aspect of our health. The good news is that it has outlined some very basic things that we can all do, no matter what our constitutional type, in order to maximize the strength and efficiency of our metabolism.

"Eat clean food as much as possible.
Fast once per month"
~ *Godumai Kshirsagar born 1923, India (This woman never went to a restaurant once in her entire life!)* ~

Tips to Optimize Digestion

Vegetarian

In today's environment, it is hard to find animal products that are free of toxins. If you want to delay the onset of aging by way of avoiding the accumulation of pollutants, then choose a vegetarian diet.

Fruits and Veggies

Nothing could be better. In fact, some studies show that fruits and vegetables help slow the aging process of the nervous system and support the youth of the physical body as a whole.

Careful Selection

Pick your food according to your constitution and the current season. Fresh and local produce is preferable. Shop at open air Famer's Markets if you get the chance. If you must shop in the supermarket than avoid all processed food with artificial coloring, flavoring or preservatives.

Skillful Preparation

Prepare your food freshly every day and make it with love. See the beauty in your food as you cook. Notice all the colors, shapes, textures and smells.

Mindful Eating

Consume your food with awareness. Make sure that you are not eating on the run, while watching television or during a heated discussion. Enjoy your meal in a quiet, clean, stress-free and friendly atmosphere.

Now it's time to get specific. We all know that one size diet does not fit all. The three constitutional types need different kinds of food, individualized portion sizes and very specific qualities of nutrition in order to thrive. Granted, it's always good to get your diet customized according to the current state of your health, but take these guidelines as general, go-to standards for each of the three biological constitutions. If you follow these basic rules, then you'll be preventing ill health for yourself in the future and optimizing your *lasting beauty*.

VATA

People dominated by the air element tend to like dry, rough and crunchy foods like crackers, popcorn and salads. This is a problem because they need more grounding foods that are warm, soft, sweet and moist in quality. They need flavors that are: sweet (naturally), sour and salty – not astringent, bitter or pungent (spicy). If you have an air dominated constitution, then you need to make sure to: (1) thoroughly cook your food, (2) consume it warm and (3) add a little good quality fat, like ghee, to moisten up your meal. Remember, the key is to make your food nourishing.

PITTA

To maintain balance, people with this constitutional framework should favor foods that are more cooling in nature and which are bitter, astringent and sweet in taste. Some examples of cooling, bitter foods that are perfect for fire types might be: dandelion greens, bitter melon, coconut, cucumber, cilantro or white fish. Contrarily, fire people should steer clear of pungent, salty and sour foods. Heating foods like: red meat, tomatoes, potatoes, citrus, yogurt or fired and spicy foods of any kind, should be avoided at all costs. Remember, the key for your nutrition is that is it cooling.

KAPHA

These types need the kind of food that will stoke their digestive fire. Foods that are light and spicy are the perfect medicine for an water person's slow digestion. Their nature however, will inevitably drawn them towards overindulgence in sweet treats and heavy foods like ice cream, cookies, cakes and pizzas. The journal of the *Proceedings of the National Academy of Science* recently stated that "incorporating a low-calorie diet… into one's lifestyle may slow the mental and physical aging process" and water types need to pay special attention to this. Remember, the key for you is cleansing food.

Digestion & The Elements

Dosha	Digestive Predisposition	Evacuative Predisposition
Vata	Weak	Constipation with straining (dry)
Pitta	Strong	Loose, sometimes burning
Kapha	Sluggish	Infrequent (slow)

Diet & The Elements

Dosha	Preferable Qualities of Food	Preferable Tastes in Food
Vata	Warm, moist and soft	Sweet, sour, salty
Pitta	Cool and soft	Bitter, astringent, sweet
Kapha	Light, dry, easy to digest, small quantities	Pungent, astringent, bitter

Exercise

If we don't move then we sacrifice our vitality. If we relinquish our vitality, then we abandon our pursuit of the self-mastery of beauty. If we want to embody *lasting beauty*, then we have to be in our bodies! A woman who has *lasting beauty* has grace in her movements and confident posture no matter what her constitution. She has a healthy heart, proper circulation, good muscle tone and great energy because she incorporates movement that is appropriate for her constitution into her everyday life. She moves, stretches and breathes into her physical vessel so that it becomes a healthy, vibrant expression of her beauty.

VATA

Exercise needn't be excessive for you. The best forms of movement are gentle, non-vigorous practices like yoga, qigong, tai chi or walking. Avoid strenuous movements that are hard on the joints like jumping, jogging or rambunctious forms of dancing. Instead, focus your efforts on exercise and movement that feels calm, gentle and nourishing. These forms of movement will support your strength and build your endurance in a way that is appropriate for your constitution. Plus, *the Frontiers in Aging Neuroscience* journal recently stated that incorporating walking into our daily regimen "may help prevent cognitive degeneration."

PITTA

Your constitutional type tones easily and excels at sports. Although you have natural athletic abilities, it is important to not overdo it! Overall, exercise which is moderate (not too gentle and not too intense) is best for you. Activities like swimming, dancing, biking alongside a stream or hiking in the shady forest would be perfect for you. Favor exercising in the outdoors if possible, but only in the early morning or evening, since the mid-day sun will cause you to overheat.

KAPHA

Out of all the three elements, earth-water is the strongest physically. Naturally, you've been endowed with a constitution that excels in endurance. You might not be the fastest runner on the team, but you sure can last the longest! Water-types, because of their more stout and bulky frames and ability to withstand physical stress, are well suited to sports like football, wrestling, boxing, weight training, long distance running, water polo, cross country skiing or rowing. Regardless of the exercise you choose however, make sure that it is rigorous! Your constitutional type, if imbalanced, can tend towards inertia, laziness and sluggishness, so do your best to combat that inclination with vigorous, intense exercise. If your motivation falters, create a set goal that you can train hard to work towards.

Sleep

If you've ever missed out on sleep then you'll know the effect that it has on your beauty. Not only does it leave you with puffy bags and dark circles under your eyes but dry skin and an irritable mood! Clearly, this does not help either or inner or our *outer beauty*.

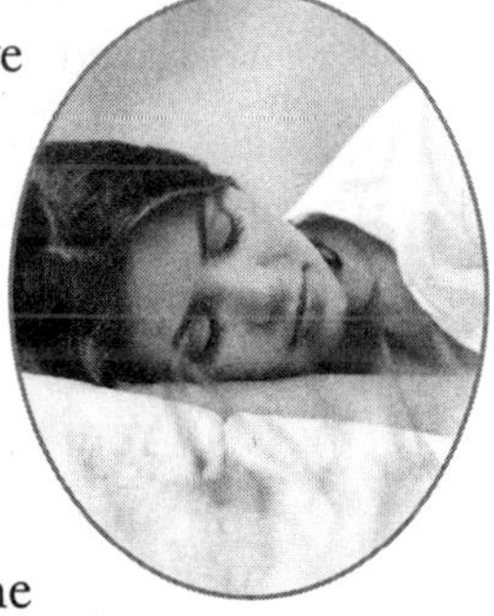

Like diet and exercise, caring for our sleep requires an individualized approach for optimal results. That's why we'll look again at each of the three elements and their specific needs and challenges around sleep. One thing is for sure however, all three constitutions can benefit from two very important rules:

Keep sleep habits regular
Get to bed by 10pm

Even if you just go by these two things alone, you'll find that likely your sleep, mood, health and thus overall beauty, shape up for the better. But now, let's take a deeper look at the special circumstances needed by each elemental body type in order to maximize the quality of their beauty rest.

> Women should avoid "an excessive lifestyle.
> You only have one body and one life."
> ~ Pauline Mitterhammer, born 1926 Vienna, Austria ~

VATA

If this is your constitutional type than you generally could use more rest. It's challenging though, because out of all of the three elements, yours is most prone to insomnia, restless and turbulent sleep. and waking up too early in the morning (anywhere from 3:00am-5:00am). Your nervous system is naturally more active and you need to make a special effort to sooth and calm it so that your sleep improves. One great way to do this is to practice full body Ayurvedic oil massage. See page 155 for instructions.

PITTA

Your ambition to save the world and finally finish that project you've been working on tends to strike you at about 10pm at night. That's when you get your "second wind" and let your night owl loose! But you especially, must resist this temptation. It is too depleting and aggravating for you to be up working on your various endeavors or partying out on the town until the wee hours of the morning. If you continue in this habit you risk developing insomina. Take care to wind down and allow yourself to get sleepy well before 10:00pm.

KAPHA

You have a tendency to oversleep. The heavy and static qualities inherent in the element that predominates your constitution make it so that sleeping is an easy and tempting pass time for you. If you want to balance your body and promote your natural beauty, you need to avoid excessive sleep and snoozing late into the morning. Your body does very well to wake up early in the morning and get no more than 8 hours of sleep. Any more than 8 hours and you may wake feeling lethargic with sluggish energy all day. To remedy this, upon awaking it is best for you to immediately do vigorous early morning exercise. Not oversleeping or sleeping in and getting moving right away, are the things you need to balance out your sleep habits.

Healthy Inner Landscape

Healthy Body & Healthy Mind

=

Healthy Inner Landscape

The body (physiology) and mind (psychology) are the two fundamental zones of the inner landscape, or "backyard," as we've elucidated. Each of these micro-environments within the greater landscape of your inner world, are multifaceted. In being so, each is deserving of its own intimate attention and fine tuning in order to render the area mastered. I encourage you to move one step at a time, focusing your efforts on the aspects of the mind and body that speak most to you and which you feel will have the greatest impact on your *lasting beauty*.

The Outer Landscape

The outer landscape is our front yard, or the public part of our lives. It encompasses everything that is external to the inner functioning of our mind and body. Our outer landscape dictates our relationships with those things outside of ourselves, like the people in our lives and the places where we live. Like the inner landscape, the outer landscape also has two different micro-environments which combine to make up the character of the outer landscape as a whole. The first sub environment of the outer landscape nourishes the social connections we harvest within our communities. The second zone of the outer landscape monitors our inexorable interaction with Nature's seasons and Her various climatological changes.

Outer Landscape: The Social Environment

In Ayurvedic medicine there is an idea that the qualities of our relationships impact the essence of our vitality or *ojas*. What this means is that if we have loving, joyful and healing relationships in our lives, then health in our body, mind and spirit will follow. That is a powerful statement to the importance of the social environment of the outer landscape. This area of our lives has the power to completely transform our health, longevity and beauty if we chose to let it.

Helpful

Open your eyes and look around you - you'll always find opportunities to pitch in and assist someone who needs a hand. Best is, you'll be pleasantly surprised at how rewarding it feels!

Whether the social activity involves school, work, church, family or friends, we have to make sure that it supports our *lasting beauty* by building our vital essence, or *ojas*. Sometimes the atmospheres of work or school can feel strained and tense and can become a daily cause for distress. If this is the case, we need to consider completely uprooting our social environment and planting new seeds in its place. Continually being surrounded by toxic social interactions becomes poison in our bodies and minds and needs to be avoided at all costs. However, if we can cultivate the relationships in our lives to be real, substantial and meaningful, then we will start to feel the mental, emotional, spiritual and physiological benefits of a strong social support system.

Additionally, it is interesting to note that growing a thriving network of social connection in our *outer landscape* is an impressive way of nourishing the micro-environments of our *inner landscape* as well - both our front and backyards are part of the same home! So I've provided several options for planting and ripening the seeds of a meaningful social environment. If you feel so inclined to experiment with any of them, by all means, it doesn't hurt to try!

The Social Environment

=

Community

Giving to others gives us a sense of happiness and satisfaction and it refines and strengthens our inner beauty. There are opportunities to serve all around us. We can do small acts of kindness for our neighbors, like picking up a piece of trash that has been left behind or letting a car go in front of us on the freeway. We can also volunteer in community service project or contribute to larger-scale humanitarian efforts in our country or abroad. Whether great or small, these acts of service allow us to actively participate in the goodness of humanity.

Through service we connect with our brothers and sisters in a deeper way. We are reminded that God often allows us to be the answer to someone else's prayers. By giving back to the community, we allow ourselves the privilege of being part of the solution. Plus, when we set an example of servitude, we allow others the honor of following suit. And that's how the whole world becomes a better place.

Spiritual Community

Satsanga is the Sanskrit word for spiritual community. There is no better place for you to connect with others than in a setting which fosters your individual spiritual growth.

Join a Club

Sharing common values with others is a fabulous way to connect and share ideas! Try holding an event or workshop on the topic of your interest. It's fun and easy to be around a group that collectively agrees about certain hobbies, or values as you do.

Get or Give Regular Massages

If talking over dinner isn't really your thing, then healing touch is a wonderful way to connect without words. Much meaning can be conveyed through loving touch. So find a buddy that you trust and arrange for a massage exchange, or simply schedule weekly massages for yourself in order to augment the degree of connection in your life.

Outer Landscape: The Climatological Environment

The final micro-environment we have left to explore in our outer landscaping, or the front yard, of our beautiful home is the area of our relationship with Nature. Ayurvedic medicine beautifully describes our interaction with Nature by stating that we are a microcosm of the greater macrocosm of all of Creation. Indeed, as we have seen, Nature exists within all of us in the form of the five elements. As we are a part of Nature then, we are undeniably affected by Her cycles and seasons. Therefore, the dynamic between our own individual Nature and the greater natural environment, is what this portion of our outer landscape is all about.

The Climatological Environment
=
Nature

This is where Ayurvedic medicine comes into play. Fundamentally, Ayurveda sets out to harmonize our inner Nature with the greater, climatological Nature. It understands that whatever is happening externally in the natural environment also impacts us internally by changing our physiology. That's why if it is cold, we naturally seek warmth and if it is too hot, we go to find the cold. Ayurveda is based upon this principal of *opposites balancing each other.* You can easily apply this idea to your daily life too. All you have to do is understand the relationship between your unique constitution and the season at hand.

Dosha	Associated Season (Similar Qualities)
Vata	Fall
Pitta	Summer
Kapha	Spring

Since part of maintaining lasting health and beauty is understanding the dynamics of your personal relationship with nature inside and out of you, let's take a look at some specific, constitutionally based examples of how this really happens.

VATA

If you are an air type, then the fall is the season which you'll have to work extra hard at maintaining balance. The fall air is dry, cool, rough and windy – all the qualities which you already have in excess. You'll need to manage your diet and lifestyle so that they contain ample amounts of the opposing qualities of: moisture, warmth, softness and stability instead.

PITTA

If you are a fire type person and choose to eat spicy Indian food in the middle of a hot summer day, you might start to become aggravated by all the heat inside and outside of your body! You'll become irritable, quicker to anger, and might even break out in a rash! So can you see jumping in a cold, fresh water lake would feel relieving to you? Well, that experience of relief is Ayurveda in action. Ayurveda takes the qualities that are in excess in the internal and external environment (heat in this case) and balances it with the opposite quality (cold).

KAPHA

If you have an water constitution, the spring time will be most challenging for you. During this season the water is laden and heavy with moisture from all the rains. It exacerbates the already sodden nature of your body. Therefore, it is your job to rekindle your internal heat and speed up your metabolism so that the dampness of the season doesn't get you down!

What do you think is an absolute for success in life?

"Go with nature and you won't go wrong!"
~ Fruma Kit Endler, born 1920, Russia ~

Deciding to live in sync with Nature is probably the single best thing you could ever do for the health and well-being of both your inner and outer landscapes. So in order for you to start incorporating this now, I've outlined some ideas that can help. Here are some traditional Ayurvedic treatments that work beautifully to remedy our less than perfect cooperation with Nature so that we can maintain *lasting beauty*.

Panchakarma

Pronounced *"punch-a-car-ma,"* is an incredible, ancient and effective method of detoxification and rejuvenation. It is designed to cleanse the body of any impurities that have accumulated as a result of living out of accordance with Nature. Panchakarma is a highly involved and individualized process lasting anywhere from 7 - 42 days. It consists of various therapeutic modalities administered daily, along with a special fasting diet and medicinal herbs. Panchakarma is specifically indicated at the start of the fall and spring for seasonal detoxification twice per year. If preformed regularly, it will not only prevents illness, restores balance and cures disease, but it also promote longevity. Removing the burden of toxins from the body and restoring it to Nature's intended balance, adds both years and youth to our lives. For more information about *panchakarama*, please visit AyurvedicHealing.net.

AYURVEDIC BODY TREATMENTS

Ayurveda is filled with therapeutic body treatments designed to enhance beauty, longevity and the harmony of the elements within the body. One Ayurvedic body treatment, called *abhyanga*, involves a full body warm oil massage and is described in detail on page 155.

LIST OF TREATEMENTS FOR YOUR SKIN AND BEAUTY	
Udvartana	Exfoliating scrub with oil and herbs
Udgharshana	Mild exfoliating scrub with dry herbs
Udsadana	Abhyanga with smooth paste of herbs
Swedana	Whole body steam with herbs or Essential oils
Pinda Sweda	Massage with warm rice boluses, herbs and milk
Valuka Sweda	Massage with sand bags and herbs
Gharshana	Gentle exfoliation with silk gloves

You can rest assured, that no matter which Ayurvedic treatment you choose, they will all be personally tailored based on your unique constitutional make-up and the seasonal influences of Nature.

"EVERYBODY SHOULD FOLLOW THEIR BIOLOGICAL CLOCK"

~ Vijaya Lele born 1935, India ~

Protect

To maintain beauty we have to offer ourselves some level of protection against the harsh elements and excessive stimulation of our environment. If we live in a dry area we need to moisturize, if our neighborhood is too noisy we have to wear ear plugs and play soothing music, or if there is pollution in the air we need to get an air purifier in our home. In doing this, we take care not to harm our bodies or overwhelm our senses. When ensure that our environment is clean, clear and peaceful, then we preserve the beauty that we were naturally born with. In other words, when we optimize the climate of our lives, then our body doesn't have to fight an uphill battle to stay healthy.

The best way to do this is to use the science of Ayurveda to learn how to make dietary and lifestyle changes that oppose the ubiquitous qualities of elements that are dominant in your climate. In summer avoid exposure to the sun, in the winter make sure to reduce stagnation with regular exercise and in fall, apply your oil regularly and shield yourself from the wind.

Daily Routine

Working with the power of Nature to maintain health at all levels is fundamental to *lasting beauty*. Fortunately, Ayurveda has done the heavy lifting for us in this regard. Through antiquity, teachers of Ayurvedic medicine deeply observed the forces of Nature and compiled for us detailed daily routines. We can follow these routines in order to maintain harmony with Nature external as well as our personal, internal Nature. In that manner, the routines are both seasonally and constitutionally specific and can be followed in earnest to either prevent illness or reverse disease.

What is your advice to empower young women?

"Try to start early and find a routine for yourself. Never give up."
~ Pauline Mitterhammer born 1926 Vienna, Austria ~

Conclusion

Life as we know it can often feel like a blur of social, psychological, environmental and physical realities all converging to give us our unique experience as human beings. It is possible however, that instead of the regular haphazard confluence of all of these facets, we approach the picture of our lives with mindfulness. With awareness, we intentionally weave each aspect together until we create a beautiful tapestry that we recognize as our lives. That is aim of the *lasting beauty* lifestyle – to give each and every part of our lives dedicated attention and specific intention so that they can all collaborate together to showcase the best version of yourself as pure and enduring beauty.

The *lasting beauty* lifestyle sets the foundation for longevity and happiness in anyone who chooses to invite its wisdom into their lives. It is choice that is accessible to everyone. You just have to be willing to take control of your habits and reshape them so they adhere to the time-tested principals of natural living. In essence, these tenets of health set forth by Ayurvedic wisdom, are anti-aging strategies that uphold youth, vitality, health, grace and beauty well into the seasoned years of life.

Now, getting back to our analogy of the home with the front and backyards, we can now better envision how each specific micro-environment and all of their individual subcomponents, are vital to the overall health and well-being of our lives as a whole.

The Landscapes of Lasting Beauty

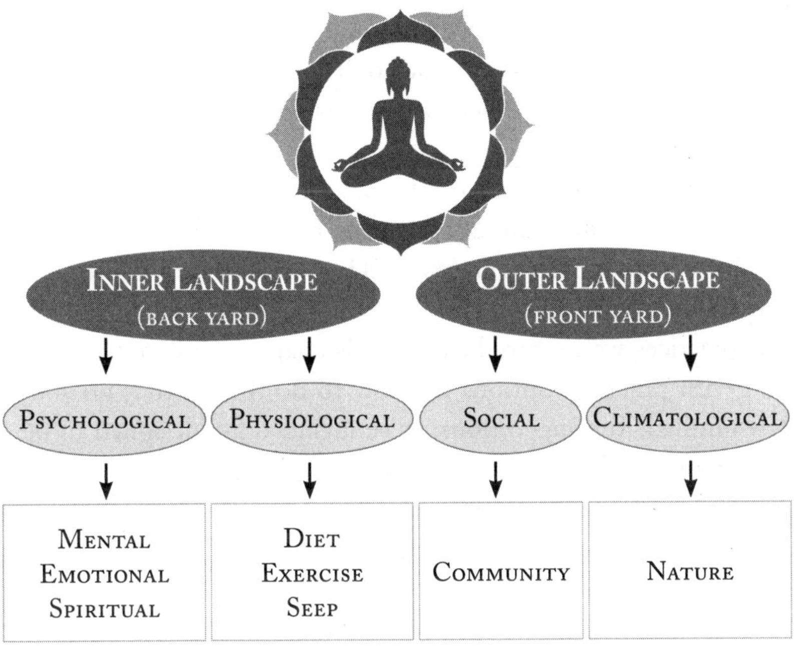

Depending on how we care for our inner and outer landscapes, our home could either be teeming with life and vitality or overwhelmed with weeds, and parasites! Then, even if one area of our lawn is gorgeous but the other is still left disheveled, the total view of the house becomes tainted. Plus, say for instance that the one area that infected with a worm or virus is left untended. Soon enough, the other beautiful areas surrounding it will catch the bug too. At the end of the day, the health of the both the front and back landscapes in addition to all the different micro-environments are at stake. You see, every part of the garden is connected to the others and they all affect each other. No one micro-environment or landscape exist in isolation from the other. We make distinctions between them only for the sake of linear comprehension and theoretical coherence, but the reality is they are all different sides of the same coin. Our inner and outer landscapes collectively make up an entire ecosystem of coexisting parts. The resilience and strength of the ecosystem depends on the robustness of each of its parts. Their sum interaction is what determines whether we'll posses *lasting beauty* or be subject to slow deterioration.

Living into the mastery of beauty means that we take every opportunity to offer mindful attention to each aspect of our home. Taking care of ourselves at this level is a spiritual act of devotion to our highest Self and thus nourishes our endless beauty. The various practices we've introduced in this chapter are here to provide you with practical options for how to do this so that no soil is left untilled. The suggestions we've included are designed to be a launching pad for you, after which you can further personalize your journey. Then finally, you'll be able to jump fully and joyfully into your own expression of *lasting beauty*!

When asked if she had a daily routine

Fruma Kit Endler replied

"YES! The first thing I always do is open the blinds and windows and let in the fresh air and sunshine!"

~ Fruma Kit Endler, born in Russia 1920 ~

Action Plan For Lasting Beauty Everyday

Here's a quick summary of all the main, take-away action items for you to practice on a daily basis that will help you maintain *Lasting Beauty*. It's all about re-training your senses to be filled with good things so that you can start to see all the beauty around and within you.

- ☐ Do something helpful every day for someone else.
- ☐ Keep good company – maintain good relationships with your partner, children, neighbors and family.
- ☐ Eat the rainbow everyday – colorful, freshly prepared food.
- ☐ Hydrate yourself properly with room temperature water or herbal teas.
- ☐ Take some time off to care for yourself.
- ☐ Learn something new every day – challenge your mind.
- ☐ Laugh! Watch comedy movies or read a humorous book.
- ☐ Explore spiritual practices that help you connect and surrender.
- ☐ No matter how old you are, or what the weather is like, walk at least 20 minutes per day.

- ☐ Practice Ayurvedic oil massage daily.
- ☐ Cultivate a hobby that brings you joy.
- ☐ Be flexible and adjustable in your life – it won't always work out the way you want it to and sometimes it's good just to let go.
- ☐ Spend some time in nature.
- ☐ Get emotional support from a counselor or confidant.
- ☐ Make sure you get enough sleep so that you wake up fresh and energetic.
- ☐ Find someone or something to be grateful about every day.
- ☐ Do not entertain negative thoughts.
- ☐ Receive blessings from teachers, elders, or healers.
- ☐ Spend time looking at the sunset, sunrise, stars or full moon.
- ☐ Keep your life simple – get rid of unnecessary burdens.
- ☐ Practice mindfulness so you can feel the beauty around you!

Action Plan for Detox / Anti-Aging

Here you'll find some simple things you can do as a part of your everyday routine to reduce the burden of toxins on your body. When you do this, you will reduce the effects of aging and in turn, promote longevity. They are gentle detoxification practices that will keep your skin clear, your energy vibrant and your beauty radiant.

☐ **Eat a high-fiber diet**

Foods that are high in fiber are: oat bran, whole grains, cruciferous vegetables and leafy greens. These foods will bind to toxins and help eliminate them. Try this for seven days and see how you feel.

☐ **Drink Aloe-vera juice**

For seven days, take ¼ cup of aloe-vera juice in the morning on an empty stomach. This will benefit the health of the blood and liver, and thus will promote the purification of the skin.

☐ **Take triphala tablets.**

They simultaneously rejuvenate and detoxify. Try this for one month. 2 tabs at night before bed with plenty of water.

☐ **For seven days, fast from gluten**

You will feel a great improvement in your digestion, gas and bloating.

☐ **For seven days, try going vegetarian**

You will feel more energetic, lighter and clearer mentally.

☐ **For seven days, fast from dairy**

You will feel less congestion, your sinuses will clear up and you'll have less puffiness under your eyes.

☐ Self-Massage

Do Ayurvedic warm oil massage with Detox Oil (see page 191). It will support lymphatic drainage and improve blood circulation.

☐ Sauna or heating treatment

At least 2-3 times per week get a sauna or heating treatment. This will support detoxification through sweating and will open and cleanse the pores of the skin.

☐ Once per month, fast

Vata types should fast on warm steamed vegetables, mushy rice and hot water. *Pitta* persons should fast on fruit juices, salads and sugar-free lemonade. Finally, *Kapha* people can fast on warm vegetable soups and herbal teas.

☐ Once per month, try a caster oil detox

Pick a day where you can stay home in the morning and take 2-3 tsp. of castor oil with ¼ cup pure orange or grapefruit juice and drink in the early morning – around 6 or 7am. You can expect 3-5 loose bowel movements through the day. Fast on a liquid diet of teas, veggie soup and fresh fruit juices that day. Additionally, you may want to minimize your activities as much as possible to fast from excess sensory information. Simply meditate, do not speak and stay away from electronics.

☐ Castor oil for menses

Menstruating women can take castor oil (as indicated above) 4-5 days before the onset of her cycle. This will help improve PMS, breast tenderness, cramps, water retention, bloating, skin rashes and mood swings.

☐ DO AN AYURVEDIC SEASONAL DETOX.

Try Panchakarma 2 x per year at the spring and fall equinoxes. It is best done during the seasonal transitions as this is the time when aggravated doshas can accumulate and compromise digestion, elimination, sleep patterns, immune function, weight gain, allergies and skin eruptions. Seasonal cleansing is like a reset button to reestablish balance and restore biorhythms. Plus, I always suggest that my clients also engage in a sensory fast during their detox. This will help clear their senses, emotions and mind in addition to their body.

"TO EMPOWER YOUNG WOMEN I WOULD SAY,
FIND YOUR PASSION; TRUST THAT PASSION –
AND GO WITH IT!

~ *Sondra Jolles, born 1928 New York* ~

ENCHANTING BEAUTY

Chapter 5

THE WISDOM OF BEAUTY

Ayurveda & The Mystic Trinity

Ayurveda: The Science of *Lasting Beauty*

Being that Ayurveda is the science of life, it is also necessarily the science of beauty. There are three fundamental subtle energies which Ayurveda credits for the evolution of beauty. They are universal qualities which are the fundamental forces behind all the creation, maintenance and dissolution of the Universe. They are: *prana, tejas* and *ojas.*

Prana	is the Nature's intelligence pervading everywhere in the universe. It is the initial essence of creation.
Tejas	is the expression of radiant light that transforms food, nutrients and all experiences into the cellular structure.
Ojas	is cosmic glue that holds and binds everything together.

Prana is the force of Life, Tejas is the force of Light and Ojas is the force of Love

Since we are all inherently a part of Nature, these three subtle energies exist within us and their presence manifests in unique ways:

- When we are full of prana, we experience a sense of vitality, clarity, calmness, and health.
- When tejas is strong within us, we have a good metabolic fire which allows us to have a clearer perception of the world around us and see things for what they really are.

> When ojas is robust, we have a natural glow and luster that are testimony to a life full of health – with a strong immunity, and happiness – with a delightful demeanor.

What is most important to remember is that when we live in harmony with the Self, we support the smooth flow of our energetic *prana*, *tejas* and *ojas*. Together these three components of our health modulate our vitality, strength and longevity and thus, beauty.

To expound upon this, Ayurveda has provided us with an all encompassing description of beauty that in a few simple words expresses the essence of this book. It sums up the three levels of beauty: inner, outer and lasting and how to achieve them when it says, ***"Shubhanga Karanam Sundaram."*** So that you can get a sense for the exact translation of Ayurveda's take on beauty, here's a breakdown of the words in Sanskrit.

Shubhanga Karanam Sundaram

Shubha - Auspicious
Anga - Body / Mind
Karanam - Transformation
Sundaram - Beautiful

Combined, these words express that true beauty involves the transformation of all aspects of body and mind to the most auspicious level. To put it another way, Ayurveda says that the secret to true beauty lies within our ability to attain harmony within the Self. A life that is lived as a reflection of our highest Self, is a life filled with beauty.

There are two subtle mechanisms within the body that Ayurveda credits for the evolution of beauty or the auspicious transformation of mind and body. These are: *prana* and *ojas*. You can think of *prana* as the breath of life that lies within you and *ojas* is the sustenance that contains that breath. When we live in harmony with the Self, we support the smooth and fluid flow of *prana* and encourage the production of our subtle vital essence, *ojas*. Together these two energetic components of our health modulate our strength, vitality, longevity, and thus, beauty.

In the end, that has been the aim of this book– to give you the tools and the guidance that you can use to achieve harmony within your mind, body and spirit. As you do so, you rejuvenate and protect your *prana, tejas* and *ojas* so that you can enjoy a lifetime of beauty. This kind of *lasting beauty* that Ayurveda describes is available to anyone so long as they follow the sequence of nourishing their beauty from the inside, out. Steadily moving from the cultivation of *inner beauty*, to *outer beauty* and then finally, to *lasting beauty*, ensures that there is no stone left unturned along your journey to mastering beauty.

1. ACKNOWLEDGE YOUR INNER WORTH
   Reawaken, rediscover, and restore your Inner Beauty.
2. ACCENTUATE YOUR *OUTER BEAUTY*
   Care for your physical body
3. MASTER *LASTING BEAUTY*
   Live a balanced, joyful life in harmony with your Self

Every step of the way counts – there are no short cuts, no speed trains or supersonic planes that will get you there any faster. If we distill the meaning of inner, outer and *lasting beauty*, we find that they all converge at one final point –love. Developing real beauty that lasts is a lifelong process of diving deep within ourselves to uncover the love that we need to transform our minds, bodies and spirits.

Satyam Shivam Sundaram : The Mystic Trinity

When asked for her words of wisdom, *Jane D. Murphy, MFT of Altadena CA, born 1931, replied that in life,* "Mystery is in. The plans are out. Everyday, I walk into the mystery."

Satyam

In ancient Hinduism there is a said to be a mystic trinity that encompasses the nature of ultimate reality. The first of the three in the trinity is known as *Satyam*, or Truth. *Satyam* doesn't just mean avoiding little white lies - it takes the concept of Truth to a whole new level. What *satyam* entails is clearing your mind of all preconditioned prejudices and ideas that threaten to taint your vision of Absolute Truth. *Satyam* thus, can be seen as freeing the mind of its illusions so that nothing remains but the Truth.

Think about some of the judgments or preconceived and likely inaccurate notions your mind may be harboring surrounding your level of beauty. Could it be that deceitful thoughts, beliefs and ideas like: "No one will ever love me because I'm too fat," or "If only had her figure, and then I'd be beautiful," run through your subconscious mind? How is the Truth of who you really are and where your beauty really lies clouded by the constructs of your mind? If we want to sincerely discover the Truth, then first we have to identify the lies.

When we quiet the mind enough to look deeply into ourselves and experience *satyam*, we realize that the Truth is in fact not that we will never be good enough. In Reality, the Truth is that we are whole, perfect and worthy right here and right now, just as we are. Thus, when we are in contact and understanding with *satyam*, we touch the Truth of our *inner beauty*.

Shivam

The second of the three in the trinity is *shivam*, or Virtue. *Shivam* is the expression of *satyam* (Truth) in action. In other words, after experiencing the knowledge and light of the Truth, we naturally act in a way that is different and more Virtuous – that is *shivam*. The qualities of our actions that embody goodness, purity and sincerity come from the source of Truth. Divine virtues then, are essentially Truth manifest. When we seek to cultivate our *inner beauty*, we aim to enhance the *shivam*, or the divine and right virtuous within ourselves. As you can see though, developing these qualities of *inner beauty* depends first upon our understanding of Truth. Hence *shivam* is the second, not the first, facet of the sacred and mystic trinity.

Sundaram

The third and final factor of the mystic trinity of reality is *sundaram. Sundaram* means ultimate, universal beauty inherent in pure consciousness. This is the kind of beauty that can only be seen with the eyes of Truth. *Sundaram* is the experience of connection with the beauty of the Soul of the world, or the oneness that exists within everything. It is the kind of beauty we encounter when we are fully present in the moment. Think back to the first pages of this book and the morning hike that brought tears to your eyes. That is the experience of *sundaram*.

Together, these three aspects of the ultimate reality, according to Hindu mystics, perfectly express the wisdom of real beauty. So as we end our time together, I'd like to leave you with this phrase to remember:

SATYAM SHIVAM SUNDARAM

MAY IT ALWAYS REMIND YOU OF THE TRUTH OF BEAUTY AND THE VIRTUES THAT INHERENTLY LIE WITHIN IT. IF YOU FIND THAT YOUR MIND EVER FALTERS AND FORGETS THE NATURE OF REAL BEAUTY, THEN JUST THINK BACK TO THIS SORT PHRASE AND REPEAT ITS SCARED WORDS UNTIL THE SOUNDS RESONATE DEEP WITHIN YOU AND RESTORE YOUR MEMORY.

Appendix

Resources

Ayurvedic Body Treatments & Skin Care

Ayurvedic Healing Inc.
Dr. Suhas Kshirsagar (Ayu MD, India)
Dr. Manisha Kshirsagar (Ayu, BAMS, India)
3121 Park Ave., Suite D, Soquel, CA 95073
Tel. 831-432-3776
www.AyurvedicHealing.net

The Chopra Center for Wellbeing
Deepak Chopra, MD
2013 Costa Del Mar Rd.
Carlsbad, CA 92009
Tel. 760-494-1639
www.chopra.com

Kerala Ayurveda Academy
46500 Fremont Blvd., Suite 702
Fremont, CA 94538
Tel. 888-275-9103
www.ayurvedaacademy.com

The Art of Living Retreat Center
639 Whispering Hills Road
Boone, NC 28607
Tel. (828) 278-8112
www.artofliving.org

Pratima Skincare
110 Greene Street, Suite 701
New York, NY 10012
Tel. (646) 429–9164
www.pratimaskincare.com

Serenity Spa Sacramento
3984 Douglas Blvd. #150
Roseville, CA, 96661
Tel. (916) 797-8550
www.serenityspaonline.com

Ayurvedic Products and Herbs

Ayurvedic Healing Inc.
Dr. Suhas Kshirsagar (Ayu MD, India)
Dr. Manisha Kshirsagar (Ayu, BAMS, India)
3121 Park Ave., Suite D, Soquel, CA 95073
Tel. 831-432-3776
www.AyurvedicHealing.net

The Chopra Center for Wellbeing
Deepak Chopra, MD
2013 Costa Del Mar Rd.
Carlsbad, CA 92009
Tel. 760-494-1639
www.chopra.com

Maharishi Ayurveda Products
1680 Highway 1 North, Suite 220
Fairfield, Iowa 52556
Tel. 800-255-8332
www.mapi.com

Mountain Rose Herbs
PO Box 50220, Eugene, OR 97405
Tel. 541-741-7307
www.mountainroseherbs.com

Banyan Botanicals
6705 Eagle Rock Ave. NE,
Albuquerque, NM 87113
Tel. 800-953-6424
www.banyanbotanicals.com

Ayurvedic Education

Ayurvedic Healing Inc.
Dr. Suhas Kshirsagar (Ayu MD, India)
Dr. Manisha Kshirsagar (Ayu, BAMS, India)
3121 Park Ave., Suite D
Soquel, CA 95073
Tel. 831-432-3776
www.AyurvedicHealing.net

American Institute of Vedic Studies
David Frawley and Yogini Shambhavi
P.O. Box 8357, Santa Fe, NM 87504-8357
Tel. 505-983-9385
www.vedanet.com

The Ayurvedic Institute and Wellness Center Dr. Vasant Lad,
BAMS, MAS
11311 Menaul Blvd. NE
Albuquerque, NM 87112
Tel. 505-291-9698
www.ayurveda.com

Kerala Ayurveda Academy
46500 Fremont Blvd., Suite 702
Fremont, CA 94538
Tel. 888-275-9103
www.ayurvedaacademy.com

Yogi Cameron
www.yogicameron.com

Lissa Coffey
www.coffeytalk.com

Deep Yoga
Bhava ram & Laura Plumb
www.deepyoga.com

References by Chapter

Chapter 1 - Beauty

Briggs, B. Overwåeight Women Tend to Earn Smaller Paychecks, Study Claims. NBC News Women's Health. N.p., 22 Oct. 2014. Web. 3 May 2015.

Merriam-Webster Dictionary. Beauty. Web. 2015. Accessed May 3, 2015 <*http://www.merriam-webster.com/dictionary/beauty*>

Chapter 2 - Inner Beauty

Benli et al. Effect of Maternal Age on Pregnancy Outcome and Cesarean Delivery Rate. J Clin Med Res. 2015 Feb; 7(2): 97–102.

Dube SR, Fairweather D, Pearson WS, Felitti VJ, Anda RF, Croft JB. Cumulative Childhood Stress and Autoimmune Diseases in Adults. Psychosomatic Medicine. 2009;71(2):243-250. doi:10.1097/PSY.0b013e3181907888

Josef Neu and Jona Rushing. Cesarean versus Vaginal Delivery: Long term infant outcomes and the Hygiene Hypothesis. Clin Perinatol. 2011 June ; 38(2): 321–331.
doi:10.1016/j.clp.2011.03.008.

Laungani N. Women's Status in Ancient India: Hinduism's revealed scriptures summon forth high regard for women. Hinduism Today. January/February/ March, 2015: 58-61.

Neu J, Rushing J. Cesarean versus Vaginal Delivery: Long term infant outcomes and the Hygiene Hypothesis. Clinics in perinatology. 2011;38(2):321-331. doi:10.1016/j.clp.2011.03.008.

Taqui AM, Itrat A, Qidwai W, Qadri Z. Depression in the elderly: Does family system play a role? A cross-sectional study. BMC Psychiatry. 2007;7:57. doi:10.1186/1471-244X-7-57.

The Marquardt Beauty Analysis Inc. Is Perfect Possible? MBA research on Facial Form and Beauty. 2014. Web. Accessed May 3, 2015. <*http://www.beautyanalysis.com/research/our-research/perfect-possible/*>

Chapter 3: Outer Beauty

Environmental Working Group. Exposing the Cosmetics Cover-up: EWG's Investigative Series on the Cosmetics Industry and Products. October 10, 2013. Web. Accessed May, 10, 2015. <*http://www.ewg.org/research/exposing-cosmetics-cover-up*>

Hari M. Sharma, MD and Charles N. Alexander, PhD. Maharishi Ayurveda Research Review Part II. Complementary Medicine International, March/April 1996; 3(2): 17-26.

Kaur CD, Saraf S. In vitro sun protection factor determination of herbal oils used in cosmetics. Pharmacognosy Research. 2010;2(1):22-25. doi:10.4103/0974-8490.60586.

Ouchi Y, et al. Changes in cerebral blood flow under the prone condition with and without massage. Neurosci Lett. 2006 Oct 23;407(2):131-5.

Rapaport MH et al. A Preliminary Study of the Effects of a Single Session of Swedish Massage on Hypothalamic–Pituitary–Adrenal and Immune Function in Normal Individuals. Journal of Alternative and Complementary Medicine. 2010;16(10):1079-1088. doi:10.1089/acm.2009.0634.

Teach Chemical Summary. U.S. EPA, Toxicity and Exposure Assessment for Children's Health. Phthalates. United States Environmental Protection Agency. Oct. 10, 2007. Web. Accessed May 10, 2015. < *http://www.epa.gov/teach/teach-summaries.html*>

Verchot, Manon. Everything you need to know about natural skin care. Tree-Hugger. June 23, 2013. Web. Accessed May 10, 2015. <*http://www.treehugger.com/htgg/how-to-go-green-natural-skin-care.html*>

CHAPTER 4 - LASTING BEAUTY

Eng-Tat Ang et al. Neurodegenerative diseases: exercising toward neurogenesis and neuroregeneration Front. Aging Neurosci., July 21, 2010.

Lo´ pez-Lluch et al. Calorie restriction induces mitochondrial biogenesis and bioenergetic efficiency. PNAS, Feb. 7, 2006; 103(6). 1768-1773.

Feature, Peter JaretWebMD. Best Foods for an Anti-Aging Diet. WebMD. WebMD, n.d. Web. 12 May, 2015.

ANCIENT DOCUMENTS REFERENCED

CHAPTER 1	CHAPTER 2	CHAPTER 3
Niti-shatak	Atharva Veda Niti Sara Rig Veda Yajur Veda	Upanishads

Acknowledgements

First and foremost, I would like to express my deepest gratitude to the most important woman in my life - my mother. Growing up, she was the epitome of beauty to me. My mother was an example of how gracefully a woman could embody her true nature and effortlessly exude enchanting beauty. Her poise taught me how to solve complex life problems and still maintain inner harmony. She, along with my father instilled in me strong morals and values. They are the true foundation of my *inner beauty*.

My heartfelt thanks to my in-laws who continue to inspire and support me. My loving, caring husband, Dr. Suhas is my best friend, who made my journey meaningful and beautiful.

He truly appreciated my inner as well as outer beauty and helped me blossom as a wife, mother and a successful businesswomen.

My son Manas is one of my greatest sources of happiness. His maturity, stability and wisdom simply amaze me. My daughter Sanika is a true Angel who never gave me any trouble growing up and created the most trusting and peaceful mother-daughter relationship. She is a role model for inner and outer beauty. I am deeply grateful for and forever blessed with my lovely family, including my brother Rajendra and his family, my brother in law Vilas and his family and my sister in law Vasanti and her family.

My deep gratitude goes to Maharishi Mahesh Yogi who gave me the opportunity to experience direct understanding of the most fundamental nature of reality. I feel so privileged and blessed be a part of the Transcendental Meditation movement for over 20 years.

I had always desired to write a book about beauty. Finally, one day a beautiful young lady, Megan Murphy walked into my life and fulfilled that wish. She was able to understand my thoughts and bring them to life through the written word. Megan's knowledge of the Vedic sciences like Ayurveda and Yoga, coupled with her extraordinary talent in writing, made the transmission of my ideas onto paper smooth and simple. Every day Megan brought all of her heartfelt dedication, brilliant ideas, sincerity and valuable skills to the table. She fully immersed herself in this project. I highly admire her abilities and I am grateful for how she enriched this book with her invaluable contribution.

Nina: what a beautiful soul. How did I get so lucky as to find a woman with such exquisite talent in graphic design and who also has a Vedic orientation? Nina is the one who made this book into a great piece of art. She laid it out so that it became a joy to look at and organized it so well that it was pleasing to the eye. Thanks for all her help and her ever-smiling attitude.

Thanks to Dr. Deepak Chopra and the Chopra Center for their generous endorsement and sincere support. Sri Sri Ravishankar ji and the Art of Living Family is a source of joy and happiness. I am very grateful for Mount Madonna Institute and Kerala Ayurveda Academy for their support.

Next, I'd like to offer my best regards and blessings to my friends who have always supported me. Dr. Tom Yarema is a part of our family and I always appreciate his insights and guidance. I thank my staff at *Ayurvedic Healing* – Robin, Sherry and all our hardworking therapists – for their undying support and understanding with our busy schedules. I would also like to thank all of my patients at *Ayurvedic Healing* who have challenged the way I think and made me look at different perspectives.

A big thanks to my dear friend Charna Posin, such a lovely person! She was a great help with the interviews and continuous encouragement to proceed with this book. Her time, energy and love are much appreciated. Thanks to Carolyn Lotze who helped me with the women's interviews. Thanks to Taryn Bentley who looked over the manuscript and editing this book.

It is with great gratitude that I offer my thanks to all the women who were kind enough to share their life stories with me. Thank you for inspiring and motivating many young women with your message.

Thanks to all of my colleagues for spreading the Ayurvedic wisdom:

Drs. Vasant Lad, David Frawley, Keith Wallace, Jay Apte, Vivek Shanbhag, Annambhotala Shekhar, Jayarajan, Subhash & Sunanda Ranade, Avinash & Bharati Lele, PH Kulkarni and Lina Thakar. My Ayurvedic friends Shunya Pratichi Mathur, Lissa Coffey, Pratima Raichur, Swami Seetaramananda, Shanta Shenoy, Tammie Fairchild, Shankari Shapiro, Laura Plumb, Shala Worsley. They continue to inspire me with their tireless enthusiasm.

I would like to express my heartfelt thanks to everyone who shared their insights and endorsed the book Marci Schimoff, Dr. John Douillard, Yogi Cameron, Yogacharya Ellen Grace O' Brian (Uma ji), Dr. Sheila Patel, Dr. Mona Saint, Lissa Coffey, Kimberley Snyder. Thanks a bunch. A big Thanks to Lotus Press team Santosh, Shanta, and Tom who helped me transform the manuscript into a beautiful polished product. Their support was invaluable.

My sincere gratitude to Shambhavi ji for her blessings. I greatly admire her as a woman who truly reflects inner and outer beauty. Her life work summarizes the essence of this book.

Last but not the least, I want to Thank all of my clients and students who have allowed me into their lives and shared with me their stories and personal journeys.

Namaste!

Glossary of Terms

Abhyanga: Ayurvedic full body, warm oil massage

Agni: Fire; particularly the digestive fire

Amalaki: Ayurvedic herb especially high in vitamin C and beneficial for the hair

Atharva Veda: One of the four primary Vedas specifying instructions for medical formulas, ceremonies and rituals.

Ayurveda: The spiritual science of life (a branch of Vedas)

Bhrajaka Pitta: a sub-dosha of Pitta which governs the metabolism and health of the skin

Chakras: Power centers in the mind and subtle body that are conduits to higher forces

Chapatti: Unleavened flatbread common to India

Chaya: Dullness or paleness in the skin

Dosha: Bio-psycho energetic force acting within the body-mind complex; encompassing one of three metabolic principals (Vata, Pitta and Kapha)

Durga: Hindu Goddess representing courage

Gharshana: Gentle exfoliation with silk gloves

Ghee: Clarified butter

Gunam: Sanskrit word encompassing the concept of inner beauty

Guru: Spiritual or secular teacher

Inner Beauty: Virtuous qualities shared with others which stem from one's own· self-love and acceptance

Kapalbhati: Pranayama exercise involving rapid chest breaths

Kali: A fierce Hindu Goddess who is said to destroys evil and illusion

Kapha: The dosha that governs bodily structure and expresses the elements earth and water

Karna Pooran: Ayurvedic practice of oiliation of the inner ear

KarnaVedham: Hindu ceremony for the piercing of the ears of a young child from twelve days to one year old

Kaval: Ayurvedic therapeutic treatment involving the swishing of oil in the mouth

Lakshmi: Hindu Goddess representing wealth and prosperity

Lasting Beauty: The culmination and endurance of both inner and outer beauty

Lavanya: Salty in taste; synonym for beauty

Madhurya: Sweet in taste; synonym for beauty

Mahabharata: Ancient Hindu epic

Maharishi Mahesh Yogi : Modern day spiritual teacher, yogi and Vedic scholar. Founder of Transcendental Meditation and Maharishi AyurVed programs.

Mantras: Words of power; sacred sounds and prayers

Manu Samhita: Special book which describes the laws of Hindu religion

Marma: Vital points on the body

Mehandi: Traditional Indian body art with henna

Menarche: The onset of menstruation

Moolabandha: Yogic posture meaning 'root lock'

Namaste: Sanskrit word and greeting used to acknowledge the presence of the Divine in another person

Nasya: Nasal administration of therapies

Nadishodana: Alternate nostril breathing exercise

Netra basti: Ayurvedic eye treatment using herbal ghee

Niti Sara: Ancient book containing a collection of different verses written in Sanskrit

Ojas: One of three vital sources of energy inherent in the universe and human body; responsible for immunity, luster and longevity

Outer Beauty: Physical beauty as an expression of healthy, vibrant physiology

PadaAbhyanga: Ayurvedic foot massage with special attention to vital points

Panchakarma: Ayurvedic detoxification treatments

Parvati: Hindu Goddess embodying the characteristics of fertility, love and devotion

Phthalates: Toxic endocrine disrupting class of synthetic chemicals

Pinda Sweda: Massage with warm rice boluses, herbs and milk

Pitta: The dosha that governs metabolism and possesses the expression of the fire and water elements

Prabha: Glow or radiance

Prana: Breath; subtle form of the life force

Pranayama: Controlled breathing exercises

Qi: Vital subtle energy as termed in Traditional Chinese Medicine

Rambha: In Hindu mythology, a beautiful queen renowned for her exquisite beauty, and talents in the feminine arts of dancing, music and love making

Rig Veda: Oldest and most primary Vedic text out of the four; scripture from which Ayurveda was derived

Rishis: A seer to whom the wisdom of the Vedas was long ago revealed

Rohini: The queen in the Hindu epic Mahabarata, who is married to the God incarnate, Krishna

Roopam: Sanskrit word for physical or outer beauty

Sahastra Chandra Darshana Shanti: Hindu celebration of the1,000th full moon, at about eighty years of age in a man or woman's life

Sanskrit: Ancient language of India in which the Vedas were transcribed

Saraswati: Hindu Goddess of knowledge and learning

Shakti: Divine feminine energy

Shiro basti: Ayurvedic body treatment involving the therapeutic retention of oil on top of the head

Shiro lepam: An Ayurvedic treatment using herbal paste on the head

Swami Vivekananda: 19th century Hindu saint

Swedana: Whole body steam with herbs or essential oils

Transcendental Meditation: A system of meditation developed by Maharishi Mahesh Yogi

Udgharshana: Mild exfoliating scrub with herbs

Udsadana: Ayurvedic massage with a smooth herbal paste

Udvartana : Ayurvedic exfoliation scrub with oil and herbs

Valuka sweda: Ayurvedic massage with sand bags and herbs

Vata: The dosha that governs all movement in the body and possesses the expression of ether and air

Vayastyag: Sankrit word expressing the concept of lasting beauty

Vedas: Ancient Indian books of knowledge presenting the spiritual science of awareness

Vedic: Of the Vedas

Vishuddha chakra: The throat chakra

Vruddha: Elder

Xenoestrogens: Synthetically derived chemicals which mimic the composition and actions of natural estrogens in the body

Yajur Veda: One of the four primary Vedas focusing on mantras in ritualistic capacities

Yoga: psycho-physical practices aimed at self-knowledge

Yoni mudra: Specific formation of the hands designed to assist in the meditation on the energy of the womb

Yoni pichu: Medicated tampon

Yoni: Sanskrit word for the vagina

Yuj': Sankrit root word meaning 'to unite'

BOOKS OF RELATED INTEREST

Ayurveda For Women

A Guide to Vitality and Health

DR ROBERT E. SVOBODA

ISBN: 978-81-7822-105-2

Ayurveda is an ancient and universal system of health and healing that can be used beneficially in any culture, in any era by anyone. *Ayurveda for Women* outlines the basic principles of Ayurveda making readers to understand their own physiological and psychological make-up, and the qualities in themselves and in their environment which promote a state of health or ill-health. It further explores the physical, emotional and spiritual realities which are unique to women. This book provides essential reading for all women interested in maintaining good health–physical, mental and spiritual–through simple, natural methods and complementary therapies.

Ayurvedic Spa

Treatments for large and small spas as well as home care to help everyone become healthy, happy, and inspired

MELANIE & ROBERT SACHS

ISBN: 978-81-7822-328-5

If you are a spa owner looking for new, authentic world-class treatments, a body worker wanting to learn methods that touch your clients on a heart level, or someone who enjoys creating nurturing rituals for yourself and family members in your own home, *Ayurvedic Spa* will guide and help you to offer and/ or achieve greater levels of beauty, peace and wellness. Ayurveda has so much to offer Spas as they mature from "beauty and pampering" to "wellness and longevity".

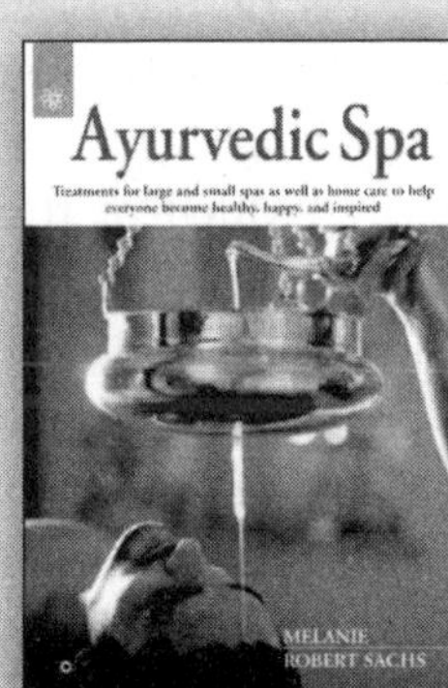

Mantra Yoga and Primal Sound

Secrets of Seed (Bija) Mantras

Dr. David Frawley

ISBN: 978-81-7822-381-0

This book is not simply a collection of Mantras or an expression of their moral significance; it is an interpretation of the philosophy and the reality of the mantric approach to intelligence and knowledge held within the sound code or vibratory pattern behind the universe itself.

The author has taken care of explaining the *Bija Mantras*, starting with the letters of the Sanskrit alphabet, and leading up to the *mantra purusha* or body of sound which is considered an important practice in mantra yoga. The application of the mantra therapy in the Vedic sciences of Ayurvedic medicines, Vedic astrology and vastu sciences, too, form an important part of the book.

Tibetan Ayurveda

Health Secrets form the Roof of the World

Robert Sachs

ISBN: 978-81-7822-327-8

Tibetan medicine was probably the first truly integrated system of ancient healing science. *Tibetan Ayurveda* provides a comprehensive guide to the four levels of traditional Tibetan medicine with a wealth of traditional health practices and teachings.

Much of the contemporary material on Tibetan medicine focuses solely on herbal medicine and acupuncture; *Tibetan Ayurveda* goes beyond these to look at other important forms of treatment such as Pancha Karma for detoxification and rejuvenation, and it is an excellent resource for anyone wanting to live a life based on the wisdom of Ayurveda.